# HOLDING BEAUTY IN MY SOUL'S ARMS

AWAKENING TO AT-ONE-MENT: VOLUME I

FAITH EXPLORATIONS
BEING TRANSFORMED IN CHRIST

KEVIN G. THEW FORRESTER

Copyright © Kevin G. Thew Forrester 2011

Scripture quotations marked (NRSV) are taken from the New Revised Standard Version Bible, copyright © 1989 National Council of the Churches of Christ in the United States of America. Used by permission. All rights reserved.

All rights reserved.
No part of this publication may be reproduced, stored in a retrieval system or transmitted in any form or by any means, electronic, mechanical, photocopying, recording or otherwise, without the prior permission of the publisher.

LeaderResources
PO Box 302
Leeds, MA 01053

Cover art: Celebration on the Mountain
© Madartists | Dreamstime.com
Back cover and end page photos © by Marlys Murray

ISBN
978-1-59518-056-8
1-59518-056-7

Also by Kevin Thew Forrester

**Awakening to At-One-Ment: Volume II**

# My Heart is a Raging Volcano of Love for You!

**Liturgical Explorations
Collects, Blessings, Litanies,
Prayers and Eucharistic Prayers**

Volume II in this series, *My Heart is a Raging Volcano of Love for You*, explores how we may express our unfolding union with God in the prayers and liturgies of the church.

Available from LeaderResources
in print and electronic file with
license to reproduce and use in worship

www.LeaderResources.org

**DEDICATED TO:**

My companions along the way,
grateful for the grace of holding Beauty

# ACKNOWLEDGEMENTS

This book is the fruit of the *LifeCycles* partnership begun in the autumn of 2001 in the Diocese of Northern Michigan. The current members of the partnership are: the Diocese of Vermont, the Diocese of Wyoming, the Diocese of Nevada, the Diocese of Northern Michigan, the Diocese of California, the Episcopal Divinity School, and LeaderResources. The essays were originally written as part of the sessions of *LifeCycles* and have been edited and rearranged for *Holding Beauty in my Soul's Arms*.

I offer my deep gratitude to my friends in the Diocese of Northern Michigan. They have supported and challenged me to explore who the living Christ is for us as we endeavor to be a Eucharistic community shaped in the waters of baptism and drawn to the fullness of life promised in both meal and water.

My faith journey has been enriched, broadened, and deepened by my Enneagram teachers, especially Helen Palmer and Terry Saracino, as well as all those who gather regularly in the Midwest to receive sacred stories of the heart, head, and body. Terry Saracino graciously reviewed and improved *Part VII, Transformation: God's Abiding Presence*.

I continue to find the writings of both Ken Wilber and A.H. Almaas some of the most creative, comprehensive, and worthwhile spiritual work being produced today. Their distinct abilities to integrate theology, spirituality, and psychology within an unfolding interfaith context of praxis, offers renewed hope to religion in the 21st century as the Spirit invites further reform: *ecclesia reformata semper reformanda secundum verbum dei* ("The church reformed and always being reformed according to the word of God.").

Over the past 17 years or so, Fredrica Harris Thompsett has become a dear friend and colleague, an *anamcara*, who reminds me of the sheer joy of theological creativity rooted in community.

Over and again I have turned to Linda Grenz, Publisher and CEO of LeaderResources, as I have researched, written, and asked for advice.

My partner in life, work, play and prayer, is Rïse, who inspires and nurtures all I do. She is a creative heart bringing life to all she touches. Miriam and Liam are the moon and the sun.

And finally, this book exists only because of my collaboration with the *LifeCycles* brainstorming and editorial team of Northern Michigan. Together over the past 8 years we have grown in our love of God, our devotion to this diocese, and our commitment to creating lifelong formation materials for Christians who guard as sacred the questioning mind and the searching heart. Life is itself a liturgy, a dance of gratefulness to the Holy Source. To these friends I offer my gratitude: Marion Luckey, Charlie Piper, Rayford Ray, Bonnie Turner, and Anita Wingert.

Kevin G. Thew Forrester

## THE ESSENCE OF DESIRE

"I did not
have to ask my heart what it wanted,
because of all the desires I have ever known just one did I cling to
for it was the essence of
all desire:
to hold beauty in
my soul's
arms."

John of the Cross[1]

# Contents

Acknowledgments .................................................................. 5
Foreword ............................................................................... 9
Preface ................................................................................. 13

## Part I   An Integral Theology as Transformative
Chapter 1   Introduction ....................................................... 19
Chapter 2   An Integral Theology ......................................... 33
Chapter 3   Theology as Transformative .............................. 39
Activities   Exploring an Integral Theology ........................ 48

## Part II   Beyond Status and Security
Chapter 4   Faint Glimmer of Empathy: Jeremiah ............... 51
Chapter 5   Love Sees no Conditions: Galatians .................. 57
Chapter 6   A Song of Utter Light: Francis of Assisi ............ 61
Activities   Exploring Status and Security ........................... 71

## Part III   Awakening to Our At-One-Ment
Chapter 7   At-One-Ment with God: Second Isaiah .............. 75
Chapter 8   At-One-Ment with Each Other: Romans ........... 79
Chapter 9   At-One-Ment with Creation: Meister Eckhart ... 85
Activities   Exploring At-One-Ment .................................... 93

## Part IV   Honoring Our Humanity
Chapter 10   Human Life is Already Divine: Ezekiel ............ 97
Chapter 11   Cross at the Crossroads: Corinthians ............. 101
Chapter 12   Love without Bounds: Mohandas Gandhi ...... 109
Activities    Exploring Our Humanity ................................ 117

## PART V     FROM DOMINATION TO WHOLENESS
Chapter 13    Blindness as Humanity's Issue: Hosea .................. 121
Chapter 14    What Kind of Clothes: Colossians ....................... 129
Chapter 15    Leaven of Freedom: Teresa of Avila .................... 135
Activities       Exploring Domination and Wholeness ................ 145

## PART VI     A COMPASSIONATE WHOLE
Chapter 16    The Authority to "Call Out": Micah ..................... 153
Chapter 17    The Way of Self-Emptying: Philippians ................ 165
Chapter 18    Enclosed in a Loving God: Julian of Norwich ........ 177
Activities       Exploring Life as a Compassionate Whole ........... 192

## PART VII    TRANSFORMATION: GOD'S ABIDING PRESENCE
Chapter 19    Development of Personality:
                     The Soul Remembers .......................................... 195
Chapter 20    Transformation:
                     Conversion in the Body Center .......................... 209
Chapter 21    Transformation:
                     Conversion in the Heart Center ......................... 217
Chapter 22    Transformation:
                     Conversion in the Head Center ......................... 225
Activities       Exploring Transformation .................................... 232

**EPILOGUE** .................................................................................. 235
**BIBLIOGRAPHY** ....................................................................... 237
**ENDNOTES** ............................................................................... 245
**ABOUT THE AUTHOR** ........................................................... 254

# FOREWORD

I learned long ago that every good journey is blessed by its resting places. More honestly, I am still learning this as slowing down does not come easily to me. Even though I know that I am living in a world thoroughly saturated with God, I do not always see life clearly. Moving too fast, I too often miss the ordinary giftedness of humanity and the sacred wonder of the natural world. Many times I forget to be compassionate to myself and to seek justice love for others. For these and other reasons, I am thankful for the opportunity to share my delight in this perceptive guide to on-going spiritual transformation. I will read it several times over, taking pleasure in its invitation to appreciate God's infinite embrace.

Kevin Thew Forrester's *Holding Beauty in My Soul's Arms* is a book for many, if not most, of us on the journey toward deeper spiritual formation. It offers a resting place, a reflective learning place where we may pause and savor at our own pace the riches of scripture, tradition, and reason as well as post-modern psychology, ethics, cultural studies, and systems theory. Familiar stories, presented in informative and provocative ways, take on greater vibrancy. Narratives of saints, ancient and modern, hold up reflections of human transformation. As we move into an unknown future, foundational theological questions about how we perceive ourselves and God are candidly and plainly opened up. It is in the *doing* of theology – reflecting upon our experience and that of wider communities – that we find nurture, insight and guidance toward Christian transformation.

Many ages and stages of travellers will find substance in *Holding Beauty in My Soul's Arms*. Those who have been dipped into or sprinkled with the sustaining waters of baptism and are newly aware of buoyant resources of baptismal theology, will find refreshing strength for the journey.

Those who wish to dive deeply and swim with the mystics who offer "profound experiential knowledge of God" (page 13) will, I believe, find that they also surface with renewed gratitude.

Those of us who wish to swim justly aligned with others will discover the truth of Evelyn Underhill's perceptive definition of spirituality as "education for action."

Those exploring new, emergent, and fresh expressions of "church," and those with thirsting souls will find in these pages a spiritual audacity that embraces the whole of reality.

Curious Christians, seekers, and newcomers to spiritual adventures will also find tools to aid their discoveries. One of the best supportive aids to the spiritual journey, the Enneagram, is explored in this volume. This tool, with its holistic embrace of nature and nurture, can in time and with practiced awareness help us be the leaders God would have us become. If this is your first exposure to the spirituality and psychology of the Enneagram, I invite you to continue to explore this resource as a companion in spiritual awareness.

*Holding Beauty in My Soul's Arms* draws upon and carries forward the pedagogy and essays originally presented in *LifeCycles*, an Episcopal process of adult education and group formation. Building on this communal heritage, I too am drawn to discuss with old and new friends, the insights I find in these pages. Ideally readers of this volume would benefit from discussing this text with other travellers.

At last here is a volume that treats spirituality and faithful living with the conventions and knowledge of post-modernity. In refusing to mistake a part for a whole, or to enshrine separation and division, but rather to dissolve illusionary walls that separate us from a God of infinite possibilities, this is a courageous book. Thank you, Kevin, for your wisdom and guidance.

Will we allow ourselves to be supported, freed from fear, living, loving, playing and from time to time resting deeply in the refreshing and moving waters of baptismal identity? *Holding Beauty in My Soul's Arms* bids us respond, "We will, with God's help."

Fredrica Harris Thompsett<br>
Cape Cod, Massachusetts<br>
Mary Wolfe Professor of Historical Theology<br>
and faculty emerita, Episcopal Divinity School

"'Dig here,' the angel said ---
'in your soul,
in your soul.'"
John of the Cross[2]

# PREFACE: ALL IS ONE IN GOD

We awaken to our at-one-ment with God and creation as we realize, in the words of Meister Eckhart, that 'God's ground is my ground, and my ground is God's ground.'³ This gracious divine common ground is the source of life itself.

To speak of *my* ground as God's ground is to recognize that every creature is alive because the Center of its being is the Divine Holy Source. As the Holy Source, God's saturating presence manifests in time and space as the abundant life of creation. Life itself is a supernatural chorus that echoes in praise of God's sweet goodness. God's abiding gracious presence draws forth a marvelous doxology from Angelus Silesius, a 17th century German mystic:

> *God is more in me than if the whole sea could in a sponge wholly contained be.*⁴

We can recognize the sea as symbolizing the pervasive waters of baptism. There have been times throughout the course of history where Christians have sought to control and contain the sea as a defensive moat against a fallen, corrupt, and threatening world. In fear, the church has all too often attempted to withdraw the spacious waters of baptism into a watery border protecting God and altar table from defilement. Fear invariably contracts the human soul and rigidifies the community of faith, placing the heart and mind and body on the anxious defensive.

In the wake of such defensiveness, baptism can be reduced to a 'sacrament' of division and exclusion, due to our fear of protecting God and safeguarding the purity of the believers. Too often the waters are troubled by egoic fear only, not eternal divine possibility. Too often the waters are controlled and contained as a moat to keep people separate and away, not the healing pool of Siloam opening our blind eyes.

But our Holy Source is the Beloved, who continually invites us to have the courage to wade in and remain a student with a beginner's mind (as the Zen masters would say). Where fear would invariably draw our souls into contraction, God invites us to step into the water and allow the waves to draw our vision ever outward. Without doubt, water can be used as a defense. But water can also buoy our courage. The waters of baptism invite us to let go and discover that sin has not to do with our essential badness, but with our continual blindness to our gracious divine goodness. We are beckoned to relax and drop down into the deep pool of Wisdom that is our very soul and be guided by the Holy One eternally present and inviting us forward. '[F]or all things come of thee, and of thine own have we given thee.' (1 Chronicles

29:14b, *NRSV*). All, not some. All is one in God. All is united in Christ. All life flows from the one water, the one God.

**FONTAL LIFE**

Wisdom for wading in these waters is to be found in our scriptures and the lives of the saints and mystics. By 'mystic,' I borrow from the work of the Jesuit theologian, William Harmless, who speaks of those who have a 'profound *experiential* knowledge of God or of ultimate reality.'[5] Although it is true that the mystics 'rarely address social relations,' theologian Catherine Keller reminds us that they certainly do 'articulate a bottomless freedom that in context was judged intolerably dissident.'[6] Here we discover stories, which is to say a theology that transform the inclination of fear to withdraw, divide and separate.

Fortunately, the sea of Divine Presence can neither be controlled nor contained. God, as the American philosopher Ken Wilber is fond of saying, is always already present as our common ground. At-one-ment is what we describe as a 'given.' Its reality is never in question and is the fundamental reality confirmed in baptism. Baptism reaffirms the abiding truth of our existence – we live and move and have our being in the Beloved. 'All things come of thee, O God.' Baptismal initiation offers us new life.

In early Syriac Christianity, Jesus was known as the 'Life-Giver' (Ihidaya). In contrast with the primarily negative approach to redemption expressed in the Greek New Testament, the Syriac New Testament chose words embodying a distinctly positive approach. Gabriele Winkler points out that in the Syriac New Testament 'the equivalents for the Greek verbs meaning 'to deliver,' 'to redeem,' 'to save,' are not used; instead they are rendered in Syriac by the terms 'to give life,' 'to make alive,' 'to cause to live.'[7]

Jesus emerges from the waters of baptism in the Jordan as the Life-Giver. He is the Life-Giver because he has awakened to his unity with God and creation. In the Syriac text Jesus is 'the unified one'. Jesus reveals the path of life because he directly experiences and knows his union, his at-one-ment, with God and creation.

Baptism is a sacrament of initiation that invites us on the life-journey of living from our common true Center – union with God and one another. The contemporary mystic Bruno Barnhart, in *The Future of Wisdom*, describes this as fontal life. Baptism confirms the deepest and widest truth about life – we are, we exist, in and through and of, the divine saturating Presence. We begin to realize for ourselves and speak a theology consonant with the reality experienced by Marguerite Porete – 'and because He is everywhere, this Soul finds Him everywhere. All things are fitting for her, for she does not find anything anywhere but that she finds God there.'[8]

In *Holding Beauty in My Soul's Arms,* drawn from essays written originally for the *LifeCycles* formation process, we explore what it means for our lives to be lived from our divine common ground. We revisit some of the pivotal self-defining stories of the scriptures and the lives of the saints and mystics, seeking their meaning for us when read from the experience and wisdom of our gracious at-one-ment.

We begin by developing an 'integral' theology, which is a theology that recognizes the graced core of creation and deliberately respects, receives, and converses with the various disciplines that study four dimensions of existence: individual and collective, internal and external. We then practice this integral theology as we discover anew how the Hebrew and Christian scriptures, along with the stories of the saints and mystics, invite us to be transformed, awakening to the truth of our common ground. In this ground we are one in Christ.

*Holding Beauty in My Soul's Arms* is an invitation to discover that the baptismal waters dissolve illusionary walls separating sacred and profane, pure and impure. Along with Nicholas Cusa, the 15th century German mystic, we are invited to discover our own prophetic and dissident voice: 'God…is the enfolding of all in the sense that all are in God, and God is the unfolding in the sense that God is in all.'[9] We realize that health and wholeness is not a matter of ritual purity, but of primordial unity confirmed in baptism. We, like Jesus, are transformed into life-givers, because we directly experience our at-one-ment. Theology itself becomes a language that satisfies and enlivens anew. We are courageously drawn out again into the deep, where the grace of God invites marvelous discoveries, none more breathtaking than the realization that we, too, are beloved. Our souls awaken and know God as surely as the taste of fresh water on the tongue.

# PART I

# AN INTEGRAL THEOLOGY AS TRANSFORMATIVE

"the Word of God,
Jesus Christ our Lord, who,
because of his superabundant love,
made himself what we are
in order to make of us what he is."
Irenaeus of Lyons[10]

> *For what is more desirable to God's precious one than to be divinized,*
> *that is for God to be united with those who have become god*
> *and by his goodness to make everything his own.*
> Maximus the Confessor[11]

There are many different ways to do or to define theology. Each way has its own truth as well as its own blind spots. For some, theology is a kind of sacred science, focusing the intellect upon God, or the scriptures, or creation (or a combination of these). One of the theological giants of the 20th century, Karl Rahner, defined theology as 'the *science* of faith.' Others view theology less as a science and more as a kind of art, such as biography, creative storytelling, or the drama of worship and liturgy. Each approach to theology says something about what theology is, but also something about the theologian who is doing the theology (... an academician, biblical scholar, liturgical artist, storyteller, etc.).

# CHAPTER 1 – INTRODUCTION

**A Description of Theology**

Each approach and every definition is partial. None of the above ways of doing theology is wrong, yet each is incomplete. As human beings, we all struggle to know God in the context of our daily lives. St. Augustine describes us as creatures whose hearts are restless until we rest and enjoy ourselves in God (the meaning of 'shalom'). Any particular theology is simply one of the guides leading us to that place of rest and enjoyment within God (others include such diverse expressions as meditation, worship, lives of compassion and justice). We will approach theology as an act of reflection undertaken together in community. We can reflect on any experience – our own as well as others'. We reflect on these experiences together, drawn to see more clearly

- ➢ *who this God is* who is in our midst,
- ➢ *how this God* is present in our midst,
- ➢ *who we are* who seek this God,
- ➢ *what difference* this God and our community make in our lives.

As we reflect on our life experiences, the Spirit of God transforms us. It is as if we are traveling like the disciples on the road to Emmaus. Our hearts are burning within, and so we ask our questions, struggle with the responses, laugh, cry, and hope together as we journey. This life journey is the doing of theology. The scope of theology is thus boundless. We can reflect on just about anything and everything – friendship, death, peace, war, oppression, liberation, sexuality, power. If we can name something, we can reflect on it and struggle with it in the light of our faith; all along the way, God is with us, transforming us.

This particular understanding of theology implies that we are all theologians – each and every one of us. We are all struggling to know God in the context of our lives, broken and beautiful. Any given theology is simply a guide, leading us to that place of shalom within God.

To shift our metaphor slightly, theology is able to guide us, because it is telling the story of what we see. But we need to learn *how* to see. The greatest obstacle we encounter to seeing is nothing 'out there,' but our very own self – our own ego. Our ego does not want to let go. It likes believing it is on top and in control. Spiritually speaking, we thus find ourselves kneeling before the twin gods of status and security.

As we shall see in *Part II, Beyond Status and Security* – through our explorations of Jeremiah, Paul and Francis – status and security play a central role in their faith journeys. There is almost no end to which human beings will not go to destroy a threat to security and status – even invoking the name of God to justify the sacrifice of other human beings

**Theology as a Communal Action**

To say that theology is something each of us does is only part of the picture. One of the earliest names given to the gathered followers of the way of Jesus was 'the body of Christ.' To be a disciple, a student, of the way of Jesus, was to be someone who entered into relationships with others. These baptized formed, as Paul's letter to the Galatians tells us, *a new kind of family* – a family of sisters and brothers holding one another in mutual regard. All of this is to say that to be a Christian is to be a member of a community – a communion. We cannot be Christians apart from another. We are the body of Christ. Because we *are* the body of Christ, *we* are also theologians. We seek to understand ourselves, our community, creation, and God, *together*. To do theology is to do something together and in partnership.

What we do together in our theology is reflect as a community upon our experiences. The church reminds us that this community extends into the past as well as the future. We are a community, or a communion, of saints – past, present, and future. This is one of the primary reasons that theology is an act of reflection that draws upon the wisdom of persons in history, as well as persons beyond our own particular congregation, denomination, or even faith. We are not in the struggle of life alone, but surrounded, as the scriptures say, by a great cloud of witnesses. We endeavor to *see* more clearly *who and how God is in our midst as well as who we are and how we are.*

In *Part III, Awakening to At-One-Ment*, we explore three of the witnesses who surround us – Second-Isaiah, Paul and Meister Eckhart. Each invites us as a community of faith to see through the false bondages that divide and separate. Second-Isaiah sees our At-one-ment with God. Paul sees our At-one-ment with each other. Meister Eckhart sees our At-one-ment with creation.

# ~SCRIPTURES~

**Resources for Reflection – Scripture(s)**

If one is a biologist, some version of evolutionary theory provides the fundamental resource for reflecting upon the data. If one is a physicist, there are certain 'laws' of physics (such as those pertaining to thermodynamics) that guide inquiry and conversation. Every discipline has primary resources to which it turns to help it make sense of what it studies. These resources, for good and for bad, often determine what we are able even to see. There was once a time when those who studied the land and the sea were convinced that the horizon was where the earth dropped off, since the known 'laws' declared the earth to be flat. Prior to Copernicus, the prevailing laws of astronomy stated that the sun and stars revolved around the earth. One's resources, therefore, cannot only help to reveal reality, but they can also at times obscure and hide. The same is true for theology.

In theology, we also have resources upon which to draw as we reflect upon our experiences (or theologize) in life. Since Richard Hooker, one of the great theologians of the Elizabethan era (16th Cent.), Anglicans speak often of theology drawing upon the wisdom of scripture, tradition, and reason. Let's take a look at each, beginning with how we draw upon the scriptures (a helpful introduction may be found in the *Pocket Bible Guide*, by Linda L. Grenz).

**Dictated by God.** According to this view, God dictated, word for word, phrase by phrase, the entire contents of the Bible. Here there is no room for error or fallibility. Every word and fact is correct and true. The author is God, and human beings are passive vessels used by God. Not only does Scripture instruct us about God, but it also has much to say about such subjects as geology and biology. Scripture is understood as being *inerrant* because its source is an infallible God.

**Inspired by God.** The Spirit of God inspired or guided the many different writers to pen the ancient orally transmitted stories. Human persons were not passive vessels but cooperated with the Spirit, drawing upon their own strengths, limited by their own weaknesses. There are mistakes in the scriptures, but they are seen as minor and having little or nothing to do with who God is revealed to be.

**Grounded in God.** The scriptures are written by human beings created in the image and likeness of God. Human persons were not passive vessels but actively and willingly drew upon their God-given gifts to write what they felt called by the Spirit to write. Scripture itself is a text where human ignorance, prejudice, anger, greed – that is, human brokenness – is part of the stories. Passages of scripture at times conflict, images of God and community evolve and change, and there are errors to be found. Yet, *in it all*, God is present and inviting the community into fullness of life. The scriptures are not meant for teaching geology, biology, astronomy, etc.

Every theology has biases. We will be utilizing a theology drawing upon the scriptures as **Grounded in God.** Scripture is understood as a collection of stories that we, as Christians, hold as especially sacred. In and through these stories we are able to discover how others laid claim to the presence of God in all facets of their lives. Within the scriptures we have stories describing who God is and who we are as the people of God. Not all of the stories are necessarily consistent with each other, but all have the gracious capacity to invite us into a reconsideration of who we know God and ourselves to be. We draw upon the scriptures as a resource-companion, not as an answer-book. The stories disclose a God persistently inviting us into a journey where we learn to trust in God's abiding presence and envision a life where all are free to live in the Spirit. We look to our forbears, such as Abraham, Sarah, and Hagar, as companion-sojourners. Their lives give us hints of who God is, who we are, and where we might be going.

Because we draw upon the scriptures as writings **Grounded in God,** we are not only free to use our entire mind, body, and heart, to make sense of them, but we have a responsibility to do so. Over the past 100 years the field of biblical criticism has flourished and grown. Criticism, as it is used here, does not mean to 'criticize' something as being wrong. Rather, it means we use our God-given talents of reason, imagination, and inquiry to grapple with the scriptures as a guide for creating a common life embodying love and restoring justice and wholeness. When, in doing theology, we turn to the scriptures, what we are trying to do is draw from their stories pictures of three different, but related, worlds.

## Three Distinct Worlds of the Scriptures

### The world behind the scriptures
This is the world in which an original author, such as Isaiah or Ezekiel, lived. We want to know as much as possible about this world and how it influenced the author. Drawing upon such diverse disciplines as agriculture, economics archaeology, political science, developmental psychology, ancient languages, etc., scholars ask: What was Jerusalem like as a city during the time of Ezekiel? What was the economy like, and how were people employed? What was the political system, and who had the power? How were families structured? Where did families live? What was even considered a family? How did people worship? Were there many gods or only one? What did people mean by 'God'? The goal is to piece together a mosaic of the ancient world of the biblical authors.

### The world of the scriptures
Now we are looking at the texts of the Bible itself. One of the challenges before theologians is the actual piecing together of the sacred texts *because we don't have the original manuscripts!* What we have are copies of copies of copies. And over time, with so much copying being done, changes and errors occur. The goal is to reconstruct a text as close to the original as possible. This is called 'textual criticism.' Scholars pore over documents in Hebrew (the earliest complete manuscripts of the Hebrew Bible date to the 10th century CE) and

in Greek (the most important Christian Scripture manuscripts date from the 4th century CE). Scholars also must contend with such languages as Latin, Coptic, and Syriac. The Dead Sea scrolls have proven to be an enormously helpful discovery. Textual critics assemble all these texts and begin their work of piecing the fragments together. Their task is complicated by the fact that sometimes they are reconstructing a poem, or a song, or a code of law, or a proverb, or a parable. Literary criticism, source criticism, form criticism, rhetorical criticism, reader-response criticism – these are some of the tools theologians draw upon to piece together the scriptures we read in our Bibles.

**The world envisioned by the scriptures**

As followers of the way of Jesus, we live for the reign of God that has been born in our midst, yet is still being born in and about us. In order not to misuse the scriptures, we need to know the historical world behind a given book or passage. But that is not enough. We also need to know what the original author was saying to an original audience. But *that* is not enough. Our history and experience are also important as they help to prevent us from stretching the meaning of a text too far – for example, claiming that the creation stories in Genesis require we reject evolutionary science and believe in a world only 4,000 years old.

We do not live in the time of Ezekiel, Jonah, Matthew, or Paul. We seek our way in the early part of the 21st century. We are drawn to investigate and discover both the world *behind* the scriptures and the world *of* the scriptures because we see in them resources for creating with God a better world for today and tomorrow – the reign of God. And so, as theologians, we ask: What might the scriptures mean for us today? Who are they calling us to be? How are they calling us to live? Where are we to find God in our midst now? How do any of the stories relate to our unfolding life-stories today?

The scriptures are not dead words of the past, but living, breathing words. Through our conversation with them, God invites us into the divine vision of a new world – the reign of God. Because the scriptures are alive and dynamic, in *Part IV, Honoring Humanity*, when we read the ancient books of Ezekiel and Corinthians, as well as listen anew to the life of Mohandas Gandhi, we do so not simply for historical knowledge but as a resource to discern the kind of world God is inviting us to build together in Christ.

# ~TRADITIONS~

**Resources for Reflection – Tradition**
**Where Do We Begin?**

Where on earth do we begin to turn, as theologians, to get a handle on the meaning of creation and history? -- A 14 billion year old creation; a 200,000 year old human species; a Jewish and Christian journey that is over 3,500 years old.

How do we even to start to tell the story? The stories? We have to talk about *many* stories don't we? Millions and billions of people and all of creation are involved.

Theology is all about the telling of stories – the story of God, the story of humanity, the story of creation. And there are so many different ways, or traditions, of telling these stories. These traditions aren't static. They are living and breathing, embodied in human beings of particular times and specific places -- doing something and saying something, in interaction with someone else. All of this is very dynamic. The Latin word for 'tradition' captures this dynamism well – we are handing something on, but this is not simply some 'thing': it is flowing river of life itself.

To be a theologian is to be a member of a community that reflects upon experience. This act of reflection is transformative – it changes us. We endeavor to see or envision more clearly who God is and how God is present in our midst as well as who we are and how we are to live in God's creation. Different communities remember and retell the stories of what they have experienced and seen. As these stories are told, and invite new communities to have similar experiences of God and themselves, the stories are retold, and in the process not only are the communities transformed, but so are the stories. As time passes, communities develop distinctive and characteristic stories. In other words, traditions develop. For example, look at the stories of Jesus told by the communities of Paul and compare and contrast them with those told by the Johannine communities (Jesus, the Human from Heaven) or those of Matthew (Jesus the Jewish Messiah) and Mark (Jesus the Suffering Son of God).

To be a people of traditions is to acknowledge that we are a people with many, many stories to remember and to tell. Even more, the stories we tell also tell us who we are and who we might become. (Remember the Jews telling the stories of Genesis during their captivity in Babylon? Such a telling of the origin of their life from the Creator was a bold act of defiance and hope in the face of deportation and servitude in Babylon. Telling the story changed the people and hope was reborn.) Theology explores and reflects on these traditions, endeavoring to draw from them pictures of three different, but related, worlds.

**First World: The World Behind The Tradition/Story**
This is the world in which the original storyteller, such as Paul, or Mary Magdalene, or Teresa of Avila, or William Temple, lived. We want to know as much as possible about this world and how it influenced the storyteller. So, for example, if we allow a prayer to collect our attention: "We are a community gathered and sent forth by God; to encounter our story; to be

washed and renewed; to be fed, with thanksgiving; and to celebrate and serve the reign of God." This prayer can focus our inquiry and prompt us to ask questions such as these, to decipher the world of a Mary Magdalene and the gospel written in her name:

- What were the traditions of gathering in Palestinian culture during the first century in which Mary Magdalene lived?
- What were the traditions of sending forth in first century Palestine? What did it mean to be sent forth? Were women sent forth as emissaries or disciples? Were people sent forth in groups? Did women and men ever go forth in pairs?
- Who were the storytellers? Who was not allowed to tell the story? Who was allowed to listen to the story and in what context? (publicly? in crowds of mixed or single gender? In crowds of Jews and/or gentiles?)
- What were the traditions of washing and bathing? Was Mary or any other women 'washed' or 'bathed' into the way of Jesus or of John the Baptist? What might this ritual have meant? Did Jesus wash or bathe anyone?
- What were the traditions for being fed? What was the meaning(s) of hosting a meal in first century Palestine? Was the meaning influenced by Greek or Roman or Egyptian cultures? Were women ever hosts of meals? Would women bless meals? Who was invited? Were some classes of people excluded?
- How have such actions and the stories and traditions generated by them embodied the celebration and service of the reign of God?

To help us respond to these questions, we also need to ask some broader questions, raised by such disciplines as archeology, economics, political science, agriculture, comparative religion, ancient languages, and sociology. These are just some of the disciplines scholars draw upon to help us reconstruct a picture of the setting or world in which the story originally was told.

**Second World: The World Of The Tradition/Story**

Now we are looking at the text of the story itself. One of the challenges before us as theologians is the actual piecing together of the story *because oftentimes we don't have the original manuscript!* What we have are retellings of retellings of retellings. Over time, with so much retelling being done, changes occur. The goal here is to reconstruct a text as close as possible to the original story. This is called 'textual criticism.' Here we rely upon the work of scholars who pore over documents in the original language, which might be Hebrew, Greek, Latin, Syriac, Russian, German, Italian, Arabic, etc. The textual critics assemble all these texts (drawing upon the tools of literary criticism, source criticism, form criticism, rhetorical criticism, reader-response criticism) and begin their work of piecing the fragments together into the most ancient form of the story possible. The end result is a reference point for us to assess how communities have changed the story in their retelling. What have they changed? Why have they changed the story? The task is complicated by the fact that some stories are in the forms of a poem, or a song, or a code of law, or a proverb, or a parable.

For example, in *Part V, From Domination to Wholeness,* we will explore the life of Teresa of Avila, who was a prolific writer. Through the critical work of textual criticism, we now know that the church published editions of Teresa's writings that removed important selections in which she laid before the oppressive church and society an alternative vision of Jesus' view of women. Except for the first sentence, the entire passage cited below was not included in the second editing of the *Way of Perfection*. Even today it is often omitted from Spanish editions of Teresa's writings.

> Nor did you, Lord, when you walked in the world, despise women; rather, you always, with great compassion, helped them. And you found as much love and more faith in them than you did in men. Among them was your most blessed mother...Is it not enough, Lord, that the world has intimidated us...so that we may not do anything worthwhile for you in public or dare speak some truths that we lament over in secret, without your also failing to hear so just a petition? I do not believe, Lord, that this could be true of your goodness and justice, for you are a just judge and not like those of the world. Since the world's judges are sons of Adam and all of them are men, there is no virtue in women that they do not hold suspect. Yes, indeed, the day will come, my king, when everyone will be known for what he is...these are times in which it would be wrong to undervalue virtuous and strong souls, even though they are women.[12]

### Third World: The World The Tradition/Story Envisions

As followers of the way of Jesus, we live for the reign of God, which has been born in our midst, yet is still being born in and about us. In order not to misuse the stories of history (as was done, for example, in the use of Christian stories to justify slavery and the subjugation of women in the United States and apartheid in South Africa), we need to know the historical world behind a given story and its tradition. (What led Teresa of Avila to establish convents in which women could be gathered and fed and sent forth? What led her to be critical of the dominating church and social hierarchies of her day?) But that is not enough. We also need to know what the original storyteller was saying to an original audience. (What are the actual speeches and writings of Teresa? Where did she deliver them? Who was invited to listen? What language did she use to write and to speak?) But that is not enough. History and context help to prevent us from misusing a text – for example, we now know that Teresa had to write in such a way as to avoid condemnation and execution by the Inquisition. Many of her passages, in which she seems excessively humble, are actually rhetorical gems, where she simultaneously exposes the abuse of power by the church hierarchy.

We do not live in the time of Mary Magdalene, Paul, Teresa of Avila, or William Temple. We seek our way in the early part of the 21st century. We are drawn to investigate and discover both the world *behind* the stories and the world *of* the stories, because we see in them resources for acting today, thereby creating with God a better world for today and tomorrow – the reign of God. And so, as theologians we ask:

➢ What vision of the reign of God might Teresa of Avila's stories of the way of Jesus hold for us today? How does her story invite us to critique the abuse of power by church leaders and civil leaders?
➢ When Teresa sends forth her sisters to found new convents, what might that mean for us today? How and when do we go forth? For whom do we go forth? What vision of the way of Jesus do we carry?

Teresa created convents where women could learn, pray, and develop leadership skills. Who are those today, in our own cultures, who need a place to gather safely and be fed in mind and spirit, as well as body? How do we respond?

History is not a dead word of the past, but living and breathing in us and all creation. Through our conversation with the stories of our ancestors, God invites us into the divine vision creating a new history – the reign of God. As theologians, we listen and retell the stories of tradition, not simply for antiquarian knowledge, but as a living resource to discern the kind of life God is inviting us to build together in Christ.

## ~Reason~

**Resources for Reflection – Reason**

Scripture, tradition, and reason are the three principle sources Anglicans traditionally draw upon when doing theology. We do this as people situated in a certain time and place, as creatures of history/tradition and culture. Reason can have a critiquing role, helping prevent fundamentalism with respect to both scripture and history. For instance, Christians have always had a tendency to accept the scriptures uncritically, using such approaches as 'proof-texting' – citing words and passages out of context to support a position – or invoking historical precedent as if it possessed absolute authority simply by having happened earlier (called '*historicism*').

How can we draw upon reason in a constructive or positive sense? Narrowly speaking, reason is our intellect. In this sense, reason is like using concepts. However, this is not the only way we 'reason.' *In a broader sense, reason is a way of referring symbolically to the entire self, created in and through the Spirit of God.* Like Jesus, each one of us is Spirit-become-flesh. God's Spirit is the wellspring of the human spirit, or self (often referred to as the 'soul'). In this broader sense, intelligence includes the head, heart, and body. *When we 'do' theology, we bring this entire self* into the act, whether we are aware of it or not.

To understand what we mean by 'reason' or the self (we will use these words interchangeably below), we need to take some time to situate ourselves historically relative to Modernity and Post-Modernity.

## Modernity & Post-Modernity

Many cultural commentators describe the West as being in the time of Post-Modernity, and to speak of Post-Modernity implies the prior existence of something called Modernity. Roughly speaking, historians date the birth of Modernity with that of the Enlightenment, or the Age of Reason – which is around the beginning of the 18th century.

## MODERNITY: REASON AS INSTRUMENTAL
### Modernity's Gifts

After almost 900 years of the 'Middle Ages,' often referred to as the 'dark ages,' a small but influential group of Europeans began to experience the power of reason to observe, measure, and verify. The result was a Western European culture reborn through the *light* of reason – hence the term, en-*lighten*-ment – beginning in the 1700's. Reason, not superstition or magic or the will of the ruler ('might makes right'), was now the source of truth. Truth became primarily a matter of observed, objective, and universal, facts – discovered by intellectual inquiry. The human sciences became the epitome of the exercise of reason, replacing theology as the 'queen of the sciences,' and also the church as the font of truth.

Eventually the 'hard' sciences of objective facts and universal truths emerged to rule the academy: biology, anatomy, physics, chemistry, astronomy, mathematics, etc. Observe, measure, verify. Repeat. *Everything* could be studied by being reduced to an object of observation, measurement, and verification. Many of the leading thinkers of Modernity were *Deists*. The Divine was reduced to the 'clockwork god' or 'the watchmaker god.' The creator simply set the laws of nature in motion and they henceforth operated on their own. For the first time in human history enlightened minds could discover these laws.

The gifts of Modernity shape virtually every aspect of 20th century life: science, art, political theory, human rights, and theology. As a result of the discovery of the laws of nature, people recognized that slavery was an inhumane institution, needing to be dismantled, and women's suffrage was a universal right. These changes were made possible, *in part*, because human beings had the courage to trust the power of human reason to accurately observe, measure, and verify the world.

**Shadow of Modernity**

But Modernity had no proper tools for observing the *internal* dimension of life. The scientific method of the 'hard' sciences came to prevail in much of the so-called social (or soft) sciences. As a result emotions, feelings, and values became immeasurable incidentals. The *ideology* of Modernity (and the Enlightenment) is precisely that its scientific method was calibrated to measure *only* exteriors.

Because the interior spirit couldn't be observed, it essentially *ceased* to exist. In the West, one of the practical consequences of this was that religion ceased to be a public matter and was relegated to the realm of individual private (emotional) piety. Science and religion went their separate ways, with the result that human beings were faced with apparently mutually exclusive possibilities: Darwin or religion; truth or myth; fact or value; reason or emotion; brain or mind; matter or spirit. *Duality* came to reign supreme.

The truth that the scientific empirical method could discover became the *only* truth capable of being discovered. One word for this is 'scientism' another is 'empiricism.' The paradigmatic (or model) figure of Modernity became the lab technician in the white coat, engaging in controlled experiments in the sterile lab. Reason, as embodied in mind, body and spirit, was reduced to the instrument of factual discovery.

## POST-MODERNITY: REASON AS INTERPRETIVE INSIGHT
**Post-Modernity's Gifts**

Beginning in the 1950's, Post-Modernity reacted against virtually every aspect of the age of reason. People discovered that human observation is *not* as straightforward and simple a matter as Modernity had thought. History, context, values, goals, and prejudices of all kinds are always at play when any of us observes anything. Absolute neutrality is not possible for human beings. The completely objective lab technician does *not* exist.

The reality of the role of prejudice became starkly evident in the 1940's through the 1960's. Supposedly objective scientists were enlisted by Hitler and Stalin as well as by the Western powers. Modern scientists researched and constructed atomic weaponry. The scientific method was used to justify the Tuskegee experiments that mutilated African-Americans in the name of research. The Algerian and Vietnam wars created cultural confusion and conflict. And we discovered that the 19th century anti-slavery movement as well as women's suffrage of the 1920's had eliminated neither racism nor sexism.

Facts were not so neutral after all. It seemed that scientists often saw what they went looking for. On the most elemental level, that of quantum physics, Werner Heisenberg (1901-1976) discovered (relying upon the scientific method) that 'The more precisely the position [of an electron] is determined, the less precisely the momentum is known in this instant, and vice versa.' Ken Wilber describes the discovery of this Heisenberg Uncertainty Principle: 'There is no way around this fact. Because one small particle will always move another small particle, any act of measurement will interfere with what you are trying to measure. A small particle's location, to some degree, will always be 'uncertain.'"[13]

This means that the more we may know where something is, the less we know about where it is going. A basic assumption of physics since Newton had been that a 'real world' exists utterly independently of us, regardless of whether or not we observe it. Heisenberg's discovery confirmed how *inter*dependent reality is. He was not saying, as some assert, that reality is simply the creation of the human mind. Rather, the human mind is an integral part of reality and it affects, in unpredictable ways, the unfolding story of the universe. What the scientist saw and measured did indeed depend upon what the scientist was looking for.

Post-Modern cultural theorists had their own counterpart to this quantum discovery on the macro-level of human affairs. Their 'deconstruction' of Modernity ruthlessly stripped away the veneer of neutrality of art, history, cultural studies, political science, etc., to reveal self-interested individuals and cultures at play.

In Post-Modernity there is no longer a single history of the United States of America 'out there' to be known. Rather, there is history as creatively told by numerous distinct groups, such as women, African Americans, Mexican Americans, Cuban Americans, Native Americans, heterosexuals, homosexuals, etc. Each person, each group, has their own interests or prejudices, and thus sees different facts and tells different truths. As these particular stories are told, they take apart, or deconstruct, the previous story that 'everyone took for granted' (such as Columbus *discovered* America). Reality is not discovered; it is constructed by human thought.

Interpretation, not facts, became the key to understanding human beings. Even more, in the end, according to Post-Modernity, there are no facts out there to discover; interpretation is *all* we have. Human beings create all the elements of the story told. We do not discover them. No universal truths exist; there are only partial interpretations that we are continually creating.

What Post-Modernity discovered is that the human community is where meaning is created. Since there are many different communities, there are many shades of meaning to convey. As a result, dialogue becomes of paramount importance. Each single community can only have a partial thread of the larger unfolding story being created by the multiple communities of this world.

## Shadow of Post-Modernity

Post-Modernity exposed the naiveté of Modernity's scientific method. There is no such thing as a *bare* fact. Every scientist, as a human being, brings an agenda to every inquiry. The knowledge we obtain about anything is always constructed from a context: a past, a present, a hoped for future. But – and this is critical – simply because all knowledge is contextual does not mean that we do not know anything about the real world. In other words, yes, human interpretation is always at work whenever we know anything. That does not mean, however, that facts do not exist. For example: if you drop a knife on your hand you will cut it open. This is true whether you are black, white, homosexual, heterosexual, northern hemisphere, southern hemisphere, 21st century or 10th century BCE The fact is you are now cut. What the act of injuring your hand *means* for you, for others, etc., is a matter of *interpretation*. But the *fact* remains as a *fact*.

The ideology of Post-Modernity results in a cacophony of interpretations. This cacophony is sometimes called 'relativistic pluralism.' In relativistic pluralism each and every voice has as much right to its interpretation of reality as anyone else: the Klu Klux Klan, the Girl Scouts, Al Quaeda, the Sierra Club, La Cosa Nostra, and Young Republicans. Each group offers an interpretation claiming its right to the story as it is perceived. There are no facts, no sense of objective truth, to make a claim on the subject's own ego. There are no universal standards.

# Chapter 2 – An Integral Theology

Where do we as theologians go from here? Are we left in an either/or dilemma? Must we choose: Fact or interpretation? Or, is there a way to draw upon the insights offered by both Modernity and Post-Modernity?

What we need is an integrated understanding of the self or an integral theology. All too often today we have a situation somewhat akin to the proverb of the blindfolded people and the elephant. Each discipline (such as psychology, biology, cultural studies, or systems theories) only has hold of one part of the body and yet is utterly convinced that it has the entire creature. What if we removed the blindfolds and discovered that the self is a much more complex creature than originally thought and that *each* discipline has *an* insight? For a picture of the whole to emerge theology needs to draw upon and *integrate* each perception.

American philosopher Ken Wilber is at the forefront of developing an integral theory that acknowledges the wisdom found in psychology, biology, cultural studies and systems thinking, for example, without choosing between them.

What Wilber has done is identify four basic areas into which all the different disciplines for studying life can be categorized. He calls these four areas 'quadrants'. None of the four quadrants is more important than the others and all of them are interrelated. We don't have to choose science over religion, or spirituality over biology. As we will see shortly, the four quadrants can help theology situate and draw upon the contributions of Modernity and Post-Modernity, as well as much else.

**The Four Quadrants in Brief**

Although Wilber's integral approach has application across every academic discipline, we will narrow our discussion to how it applies to theology. For each quadrant there is a particular question that runs to the heart of its focus:

> Who am I?        What am I?
>
> Who are we?      What are we?

As you can see, the questions alternate between 'who' and 'what,' as well as between a focus on the individual and the collective. The 'who' question brings our attention to what is going on inside of the person or the collective, whereas the 'what' question directs us to the outside or surface of the person or the collective. Graphically, we might represent the four questions this way.

**An Integral Approach to the Self and Theology**

*individual*

| Who am I? | What am I? |
|---|---|
| Who are we? | What are we? |

*internal* — Spirit — *external*

*collective*

## Who am I?

Since the dawn of humanity, human beings have asked the question 'Who am I?' Later, psychology would re-formulate this question as 'How does my sense of 'I' or 'self' form?' This is a question that goes to the heart, or to the interior, of individual human existence. And yet neither Modernity nor Post-Modernity had the ability to adequately grapple with it.

'Who am I?' is perhaps the most ancient and pressing question of the human condition. It has persisted through the ages, especially in the lives of the mystics of every wisdom tradition. Each of us wants to know, needs to know, who we are. In *Part 6, A Compassionate Whole*, we will see how fiercely this question burns in the prophetic book of Micah, in Paul's letter to the Philippians, and in the mystical writings of Julian of Norwich. 'Who am I?' asks not only who we are as individuals, but also who 'God' is, in whose image we have been created.

In the last two centuries, depth psychology has joined the mystics in the search for inner meaning. Psychologists (such as Freud and Jung) and mystics (such as Theresa of Avila and Julian of Norwich) each, in their own way, has sought to respond to the question, 'who am I?'. Oftentimes this question has been cast in the language of human longing to know intimately our own deep, personal beauty. Depth psychology and spirituality are disciplines that help us know who we are and thereby embody our full beauty. An incarnational, sacramental theology recognizes this embodiment for what it truly is: the very flowering of the beautiful divine Spirit in history.

## What am I?

Science, that marvelous gift of Modernity, asks a second question: 'What is going on physically, bio-chemically, as the human person develops?' *What* makes it possible for the 'I' that each of us is, to develop? With this question we have left the interior world of meaning and beauty. We are no longer asking a question about 'who' but 'what'. '*What* am I?' 'What is it that makes me tick?'

Physics, biology, neurology, behaviorist psychology, are just a few of the sciences that study what it is that makes life tick. Modernity was not all wrong. Objectively speaking, we can know certain undeniable and unwavering, universal, truths about the human being. One of them is that every internal spiritual expression has an external biological or physiological correlate. When a human being has a hope or a dream or a fear, there is a corresponding firing of neurons in the brain, and hormones being released, etc.

> That thoughts and feelings can affect our health is hardly news. In the span of a few decades, mind-body medicine has evolved from heresy into something approaching cliché....the relationship between emotion and health is turning out to be more interesting, and more important, than most of us could have imagined. Viewed through the lens of 21st-century science, anxiety, alienation and hopelessness are not just feelings. Neither are love, serenity and optimism. All are physiological states that affect our health just as clearly as obesity or physical fitness. And the brain, as the source of such states, offers a potential gateway to countless other tissues and organs—from the heart and blood vessels to the gut and the immune system. The challenge is to map the pathways linking mental states to medical ones, and learn how to travel them at will.[14]

'Who am I?' and 'what am I?' go together. What we eat affects how we feel. Physical exercise can change the meditative state of someone at prayer. There is an undeniably intimate, integral connection between thought and emotions and human chemistry. This does not mean, as some scientists would like to claim, that spirituality can be reduced to biology or physics. That would be the ideology of scientism we spoke of earlier, and represents a shadow cast by Modernity.

An integral theology recognizes the importance of both questions, 'who am I?' and 'what am I'? An integral theology acknowledges *both* beauty *and* truth, interiority *and* exteriority, mind *and* brain, as interconnected manifestations of the Spirit of God.

**Who are we?**

We have discussed the interior and exterior dimensions of the *individual* self. But human beings are social creatures. Broadly speaking, this is the *collective* aspect of human existence. 'Who are we?' is a shorthand way of asking, 'Why is it that human beings are communal creatures?' Or, 'How does community even form?' This question, 'who are we?' takes us into a very different arena than our first two questions. Now the focus is on *us*. How do 'we' form community from a group of very different persons? This is a question about common values, common goals, and a *common good*.

In this quadrant of the integral approach are scholars who try to understand what the *common* good *is* that holds groups together. What is it that people value so dearly that it bonds them together to sacrifice and even die for the creation and sustaining of a *common* life: education, commerce, politics, art, medicine, leisure? We will see in *Chapter 17, The Way of Self-Emptying*, that it is this very question that is central in Paul's letter to the Philippians.

Countless diverse communities exist in our world today. Each has a story to tell about what it means to live, work, play, dream, and worship, together. If we go back to the ancient Greeks and Romans, we discover philosophers (such as Plato, Aristotle, and Cicero) who were passionately concerned about how we human beings manage to live together and find meaning in 'our' lives. Adam Smith explored community through ethics and economics. Thomas Kuhn pioneered the study of changes in science and community through his theory of paradigms. Sociologist Max Weber, the founder of modern sociology, studied religion, economics, and politics in his quest to understand how human community works.

Who am I? What am I? Who are we? These three questions, basic and as simple as they are each contain their own disciplines of study. All too often the disciplines within the different areas, or quadrants, have isolated themselves from each other. But the questions about what we understand as beautiful, true and good are *inter*dependent. Each, in its own way, manifests the Spirit of God present in life. Each question requires the attention of theology.

**What are we?**

Once again we find ourselves asking a question about 'what' makes it possible for people to function; however our context now is the collective. Our attention shifts from the interior dimension (the 'place' of values and dreams) back to the exterior dimension. A community may be committed to a common good, hold common values, and treasure a common dream, but what is the 'glue' that actually holds the good, the values, and the dream together? What makes the common good actually work?

When we looked earlier at human beings as a collective from the *inside*, what we were exploring was the 'soul' of human community. We can also look at human beings as a collective from the *outside*. Whenever we hear someone talking about *systems* theory or *systems* thinking, we are looking at the outside, the exterior, of human community. If we use the human body as our metaphor, systems are the skeleton and muscle (the glue) that hold the body together – you cannot have one without the other.

One way to think of systems thinkers is as mapmakers. They chart the interrelationships between the things (churches, schools, clubs, not-for-profits, etc.) that exist in and as community. Fundamentally, systems thinking is an extension of the Enlightenment paradigm whose method was that of observe, measure, verify. If not balanced with the other quadrants, systems thinking tends to reduce, or flatten, everything to a number.

Let us take another look at the graphical representation of the four quadrants.

## An Integral Theology

These four questions are universal -- Who am I? What am I? Who are we? What are we? Each and every human being, from whatever time and culture, asks them, in some fashion. For those of us in the Christian tradition this will come as no surprise. We are created in the image of the Triune God (the divine community) whom the Hebrew people encountered as 'I am who I am' – which is the first question turned into a statement. God is the living answer to the human question. The human, as made in the divine image, is thus a living question whose answer can only be found in the heart of God, who is also our heart (as we shall see in *Chapter 18*, with Julian of Norwich).

Through these four questions we grapple with what is most important to us, and all that is important to us. Modernity and Post-Modernity have each restricted the scope of our gaze to only a piece of the larger, integral whole. As theologians we need to learn how to be in dialogue with all four questions because the Spirit of God is present and manifest in the whole, described so well by the four quadrants. Otherwise, our theology is mistaking a small piece for the magnificent whole.

# Chapter 3 – Theology as Transformative

> Theologians mumble, rumble-dumble,
> necessity and free will,
> while lover and Beloved
>     pull themselves
>         into each other.     Rumi[15]

> All that I have written seems to me like straw
> compared to what has now been revealed to me.
>         Thomas Aquinas[16]

> Someone asks, 'Do you know the prophet Noah?'
> You may answer, 'Well, I've     read stories in school.
> I've heard legends that have come down.'
> But only someone in Noah's state can *know* him.
> Now I hear a theologian reacting,
>     'Don't get stuck in that ditch!
>         Rumi[17]

**Theology: Personal Transformation**

To do theology, we need to be engaged with the personally transformative question, 'who am I?' Otherwise, theology is like so much 'straw.' For theology to be meaningful, it must be an expression of what we have experienced, in all of its beauty. Otherwise, all our talk about God is not much more than 'mumble, rumble-dumble.'

The theologian is not someone who settles for knowing *about* God. The theologian is someone who speaks only because she knows God. '*Only* someone in Noah's state,' cries Rumi, 'can *know* him.' Without the direct *experience* the language is dry straw. The language is straw because the soul itself is parched. Theology is a living language only because the theologian is on fire with the divine presence. When we talk of knowing God, the knowledge we are speaking of here is direct, personal experience of the divine, not emotionalism. It is the knowledge Jesus has of God in his experience at baptism. Jesus knows (experiences) himself immediately as God's beloved. This experience is the wellspring of his teaching with authority; his immediate knowledge that God is always already well-pleased with him is the soul of his theology.

To follow the way of Jesus is to become a theologian like Jesus, where theology is born of the direct experience of one's own belovedness. An integral theology is a theology grounded in the mystical experience of the

Spirit. Theology is in part, therefore, a response to the divine question beating in the human heart: 'who am I?' Theology is an expression of spirituality.

'Who am I?' is a broad question that has several dimensions, such as moral, psychosocial, interpersonal, emotional and cognitive. What concerns us here is its spiritual dimension. St. Augustine reminds us that the human spirit is restless until it rests in God. Julian of Norwich teaches us that we are enclosed in God and God in us, but we do not see it. Ken Wilber speaks of the divine being always already present. The human journey, indeed the journey of all creation, is to become aware of the always already present God unfolding in and through us. We can understand theology as that discipline that speaks of this unfolding, which is the very unfolding of the theologian herself.

Theology always reflects who the theologian is. For theology to be transformative and not so much 'straw,' we, as theologians, need to be engaged in the spiritual journey. To engage wisely in the journey requires a map of the spiritual terrain. We need to be able to identify the passions/vices that drive us. We need to be able to discern what the virtues are that strengthen us to be receptive to life. We need to become aware of the different foci of attention that tend to fixate our minds and lead us astray.

**The Enneagram**

For theologians, the Enneagram offers an enormously helpful legend for navigating the soul's journey. What is the Enneagram? What can it teach us about the passions, virtues, and fixations of the mind, all of which affect the spiritual journey of the theologian? What kind of transformative wisdom does it offer?

**What is the Enneagram? Gurdjieff's Diagram**

George Gurdjieff (1877-1949) was an Armenian mystic whose own teaching was influenced by Christian mysticism and Sufism (the mystical tradition within Islam). Gurdjieff coined the term, 'Enneagram,' which means nine types or ways. 'Ennea' is Greek for nine and 'gram,' in this context, connotes way or type. Although he introduced both the concept of the 'chief feature' (which we will discuss later) and the geometric Enneagram star (see Figure A, page 40), Gurdjieff did not develop an Enneagram psychology/spirituality of personality types.

The Enneagram is a map of the spiritual journey. But it is more than one map. Since Gurdjieff, the Enneagram has evolved and offers many maps, each of which is interrelated to the others. There is an Enneagram of vices/passions, of virtues, of personality and fixations (or foci of attention), to name just three. Each map contains nine points that are affixed to the nine edges of the geometric star. The points never vary and each Enneagram map adds dynamic depth to our understanding of the spiritual journey.

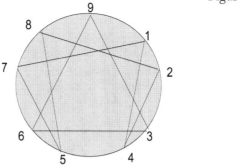

Figure A

## Early Wisdom of Evagrius: Distracting Thoughts

313 CE is a watershed year in the West. Constantine emerged as the emperor of Rome and he credited the Christian God for his victory. Christianity was drawn out of the shadows of persecution and anointed the official religion of the empire. For many, the age of Christendom also heralded the demise of the way of Jesus. Social status, not spiritual search, characterized much of the new official religion.

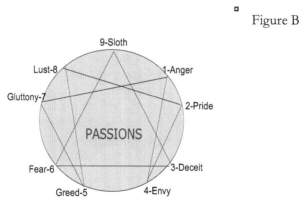

Figure B

## Enneagram of Vices/Passions/Distracting Thoughts

Slowly, but surely, many women and men began to hunger for their own direct experience of the God of Jesus. They moved to the wilderness and became known as desert monks.

Evagrius Ponticus (345 to 399 CE) was among the scores of desert monks. Originally from what today is modern Turkey, he left city-life behind and sought God in the quiet of the Nitrian wilderness. We discover through his writings that the journey of the desert monastics (also known as anchorites) was neither romantic nor smooth. Again and again these women and men encountered spiritual obstacles, which Evagrius describes as distracting 'thoughts.' The monk could not blame a corrupt culture or busy city life as the sources of these distracting thoughts. They emerged from a place none other than the monk's own soul.

Evagrius, a student of Basil of Caesarea and later Gregory of Nazianzus, Melania the Elder, Macarius the Egyptian, and influenced deeply by the theology of Origen, identified eight vices or 'distracting 'thoughts' that impede the way to God and to passionless peace of heart.' His starting point, it seems, was Matthew's rather enigmatic statement about an unclean spirit (Matthew. 12: 43-45):

> *When an unclean spirit goes out of a person it wanders through arid places searching for rest. When it finds none, it says, 'I will return to the home I left.' And upon returning, it finds its old house empty and swept clean. Then it goes and brings back seven other spirits more evil than itself, and they enter and set up housekeeping; the person ends up far worse than before. And that is how it will be with this evil generation!*

A surprise to many readers is that the first passion Evagrius lists is not that of pride, but gluttony. Through listening to the other monks, he discovered that gluttony was the kind of vice that 'incorporates' (takes into its very self) the other seven vices. In the language of spirituality, gluttony means much more than physical hunger. Gluttony is the restless and incessant hunger of the mind for more -- more and more thoughts so that the self is constantly distracted from being present here and now to God. Each of the other vices (anger, pride, vanity, sadness/avarice, lust and laziness/acedia), in its own way, distracts the human soul, orienting the mind to the past or future, away from the only place God is actually to be known: here and now.

Evagrius' list of eight vices was later reduced to seven by Pope Gregory the Great and comes down to us in the West as the seven deadly sins: anger, pride, envy, greed, gluttony, lust and sloth. We find these sins surfacing in classic literature such as Dante's *Purgatorio* and Chaucer's *Canterbury Tales*.

The experience of the early desert monastics is not unique, and in fact echoes similar experiences in Buddhism almost 1000 years earlier. Evagrius, however, not only had the patience and skills to listen to the monks relate their spiritual journeys. He had the ability to discern the underlying patterns, thereby laying the foundation for what was to become known as the Enneagram.

### Medieval Wisdom: Sufi Sensuous Surrender to the Beloved

The Spirit unfolds because she is drawn inexorably to taste who she is. 'Who am I?' is not an abstract or speculative consideration. As a lover longs for the beloved, so the self desires above all else to know who she is. The flow of the Spirit is that of unfolding. The distracting thoughts Evagrius catalogued are not unique to the desert monastics, they describe the human condition. It should not be unexpected that we find the desert spirituality of vices resurfacing centuries later, being used and developed by the Sufis.

The Sufi mystical tradition, like that of Christian desert monasticism, is quite practical in orientation. Sufis offer spiritual guidance to those desiring to know the Beloved here and now. The great Sufi mystic and poet, Jelaluddin Rumi (1207-73), wrote the poem, *Some Kiss We Want*. It exquisitely expresses the spiritual longing of the human heart:

> There is some kiss we want with
> our whole lives, the touch of
> 
> spirit on the body. Seawater
> begs the pearl to break its shell.
> 
> And the lily, how passionately
> it needs some wild darling! At
> 
> night, I open the window and ask
> the moon to come and press its
> 
> face against mine. *Breathe into
> me*. Close the language-door and
> 
> open the love-window. The moon
> won't use the door, only the window.[18]

'Close the language-door and open the love-window.' Language is important but the source of language, especially language about God (or theology), is the direct experience of divine love. The only task of the self is to open the window so that love, ever-present, might 'press its face against mine.' We don't open the door and walk through, rather we let up the window and receive the divine moon; we surrender to the kiss of the divine face. Sufi spirituality brings profound knowledge of tenderness, sensuality and surrender into what will become the Enneagram.

### Contemporary Wisdom: Gurdjieff, Ichazo, Naranjo

Evagrius identified the 'thoughts' that distract the soul's search for God; or, as the Sufis would say, that distort the direct experience of the Beloved. Similar to Evagrius, Gurdjieff recognized that every personality has a bias, which we take to be 'normal'. Our compass is skewed and we don't even know it. Our experience of the Beloved is distorted but we cannot see it.

Whereas Evagrius speaks of disrupting thoughts and passions, Gurdjieff speaks in terms of the 'Chief Feature'. He describes it this way:

> It is very important at a certain stage of self-study to find one's Chief Feature, which means chief weakness, like the axis round which everything turns....Always the same motive moves the Chief Feature. It tips the scales. It is like a bias in bowling, which prevents the ball going straight. Always the Chief Feature makes us go off at a tangent. It arises from one or more of the seven deadly sins, but chiefly from self-love and vanity. One can discover it by becoming more conscious; and its discovery brings an increase of consciousness.[19]

In the 1960's Bolivian Oscar Ichazo had the insight of associating Christianity's seven capital sins (Evagrius's distracting thoughts and Gurdjieff's chief features) to each of the nine points on the Enneagram star. He also added two more: Deception/Vanity at Point 3 and Fear at Point 6.

It is unclear as to exactly how Ichazo came to his insight. He claims to have learned from Sufi masters in Afghanistan as well as Gurdjieff's own writings. Ichazo, more than anyone, transformed the Enneagram into a 20th century psychological typology. Language sometimes differs among Enneagram teachers – passions, vices, chief features – but the central idea remains the same.

Ichazo also discovered how the types are interconnected and flow in and out of each other. He incorporated this flow-pattern into Gurdjieff's nine-pointed star through the use of arrows. With these two developments of Ichazo we have what is now called the Enneagram of Passions (see above, Figure B).

Perhaps the most important development of Ichazo is that his correct placement of the types on the Enneagram enabled teachers to *verify* the relationships among the types through interviews. The interview process meant that type description could be based upon data gathered from actual people, rather than speculation.

Claudio Naranjo, a Chilean psychiatrist, and student of Ichazo, adapted the Enneagram still further. He correlated the nine personality types with contemporary Western psychology. In essence, he brought spirituality and psychology, Evagrius and Freud, together.

> His contribution to the Enneagram successfully joined the insight and methods of a mystical path of transformation with the intellectual power of a Western psychological model....Naranjo gained his insight by interviewing individuals who were psychologically sophisticated, and who could describe their preoccupations of heart and mind. One of his Enneagrams is a

mapping of the major defense mechanism that supports each of the nine.[20]

## Wisdom of Enneagram Matures:
## Palmer and Daniel Develop Self-Discovery through Narrative

Over the last 30 years the Enneagram has evolved in different ways. Helen Palmer (who attended an early workshop of Naranjo) and Stanford Psychiatrist David Daniels have partnered to establish a unique school within the Enneagram field, centered on the personal narrative. This narrative tradition has interviewed well over 30,000 people providing an enormous wealth of empirical data to verify the Enneagram system of spirituality and psychology. In her book, *The Enneagram*, Palmer notes that she has 'made it a policy to verify an issue by presenting it to panels [groups of individuals who are all one Enneagram type] over and over again before including it within the characteristics of a type' (see Figure C)

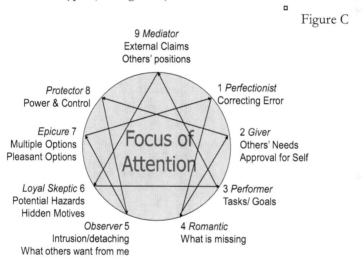

Figure C

When a trained Enneagram teacher interviews an individual or a panel the principle characteristics of a type become self-evident and self-validating. Each of the nine types has a distinct world-view which forms in early childhood, through a combination of nature and nurture. An Enneagram type, or ego, is an inevitable and necessary human development. We lay claim to our place in life and win the love we need to survive through our ego.

## Enneagram of Type: Where Attention Goes

Through exploring the work of Gurdjieff, we discover clearly how each Enneagram type has a bias; we lean in a direction we assume to be true north.

For example, the bias of the Enneagram Type 1 filters life through the lens of perfection. The mind is inevitably drawn to focus on correcting error. Out of all of the million bits of data received through the senses, the Perfectionist-1 naturally selects those bits that need to be corrected and improved. In this way the bias is reinforced and preserved: God becomes a demanding and ever-vigilant divinity who requires moral rectitude and the church reduced to a select group of the supposedly pure elect.

Through our ego, each of us perceives our world differently, depending upon both nature and nurture. Where the Perfectionist-1 focuses on correcting error and creates a God in this image, the Loyal Skeptic-6, forever fixes her gaze on the horizon searching for certainty and noticing potential hazards. God becomes the rule-maker who guarantees predictability and safety in a dangerous world. The church becomes a safe-haven, a bulwark against an unpredictable life, obsessed with orthodoxy and loyalty.

None of us is raised in an environment that holds us perfectly. Each of us, in the midst of our imperfect family environments, develops a strategy, mostly unconscious, to survive and gain the attention we need that assures us of our place in life. The Enneagram type is our survival strategy. The Perfectionist-1 is partly right, there is error in life. But that is a very small piece of the bigger picture. A life and theology constructed on such a partial vision is a basis for religious zealotry and crusades. Through the spiritual journey of transformation, the passionate anger of the '1' is converted into serenity. We see this journey in the life of the zealous Saul, fixated on routing out and even killing the unorthodox Jews. Through his conversion he becomes Paul, someone who envisions a community in which all are equal and welcome (Galatians 3:28): 'In Christ there is no Jew or Greek, slave or citizen, male or female. All are one in Christ Jesus.'

Each of us, created in the image of a loving and trusting God, is originally held in the bliss of the divine embrace. It is also true that for each of us we lose touch with this embrace and its immediacy fades into the background. In its place we develop strategies to survive and win the love we feel, sense, or think we have lost. In other words, our ego develops. The Enneagram type is the self's way of compensating, at a very early age, for the felt loss of the divine embrace.

Our Enneagram type – and no type is better or worse than another – serves us each so well in the first half of life, as we establish an individual identity, find partners, embark on careers, and start families. Sooner or later, however, the bias of our fixation results in suffering for ourselves and others, over and over again. We ask ourselves, 'Why does this continually happen?' We react by developing theologies whose concept of God is constricted by our fixations: A God who demands perfection (Perfectionist-1), demands achievement (Performer-3), demands obedience (Loyal Skeptic-6), demands power and control (Protector-8). We create churches and ethical systems driven by our vices. They do not liberate us, but on the contrary, hold us captive and dominate our lives by reinforcing our types.

Essential to the spiritual journey for each Enneagram type is the process of learning to *let go and receive the gift of transformation*. For a rare few this journey begins in their teens. But for the majority of us it commences after we have hit 'the wall' in some way, and our formerly reliable type structure is unable to propel us over one more time. Like Saul, life has thrown us to the ground, as we have become blinded by our own fixations and drives. Such a fall, however, is grace: the invitation of the Spirit can now be more readily felt and heard.

In *Part VII, Transformation: God's Abiding Presence,* we explore how if we, as theologians, are to understand who we are in our essence ('who am I?'), as an unfolding of the Spirit, then we need to learn to surrender and inquire. The Enneagram offers a detailed map of what we are to let go of. Every type needs to let go of its egoic grip and control of life. The Enneagram shows us the face of our ego, making it easier for us to become aware of when our type is driving us through life and into those painful walls.

The Enneagram does not put a person at war with herself. The wisdom of the Enneagram is that type structure is a constricted expression of our true self. Meditation is one of the essential spiritual practices for learning to let go. In meditation we learn to gaze lovingly and tenderly at our ego. We develop the practice of watching our fixations and passions arise before our awareness. We don't try to suppress them or embrace them, but gently receive them into our awareness and allow them to pass. Gradually, our fixations and passions begin to soften and fade. What arises is gracious space, space for the true self – one's true essence – to slowly emerge and be.

The Enneagram helps us, as theologians, to identify where it is we get stuck in our spiritual journey home. Coming to know ourselves is a matter of softening the various barriers that keep us from directly experiencing our belovedness, which is our true Christ-self. As we awaken to the truth that God is always and already at-one with us and all creation, our souls begin to unfold into lives and ministry of unbounded compassion.

As theologians, we will now explore some of the pivotal stories from the scriptures and saints and discover in them the abiding invitation to know life as a compassionate whole.

# ~Exploring an Integral Theology~

**Three Sources**

Theology draws upon the wisdom of scriptures, traditions, and reason (entire self), to guide its reflections and discoveries. What is your understanding of these three sources and your comfort in using each? Which do you find yourself turning to more often? Which do you avoid? Can you remember a time when you perceived an inconsistency (or contradiction) between the sources or within them (for example, divergent creation accounts in Genesis)?

**Doing Theology (a group activity)**

We can theologize about any experience, because God is always present, in some way inviting us to reflect upon and continue our faith journey. As a group, practice doing theology in community. Choose an experience upon which to reflect together, drawing upon the three resources to assist you – scriptures, traditions, and reason (entire self). It could be a decision facing your congregation or denomination, or facing your community (a piece of legislation pending or a conflict needing to be resolved in your community).

- ➤ How does each resource give you a different perspective on your experience?
- ➤ How do different members of the group draw upon the scriptures, traditions, reason (entire self)?
- ➤ Are you more inclined to 'see' your experience through one source rather than another? How is this a strength and a weakness in your perception?
- ➤ How do you see God present in your life in and through this experience?

**Use of the Scriptures in Film**

View one or two of the following films. How are *the world behind the scriptures*, *the world of the scriptures*, and *the world envisioned by the scriptures* portrayed in the film(s)?

| | |
|---|---|
| The Color Purple | Pieces of April |
| Malcolm X | Places of the Heart |
| The Matrix | The Ten Commandments |
| The Passion | |

# PART II

## BEYOND STATUS AND SECURITY

"And because all things are consonant with God,
these souls find God in all things."
Marguerite Porete[21]

> *Either we acknowledge that God is in all things*
> *or we have lost the basis*
> *for seeing God in anything.*
> Richard Rohr, OFM

Through our explorations of Jeremiah, Paul and Francis we will discover how the relationship with security, status and sacrifice plays a central role in their faith journeys. The painful historical truth is that often there is no end to which human beings will not go to destroy a threat to security and status. To justify our sacrifice of other human beings we will invoke the name of God in prayer, liturgy and song. It would appear that virtually every culture from the foundation of the world has been able to find "good" reasons to identify and then kill an 'enemy,' weaving together violence and the sacred in the dominant theology.

In Jeremiah, Paul and Francis we will encounter figures that pierced the temple veil, allowing humanity a glimpse of the true divine love which courses through the life of all creation. In the end, this emerging theology of divine compassion begins to challenge the validity that a theology of divine wrath has had over humanity's fearful heart.

# Chapter 4 – Faint Glimmer of Empathy: Jeremiah

## God's Ways Are Not Our Ways
### Violence and the Sacred

It is possible to theologize on any experience. If we can name or describe the experience, we can reflect upon it, converse with it, attempting to discover how the divine is present, and in the light of that divine presence, how best to respond. The prophets of the Hebrew Scriptures are keen observers of Israel. They are courageous observers as well, for they do not shy away from the underbelly, or the experiences of pain and suffering, endeavoring over and over again to discover how God is present and what this means for Israel's life.

Contemporary philosopher Rene Gerard points out that since the 'foundation of the world,' violence has been associated with humanity's experience of the sacred. From Cain and Abel to the present, it is impossible (at least in the West) to observe and reflect upon humanity's encounter with the sacred without talking about violence – often said to be done either by God or in God's name or for a just cause sanctioned by God. Two words which seem wedded together in the stories of Judaism and Christianity are '*Violence*' and '*Sacred.*'

Girard has been a leading voice beckoning Christianity to reconsider this presumed link between violence and the sacred. He believes that the prophets, in particular, can help us reflect in a new way about who God is and how God is present in our lives. In his book, *Things Hidden Since the Foundation of the World*, Girard describes how we are thoroughly accustomed to thinking that God sanctions and works through violence, and this unquestioned belief blinds us to something God has been trying to reveal to us since the beginning. If we are able to unveil violence, we will discover that as human beings we are crossroads of survival. We are being given a rather stark choice: violence or life. Although we often confuse them – God's ways are not our ways. The prophets, such as Jeremiah, can help us to discover a different way: the way of life, the way of God.

### Primitive Religion and Sacrifice

To appreciate Jeremiah's profound new insight, we need to understand that *many religions*, including the religion of the Hebrew people, *are* founded upon violence. As human societies became larger, more impersonal and more hierarchical, many of them adopted ritual sacrifice of animals and often other humans. Ostensibly, such sacrifices were done to secure the favor of the god(s) and/or to restore or maintain balance and harmony in the cosmos, but they also served the socio-political function of validating and sustaining the power of the leaders by invoking special religious authority.

Typically, the sacrifice was effective only for a while, and then, with the completion of a cycle of the universe or the emergence of a new crisis, another ritual sacrifice would be necessary. The god(s), the cosmos, the society, required it. Often ritual sacrifice was a kind of catharsis, whereby the people could project (or lay) their anger, hostility, desire for vengeance, upon the sacrificial victim.

Where was God perceived to be in the midst of such sacrifice? With those who sacrificed. God required human sacrifice in order to be satisfied. Abraham's 'almost' sacrifice of Isaac reflects this demand of primitive religion. The biblical references to high altars scattered throughout the land of Israel speak to the common presence of these places of human sacrifice. The alternative to such sacrifice was understood to be social chaos, cosmic disorder, and massive wars. And so, we read even in the gospels, 'It is better that one man should die than that the whole nation be destroyed.'(John 11:50) The high priest Caiaphas is simply echoing the inherited 'wisdom' of sacrificing a human victim to 'save' the nation from war and regain the peace. Again, we ask, *where is God in this sacrifice?* The conviction (that is, *theology*) held by many is that God is making the demand for sacrifice. To speak somewhat simplistically, God is the Violator and we, created in God's image, are violators. Gil Bailie puts it this way:

> ...cultures have forever commemorated some form of sacred violence at their origins and considered it a sacred duty to reenact it in times of crisis. The logic of sacred violence is nowhere expressed more succinctly nor repudiated more completely than in the New Testament, where the high priest announces its benefits and the crucifixion straightaway reveals its arbitrariness and horror. The New Testament account of the crucifixion reproduces the myths and mechanisms of primitive religion [such as the sacrifice of Jesus the victim on the cross to satisfy Rome and some of the Jewish authorities] only to explode them, reveal their perversities, and declare allegiance to the Victim of them.[22]

Bailie is describing an earth-shattering shift that deconstructs our understanding of how God is present in creation. And when does this shift happen, that we come to perceive God as aligned not with the Violator, but with the Victim? Jeremiah lies at the heart of this transformation in faith and theology.

## From Violator to Victim

The majority of scholars hold that Jeremiah began his prophetic ministry in 627 BCE, during the thirteenth year of the reign of King Josiah. His ministry continued over the next forty-five years, 'holding the record for prophetic activity.' Jeremiah prophesies during the reforms of Josiah, during the reign of King Jehoiakim (Josiah's son, 609-598), as well as through the first and second destruction of Jerusalem by the Babylonians (598 and 586). Legend has it that in the end, he was stoned to death by his own people in Egypt.

Jeremiah lived during a time of tremendous social upheaval and chaos, when things were falling apart at the seams for Israel. The temple, which was understood to be the divine sanctuary and guarantee of God's presence and protection of the people, was destroyed not once, but twice. What should the response of the people be to such brutal violence? Where was God now and what was God asking them to do and to be in response to the Babylonian invasion?

This is a major turning point in Israel's history, Gil Bailie tells us. And our question again arises: Where is God to be found? In the early prophets, such as Micaiah (see 1 Kings 22:26-28), we see a willingness to champion 'the *cause* of victims.' These prophets seem to have been willing to challenge the mighty and even 'suffered their intermittent scorn.' Jeremiah and the other latter prophets go a considerable step further. They are willing 'to actually suffer the *plight* of victims.' Jeremiah begins to see that God is to be found not in retribution, not in ritual sacrifice demanded to appease that God, angry with our moral and/or religious failure, but *in the very victims of the violence*.[23]

One of the consequences of this shift by the latter prophets such as Jeremiah is that often they are not beloved by their own people. The people have grown accustomed to vengeance as cathartic. They *want* to retaliate. It is seen as the 'reasonable' course of action. But now Jeremiah is offering another response rooted in the dawning awareness that 'God's ways are not our ways,' particularly and especially when it comes to violence. God does not divide and conquer. God embraces and forgives (70 times 7, as the gospels will later remind us). Jeremiah is courageous because the center of his identity is neither himself nor the people whom he serves. His center is God – God who is trying to speak a new word or an old word in a new way, so that people can see through the veil of violence that for so long has clouded their vision of the divine.

Jeremiah is capable of seeing God in the victims of violence because he himself is a prophet who suffers violence. And here we come to a pivotal point. Jeremiah has a revealing word to speak about God because he himself has suffered. His own suffering has begun to bring to birth in him and through him a new sensibility and awareness. Israel remains embedded within a world cowered to *divine wrath* (Jer. 1:17-19; 6:11; Lamentations 4:11). In the life of Jeremiah and the other prophets, we begin to 'see the first faint outlines of a world made morally intelligible by *divine empathy*.'[24] In Jeremiah's call we see the God-centered life of this prophet, the foreseeing of social upheaval, as well as intimations of divine empathy.

> *But you, gird up your loins; stand up and tell them everything that I command you. Do not break down before them, or I will break you before them. And I for my part have made you today a fortified city, and iron pillar, and a bronze wall, against the whole land – against the kings of Judah, its princes, its priests, and the people of the land. They will fight against you; but they shall not prevail against you, for I am with you, says the LORD, to deliver you. (Jeremiah. 1:17-19. NRSV)*

Jeremiah is a prophet precisely as a victim of his society's violence. 'Especially in the extraordinary cases of Jeremiah and Second Isaiah, the suffering of the prophet at the hands of his society *was* his prophetic message.'[25] Where is God? God is with the victims of unjust and brutal violence – whoever they may be. God is in the words uttered by the one killed in war. Violence is not what is sacred; rather the victim is the one who is sacred. God does not sanction violence. Rather, *violence sacrifices God*. This transformation in awareness, this emerging theology, is part of the legacy of Jeremiah.

Such a radical transformation in human awareness and understanding of God and us takes time to permeate into every aspect of life. The lures of violence are strong and seductive – especially when we are convinced the violence we do and the lives we sacrifice – is done in the name of good, in the name of country and religion and in the name of God.

King Josiah, who ruled during the first period of Jeremiah's prophetic activity, was considered a great king, who instituted reform of the Temple. Integral to this reform was the eradication of Canaanite religious influence including the places and vestiges of Canaanite human sacrifice. We are told in 2 Kings 23:10 that Josiah

> *defiled [destroyed] Topheth which is in the valley of Benhinnom so that no one would make a son or a daughter pass through fire as an offering to Molech.* (NRSV)

'Pass through fire' is a euphemism for ritual human sacrifice. Josiah's reform sought out and destroyed such altars (also known as 'high places'). And yet, the very means Josiah reverted to in order to accomplish his worthy goal was itself laced with violence and killing.

> *Moreover, Josiah removed all the shrines of the high places that were in the towns of Samaria, which kings of Israel had made, provoking the LORD to anger; he did to them just as he had done at Bethel. He slaughtered on the altars all the*

*priests of the high places who were there, and burned human bones on them. Then, he returned to Jerusalem.* (2 Kings 23:19-20. NRSV)

Josiah reverts to the human ways of violent slaughter. His own temple reform remains built upon a foundation of human sacrifice. The veil of sacred violence is again lowered on the people, and Jeremiah sees through it and speaks. A temple built on violence is a shrine to violence. The people are simply deceiving themselves.

> *Do not trust in these deceptive words: 'This is the temple of the LORD, the temple of the LORD, the temple of the LORD.' For if you truly amend your ways and your doings, if you truly act justly one with another, if you do not oppress the alien , the orphan, and the widow, or shed innocent blood in this place, and if you do not go after other gods to your own hurt, then I will dwell with you in this place, in the land that I gave of old to your ancestors forever and ever.'* (Jeremiah. 7:4-7. NRSV)

Israel's sacred violence eliminates God through its elimination (killing) of new victims. The people do not want to hear Jeremiah's proclamation of God's word. They want the temple and their violence as well. This is the human penchant. And so, the people now turn against Jeremiah.

> *And when Jeremiah had finished speaking all that the LORD had commanded him to speak to all the people, then the priests and the prophets and all the people laid hold of him saying, 'You shall die! ... When the officials of Judah heard these things, they came up from the king's house to the house of the LORD and took their seat in the entry of the New Gate of the house of the LORD. Then the priests and the prophets said to the officials and to all the people, 'This man deserves the sentence of death because he has prophesied against this city, as you have heard with your own ears.'* (Jeremiah. 26:8, 10-11. NRSV)

Sedition is the accusation or crime supposedly worthy of a new sacrificial victim. Divine empathy as the law of the universe is only a faint glimmer, but it is in the eye of Jeremiah and will not be extinguished. Bailie reminds us: 'Here is the prophet as critic of religion becoming the prophet as the victim of religious righteousness. Here is Jeremiah as the spiritual descendant of Micaiah and the spiritual ancestor of Jesus of Nazareth.'[26]

# CHAPTER 5 – LOVE SEES NO CONDITIONS: GALATIANS

### From Conditions to Compassion

We have been discussing the birth of a transformation in Israel's theology found in the prophecy of Jeremiah. At the heart of this transformation is the experience and awareness that God is not aligned with the violators but is to be found in the life of the victim. The victim is the presence and voice of God calling out to the violators, reminding them that the one whom they seek to sacrifice is holy. To experience God's presence in the life of the victim requires a conversion of heart, whereby we come to know God in our midst not as 'divine wrath,' but as 'divine empathy,' or, in the simple words of John's Gospel: love.

### Saul the Persecutor

King Josiah, renowned for his temple reform, reminds us of the seductive power of violence, especially when we are convinced we are sacrificing human life in the name of the sacred, or for good ends. In the Scripture narrative, several hundred years after Josiah, we come upon another zealous reformer, one Saul of Tarsus (later known as Paul). We meet him as a 'young man' in Chapter 8 of Acts, witnessing and applauding the stoning of Stephen. Luke describes Saul as someone breathing 'murderous threats against the disciples of Jesus.' (Acts 9:1) Saul has a righteous cause, and thus seems to have no qualms about sacrificing other human beings for its sake. This is not a passive interest of Saul. Rather, Luke describes him as 'going to the high priest' to ask him for 'letters, addressed to the synagogues at Damascus, that would authorize him to arrest and take to Jerusalem any followers of the Way that he could find, both women and men.' (Acts 9:1, 2)

We find a similar description of Saul's zealous character in Galatians. 'You've heard, I know, the story of my former way of life in Judaism. You know that I went to extremes in persecuting the church of God and tried to destroy it; I went far beyond most of my contemporaries regarding Jewish observances because of my great zeal to live out all the traditions of my ancestors' (Galatians. 1:13-14). Saul would not, and did not, stop short of killing other human beings in the name of preserving those ancestral traditions. Like King Josiah before him, Saul is seduced by the power of 'divine wrath,' a power giving him the authority to determine whether fellow human beings live or die. Destruction is divine work, the purpose of which is to keep the faith pure and undefiled by the followers of the way of Jesus (or, for that matter, of any other way deemed unorthodox by Saul). Saul is intoxicated by – today we might say addicted to – the experience of killing in the name of God. And like most addicts, he has to hit rock-bottom before he might wake up to the truth of God's ways.

**Paul the Proclamator**

Acts 9:3-5 tells us that as Saul is approaching Damascus, 'a light from the sky suddenly flashed about him. He fell to the ground and heard a voice saying, 'Saul, Saul, why are you persecuting me?' 'Who are you?' Saul asked. The voice answered, 'I am Jesus, and you are persecuting me.' These words are utterly astounding. Saul had never met Jesus of Nazareth, whom he knew to be long since dead. And yet, lying humbled and vulnerable upon the earth, he realizes that Stephen, along with every other person he has harassed, violated, persecuted, killed, in the name of God, has in fact been Jesus.

Fallen-Saul thus becomes risen-Paul. 'One who formerly was persecuting us is now preaching the faith he tried to destroy' (Galatians. 1:23). As the letter to the Galatians reveals, Paul still retains his zealous heart, but now he is no longer breathing 'murderous threats.' Divine empathy has risen out of the ashes of his once wrathful heart. Nothing, he now realizes, can separate him from the love of God, nor should it be allowed to try to. 'For I'm certain that neither death nor life, neither angels nor demons, neither the present nor the future, neither heights nor depths – nor anything else in all creation – will be able to separate us from the love of God that comes to us in Christ Jesus, our Savior' (Rm. 8:38-39). How could there ever be separation if each and every person is the living presence of Christ?

Saul, the persecutor, becomes Paul the proclamator. But we must see that the power of Paul's proclamation is rooted in his awareness of the pain and suffering caused by his acts of zealous sacrifice. He had been a willing persecutor, and killer, for God. He had persecuted in the name of protecting divine purity. Another way of saying this is that for Saul, there were certain strict conditions that had to be met in order for one to be considered a legitimate and acceptable Jew. The followers of the way of Jesus, in Saul's mind, failed to meet these conditions. Even more, their very presence and message undermined the ability of the Jewish authorities to maintain the conditions and hence the purity of the faith. God's holiness and the people's purity were at stake in Saul's faith, and so people had to be sacrificed – God demanded it, religion sanctioned it, society thirsted for it.

**From Conditions to Compassion**

In his letter to the Galatians, we discover a Paul who is now convinced that divine empathy neither establishes nor tolerates conditions. But, we need to ask: no conditions with respect to what? For many centuries, the essential argument of Galatians was understood to be about personal salvation. Galatians was seen as Paul's response to the questions, 'How is a person saved? How does one find a gracious God?' There was a group in Galatia called the Judaizers (Jewish Christians), who answered that one is saved by faith in Jesus Christ and doing the works of the Law. Paul countered, so this traditional interpretation goes, that one is saved by faith alone. Salvation comes only through faith.

For a significant group of scripture scholars today, however, Paul's letter to the Galatians is 'not primarily a letter about individual salvation.' Paul's concern is rather 'the condition on which Gentiles enter the people of God.' Scripture scholar, Frank Matera, describes the central issue of Galatians this way:

> Galatians is 'about the condition on which Gentiles enter the people of God', that is, what are the entrance requirements for Gentile Christians who want to be recognized as full members of that portion of Israel which believes in Jesus the Messiah? Must they adopt the cultural practices of Jews in order to enter the congregation of Israel's Messiah, the Church? Must they accept circumcision, practice specific dietary regulations, and follow the Jewish religious calendar? Or is it possible to be accepted as a full member of the Church on the basis of the faith in Christ, apart from doing these works of the Mosaic Law?
>
> Seen in this perspective, Galatians is not primarily a letter about individual salvation...But for Paul it was first and foremost a defense of the rights of Gentiles to enter the Church on the basis of their faith in Jesus Christ without adopting the cultural practices of Jewish Christians. Thus Krister Stendahl (*Paul Among the Gentiles*, 2) maintains that the Pauline doctrine of justification by faith 'was hammered out by Paul for the very specific purpose of defending the rights of Gentile converts to be full and genuine heirs to the promises of God to Israel.'[27]

There are no conditions, Paul is telling us, which we must meet prior to being accepted as God's own. Gentiles, as well as Jews, are genuine heirs to the promises of God. Women, as well as men are genuine heirs. Slaves, as well as free, are also genuine heirs. Gentiles – Women – Slaves – these are all victims of the religious system. These are the kinds of persons Saul would have previously so willingly sacrificed on the altar of religious purity. Within these persons, Paul now proclaims, is the living, breathing, Christ. Love sees no conditions justifying separation or sacrifice. Paul has become an apostle championing awareness of the living God in the victims of religion. For 'in Christ,' Paul declares, 'you are all children of God through faith' (Galatians. 3:25 NRSV). Paul's faith, rooted in his experience of God after having fallen to the ground on the road to Damascus enables him to see all as children of

God. He can see history from the bottom up, so to speak, from the perspective of those who have been made to suffer because of the human thirst for vengeance and sacrifice.

# CHAPTER 6 – AS SONG OF UTTER LIGHT: FRANCIS OF ASSISI

**Apostle of Non-Violence**

If Saul of Tarsus had never fallen to the ground, or (according to the tradition in Luke's account), been thrown to the ground from the back of a horse, Paul would not have been born. Fall or descent inevitably precede ascent into the light or awareness. At least this seems to be the case for men in the West. As women become more a part of (are inculturated into) the Western myth of success they, too, are finding this path an invariable truth in their spiritual journey.

Francis of Assisi, like Paul, fell and descended into the darkness before he ever began to glimpse who he truly was and what he was to be about in this ever-so-brief stint on earth. In the words of a contemporary Franciscan, Richard Rohr, he did not have a clue as to what was 'Really Real' until his carefully constructed plans had been shattered. The shattering allowed the light of the Really Real to penetrate his human ego. Initially, however, the light was experienced as an utterly disorienting darkness, which could either be accepted and leaned into, or rejected and cordoned off. Here we discover another constant truth about the spiritual journey: God invites – persistently and arduously – but does not control our wills.

For Francis, the inward journey begun with his fall does *not* disconnect him from the world. As he accepts and leans into the darkness thrust upon him, and descends into the depths of his soul, he is *not* taken away from others – as if the Spirit and world, soul and society, could be separated. Again we encounter another invariable truth of the spiritual journey: to journey within is also to embrace without. Soul and society are one, not two. The descent of the soul makes possible the liberating ascent into society, because only the soul which has shed the small and self-centered agenda of the ego is capable of embracing all of God's creation.

As Francis looks ever more deeply within himself, he begins to see more clearly the presence of God in everyone and everything. Francis is not a romantic idealist, but someone who knows firsthand profound suffering and loss, embraces it, allows it to teach him, and emerges convinced that love, and love alone, is the way of life. Such love is the heart and soul of non-violence, for a follower of the way of love could neither violate nor kill another. Francis fell into the darkness only to find himself and become an apostle of non-violence.

Many historians regard Francis of Assisi as one of the three most (if not *the* most) influential figures in medieval Europe (the other two being his contemporaries: Pope Innocent III and Emperor Frederick II). He was a troubadour and is credited with having composed the first piece of poetry in vernacular Italian, 'The Canticle of the Creatures.' He influenced church architecture as he restored churches and helped initiate extensive reform of church leadership. Not only did he establish his Franciscans, he also supported Clare as she began the Second Order, and then he created his beloved Third Order. He refused to be ordained a priest of privilege, choosing instead to witness to the way of Christ embodied in utter poverty and service to the poor.

### Early Years – A Playboy

Nothing in his early years would seem to foreshadow the person Francis Bernadone was to become. He was born in the town of Assisi (Italy) at the dawn of the rise of the merchant class in Europe. Francis' father, one of the wealthiest men in town, made at least two annual trips to France and Flanders to purchase wool for the marketing of his fine cloths. Francis accompanied his father, became accustomed to travel, and learned to enjoy the song and entertainment that helped pass the time. Yet, these journeys also exposed Francis to a side of life that he found most unappealing. Donald Spoto, in his marvelous biography, offers a description.

> On the roads and in the forest camps, it would have been impossible for him to avoid seeing the everyday signs of violence: fights to the death over a skin of wine, a loaf of bread or a handful of pearls; vicious killings for the sake of diversion; tortures inflicted for vengeance or sport or mere pastime...And of course, everywhere there were lepers.[28]

We might describe young Francis today as having the personality of a playboy, the *bon vivant* of Assisi – the first to gather folks for a party and the last to leave the revelry. His dance and song did not court pain and poverty, but rather filled his life so full of laughter and frivolity that he had no time to notice. If he happened into the vicinity of one of the leper dwellings (called a 'lazar house,' short for the beggar Lazarus who lay before the gate of the rich person – see Lk 16.19), 'besides being incapable of looking at them, he would not even approach the places where they lived ... and if he gave them alms, he would do it through someone else, turning his face away and holding his nose...'[29]

### Suffering Finds Francis

Francis, however, could not hide forever from the pain and suffering of 13th century life. Following his desire to be a glorious knight, he was struck down in one of the periodic battles with neighboring Perugia. He was one of the fortunate ones who 'survived,' only to be cast into a dank and dingy prison for the next year. In the endless nights of the prison, there was neither music nor dancing, there was no means to avoid the stench or the pain or the sickness. Francis contracted malaria. He waited and languished. Finally, he was released to his parents and convalesced for a full year, but he was never the same. He had fallen into a deep and dark place, and although his body was now home, his soul remained in the shadows. His usual song and cheer were now an ineffective anesthetic. He had begun to know suffering.

In 1205, about two years after being released from prison, Francis found himself taking a rest in a dilapidated old church, San Damiano, on the outskirts of Assisi. As he looked upon the cross fixed to the wall, the Christ figure spoke to his heart. Spoto describes the experience of Francis.

> In the stillness of the small church, Francis felt, as an early source described, 'different from when he had entered.' And then, 'the image of Christ crucified spoke to him in a tender and kind voice: 'Francis, don't you see that my house is being destroyed? Go, then, and rebuild it for me.'[30]

Francis understood Christ's invitation literally and undertook the renovation of San Damiano. To finance his work, he sold some of his father's precious cloth. The relationship between them quickly deteriorated, reaching the point where father hauled son before the bishop of Assisi for a trial. Francis, who had taken to dressing poorly, arrived at the trial arrayed in his father's finest clothes. When his father demanded repayment for what his son had stolen, Francis, before family, bishop, and assembled members of Assisi, stripped-off his clothes and returned them, along with the money, to his father. 'Up until now,' said Francis to a stunned gathering, 'I have always called Pietro di Bernardone my father. In the future I will only acknowledge our Father who is in heaven.' An early source describes the immediate aftermath in this way.

> His father, burning with both grief and anger, gathered up the clothes and money, and carried them home. The others present took Francis's part, moved with pity to tears that Pietro had left him there naked. The bishop, seeing Francis's courage and admiring his resolution, threw his arms open and covered him with his cloak. He realized that a great mystery lay behind the scene he had just witnessed and from now on helped and watched over Francis with loving concern.[31]

Francis, in dramatic fashion not unlike that of the very troubadours he grew-up admiring, had begun to strip away the protective layers keeping him safe and secure from the pain and poverty of the world. He would not be of the new merchant class, whose life was defined by the endless and tireless pursuit of money. From within the darkness of the dank prison and from the quiet voice of Christ in ruined San Damiano, Francis had begun to sense a new vision; which, if embraced fully, would satisfy him as no ribald revelry of youth ever had.

It is the life of Job and not a Hollywood fantasy, where having turned himself around, the saint-to-be would now know the serenity of life-in-God, which best describes the journey of Francis. The prison was not the end of Francis' pain and darkness; the prison symbolized the course Francis was to take. His freedom would lie precisely in his embrace of the dark, the dank, even the putrid.

Lepers, it seemed, had reminded Francis of everything he had always tried to deny – that life, all life, ended in death. It is said that if he passed within two miles of a leper down-wind, he would hold his nose. The stench was indeed horrible, as decaying flesh covered bodies, eating away noses and fingers. How leprosy was transmitted was unknown, which only heightened the terror of contracting it. Lepers, cast into the living hell of the lazar, were reduced to eating scraps and banging sticks to warn others to avoid their presence.

But now, Francis entered the stench and did not recoil. He 'knelt down and gave what he could: an embrace, a bit of comfort, a few sympathetic words.' And in this act of self-less love, from one outcast beggar to another, Francis began to fall very deeply into the love of God. Not only did he continue his work of restoring San Damiano, but from now on his life would be defined by his care of brothers and sisters who were lepers.[32]

## Christ in the Crusades?

Sometimes our romantic longings of youth are realized only to be swept away by confrontation with the Really Real in which we now find ourselves immersed. Francis had dreamt of being a knight, a crusader for the faith. He had grown up hearing the stories about St. Michael slaying the dragon, Percival, and the heroic exploits of the early crusades. Martyrdom at the hand of the infidel, in the cause of Christ, was seen as the pinnacle of Christian sacrifice and honor. And so, when Pope Honorius III reiterated the call to assemble for the Fifth Crusade, Francis, despite poor health and the objections of his companions, answered.

What he saw on the shores of Egypt, at Damietta, sickened and disillusioned him. Human slaughter and stench permeated everything, the crusaders anesthetized only too briefly through bouts of drinking and minutes with prostitutes shipped-in for their pleasure. Prayer and Christ seemed as distant as Assisi. The Bishop who led the crusaders, cardinal Pelagio, was more intent on personal glory than securing the holy land. He rebuffed repeated offers from the Muslim sultan al-Malik al-Kamil (d. 1238) that were more than fair. He sent his own soldiers into senseless and gruesome death.

Francis saw clearly that this was no crusade in the honor of Christ. After numerous pleas to cardinal Pelagio, he was finally allowed to undertake what most saw as a mission of suicide. He would walk over to the camp of al-Kamil and speak with the sultan of his own faith. This seemed certain suicide, for to attempt to convert a Muslim was a crime often met with death. Yet, Francis and his companion went. Again, Spoto wonderfully describes the scene.

> Reports of Francis's sojourn to the Muslim sultan al-Malik al-Kamil are found not only in medieval French and Italian Crusade records ... but also in an Islamic chronicle. These documents tell how Francis and Illuminatus left the Christian camp in early September for the headquarters of al-Kamil.

Since Francis and Illuminatus were dressed so simply, in garments similar to Sufi holy men, they were brought to see al-Kamil.

> The Muslim ruler of Egypt, Palestine and Syria, the same age as Francis, had ruled his empire's forces since 1218 and, also like Francis, was a man completely dedicated to the traditions of his faith and to its dissemination ... In brief, Francis was now standing before a profoundly devout and pacific man who also believed in One God.

Al-Kamil's advisors counseled that he should kill Francis and Illuminatus, for their clear purpose was to convert the sultan. But al-Kamil refused, moved by the spirit of Francis. 'I will never condemn you to death — for that would indeed be an evil reward to bestow on you, who conscientiously risked death in order to save my life before God, as you believe.'

> So far as we know, the sojourn was unprecedented in the history of Muslim-Christian relations. For a week, Francis and Illuminatus were the sultan's guest ... Francis may have gone to the camp with the traditional desire to convert or to die trying, but as his writings over the next few years reveal, he departed with a far different attitude. We might even say that it was Francis's own conversion that progressed.[33]

In the end, al-Kamil left Damietta. Pelagio conquered and seized the city. All that remained of the original 80,000 inhabitants were 3,000 starving and ill. After a few hours, the stunned crusaders finished their holy war by killing the remaining men and raping the women.

Once again, a deeply held prejudice was stripped away. The sultan, al-Kamil, was the man of God who sought peace. The infidel was the person of prayer, and not the Christian prelate. War had not been holy, but a hell. To put it simply, Francis found Christ in al-Kamil, not in the crusader.

Francis returned to Assisi, a failure in his own eyes. He had not died a martyr. He had not helped free the holy land. He had not converted the sultan. His own life and its ambitions seemed to be crumbling before him. Even his own order of Franciscans was charting a new course, no longer committed to his original radical call for poverty. The order had now grown large and required a leader with administrative gifts, so Francis felt compelled to hand over the leadership.

> 'From henceforth I am dead to you, but here is Brother Peter Catanio, whom you shall obey.' Then all the friars began to lament noisily and weep bitterly. Francis bowed down before Peter and promised him obedience; after that he remained a subject until his death like any other friar.[34]

### Bearing the Wounds and Joy of Christ

In the early fall of 1224, Francis began a forty-day retreat of fasting and prayer. Virtually blind, in constant pain and weakened by disease, he came before God. There were no more barriers. He had nowhere to go, no place to hide. It was almost as if he were back in the dark of prison. But this time there was a vision. The darkness held light.

> Among many other graces which the Lord bestowed upon him, there is the vision of the seraph [angel] that filled his soul with consolation and united him closely to God for the rest of his life. When his companions brought him his meal that day, he told them what had happened.

From this simple account has grown the story of the stigmata – the bearing of the wounds of the crucified Christ. Once again, Spoto's reflections are worth quoting.

> At last Francis knew the meaning of conformity to Christ in absolute poverty – to accept his own limitations, his own complete reliance on God. If he was not to be a merchant, not to join the world's struggle for material success, then he had to follow this refusal to its logical term: there were to be no visible signs of spiritual success – neither converted infidels, nor baptized sultan, nor a fraternity that remained as he had planned and formed it. He had tried to imitate the life Jesus; now, in his decline and death, in his frustrations and failures, he would follow that path all the way to the cross.

Francis bore the stigma of his culture's despised and discarded ones, and the very person who had become nauseous when two miles downwind of lepers, now bled from sores. 'Because Francis, in imitation of Jesus, had been unafraid to touch and nurse [the lepers] in their worst state, would not Francis's own leprosy have been a form of crucifixion? Was not this terrible illness a kind of stigmata?' In other words, 'The truest sign of his humanity was in his wounded, scarred body, used up in 40 years of service. It is this aspect of his life that has the most to say to us – more than the fact that he devoted himself to poverty or became a fool for Christ.'[35]

Imprisoned by his own failing body, Francis was now most free. He had come full circle to discover Christ present within all his wounds – within the dank and darkness. If Christ were present here, there was indeed no place, there was no one, in whom Christ was not alive. The darker Francis' world became, the more Christ's presence shed its light. And so it was, as Francis lay in darkness awaiting his own death, he spoke a poem, a song of utter light, which is itself a plea for peace.

> Most High, all-powerful, good Lord,
>     Yours are the praises, the glory, and the honor and all blessing,
> To You alone, Most High, do they belong,
>     and no human is worthy to mention Your name.
> Praised be You, my Lord, with all Your creatures,
>     especially Sir Brother Sun,
> Who is the day and through whom You give us light.
> And he is beautiful and radiant with great splendor;
>     and bears a likeness of You, Most High One.
> Praised be You, my Lord, through Sister Moon and the stars,
>     in heaven You formed them clear and precious and beautiful.
> Praised be you, my Lord, through Brother Wind,
>     and through the air, cloudy and serene,
>         and every kind of weather,
>     through whom You give sustenance to Your creatures.
> Praised be You, my Lord, through Sister Water,
>     who is very useful and humble and precious and chaste.
> Praised be You, my Lord, through Brother Fire,
>     through whom You light the night,
>     and he is beautiful and playful and robust and strong.
> Praised be You, my Lord, through our Sister Mother Earth,
>     who sustains and governs us,
>     and who produces various fruit with colored flowers and herbs.
> Praised be You, my Lord, through those who give
>     pardon for Your love,
>     and bear infirmity and tribulation.

> Blessed are those who endure in peace
> for by You, Most High, shall they be crowned.
> Praised be You, my Lord, through our Sister Bodily Death,
> from whom no one living can escape.
> Woe to those who die in mortal sin.
> Blessed are those whom death will find in Your most holy will,
> for the second death shall do them no harm.
> Praise and bless my Lord and give Him thanks
> and serve Him with great humility.[36]

## Invitation: Beyond Security and Status

Theology is the act of reflection upon experience. Of its very nature, it is transformative. Theology is telling the story of what we see. But we need to learn *how* to see. The greatest obstacle we encounter to seeing is nothing 'out there,' but our very own self – our own ego. Carl Jung (d. 1961), the founder of analytical psychology, describes the first half of life as all about building up our sense of self, or ego. This is the psychological process known as individuation. We 'climb the mountain' to assert our identity and strength. We gather goods, acquire security, and win status. We stake our claim before others, seeking to prove our worth to them, it is true, but even more – to our own self. This process of becoming an individual is necessary and healthy, but it represents the primary task of only the *first* half of life. The second half of life is about the *shedding* of this very ego we have so painstakingly developed. Herein lies the rub. Our ego does not want to let go. It likes believing it is on top and in control. Spiritually speaking, we thus find ourselves kneeling before the twin gods of status and security.

Status and security are quite fragile in this world. We can, and often do, spend a lifetime struggling to maintain and protect these twin gods. In their name, we sacrifice family, friends, soul and God. Sacrifice is thus intimately connected with the acquisition and maintenance of our status and security – prestigious job, respectable neighborhood, and fashionable clothes. If we keep on this course, we discover at the end that we have sacrificed our life for elusive and false gods – for an illusion of status and security. We have been seduced into sacrificing the wrong things for the wrong gods.

In our explorations of Jeremiah, Paul and Francis we have seen their relationship with security, status and sacrifice all playing a central role in their faith journeys. It seems there is no end to which human beings will not go to destroy a threat to security and status – even invoking the name of God to justify the sacrifice of other human beings. Although the names and faces change, every culture from the foundation of the world has always found good reasons to identify and then kill an 'enemy.' Violence and the sacred have customarily been woven together in theology. And this theology has veiled the true nature of God.

In Jeremiah, Paul and Frances we have encountered figures who pierced the temple veil, allowing a glimpse of the true divine love which courses through the life of all creation. This theology of divine compassion challenges the validity, the stranglehold that a theology of divine wrath has had over humanity's fearful heart. Jeremiah is one of the first to lead us into a new theology – teaching that it is the victim, not the violator, with whom God is to be identified. (This does not mean God is not within the violator, but that God is neither the cause nor the justification of the violation.) Paul, in Galatians, dismisses all categories devised by human beings that separate us from one another and God. These violate our common life in Christ. Baptism reveals that God's grace precedes and thus dissolves all the conditions we name as prerequisites for receiving complete acceptance by God. Saul the persecutor is transformed into the advocate of all. But before Jeremiah and Paul can even begin to glimpse God behind the temple veil, they themselves must experience falling down, suffering, and letting go. It is as if their very act of falling rips the veil in two, allowing sight of the true face of God. (Recall Luke 23:44-46.)

There is something beyond our desperate, fear-filled grasp for security and status. But we cannot seem to see it from on high. Our egos need to be grounded. Francis is cast into the dungeon of Perugia. In the failure of his original ambition, he experiences freedom for the first time. Francis teaches us that the freedom to be who we are called to be, and the ability to see the Really Real (the reign of God), comes at a cost. We must let go of all that we have embraced in our hearts as gods. Francis the playboy only discovers God thru the loss of his twin idols, status and security. Separated by religion, culture, and centuries, the message is yet the same, and it echoes and deepens the theology of Jeremiah and Paul. For us to see God, and to discover our true selves, we have to sacrifice our egos, and let them die. Then, and only then, do we experience resurrection – the radiant beauty of all creation in the midst of loss and death (Francis). Life is not about 'me' but about *us* living in God – all of us.

Loss and death come in many guises. A friend dies from aids-related complications. A migrant worker is denied access to health care. A child is killed by a drunk driver. A divorce. Loss of job. A brother is sentenced to death by lethal injection. A country goes to war. Jeremiah was rejected by his own people. Paul was thrown to the earth, lost his standing in the Jewish community, and was martyred. Francis was literally thrown in jail and suffered numerous deaths throughout life (gastritis, blindness, leprosy, poverty, sense of failure). Within our Western culture such losses are counted as a sign of a failed life. Even more, often they are interpreted (theology) as signs of God's disfavor. Yet, for these saints of the faith, such loss, even death count as nothing. The real sacrifice for each is the willingness to come down from the self-centered mountains they have climbed, to discover that the kingdom of God is within us all.

To summarize the theology being proclaimed through these lives, we might say this. We are free when we realize we have nothing to lose. Everything belongs to God. We are free from thirst to sacrifice new victims when we see we have no one to fear. Love is the law of creation. We are free to know even our enemies as friends, to escape the compulsion to demonize and 'crucify' our oppressors, when we perceive that all are God's children already. In the realm of God, enemies are no more. We are free to accept the cross of our losses, even death, without blaming others, when we are given the grace to see through the twin idols of status and security.

# ~Exploring Status and Security~

### God's Ways Are Not Our Ways: Jeremiah
### Transforming Perception of God and Self
Human awareness of 'who God is' has experienced transformation throughout the scriptures and continues to undergo transformation in our own lives and experience. What difference does that insight have for us?

### From Conditions to Compassion: Galatians
### Sacrificing Victims for a Noble Cause
Saul sacrificed Christians for what he believed was a righteous, or noble, cause. Have you or any group you have been a part of ever experienced yourself willing to sacrifice someone else for a noble cause? Describe your experience.

### Apostle of Non-Violence: Francis of Assisi
### Fear and Embrace
Francis must face what it is he most fears: He must touch the leper. The result is that he comes (ascends) to recognize God in all creatures. The descent depends upon his personality and fear. What fear might God be inviting you to face in your own spiritual journey? What impact might this have on how you see and care for others?

### Responding to Evil
In the gospels, we do not have an account where Jesus actually destroys evil. Richard Rohr describes Jesus responding to evil by controlling or absorbing it (similar to Gandhi and Francis). If this is true, what impact might this have on your life and theology (your way of seeing God present and active in creation and inviting you to live)? How do you and others you are connected with usually respond to evil? If that differs from how we would expect Jesus to respond, what would it take for that to change?

# PART III

# AWAKENING TO AT-ONE-MENT

"God became human so that we might become god."[37]
Athanasius

> *God's ground is my ground,*
> *and my ground is God's ground.*
> Meister Eckhart[38]

For most us, we only come to "acknowledge that God is in all things," after long, slow, and difficult digging within the ground of our soul. Second-Isaiah, Paul and Meister Eckhart each reveal a dimension of human spiritual awakening to Divine Presence. In the case of Second-Isaiah we have a prophet who reflects the Hebrew people struggling to see God as the one who is on the side of all victims. The songs of the suffering servant are cries from the human heart to restore wholeness, which is to awaken to our at-one-ment with God.

The letter of Paul to the Romans complements the vision of Second-Isaiah, by inviting us to awaken to our at-one-ment with each other. God has no favorites, Paul reminds the community at Rome. The young Christian community is to respect and honor its Jewish neighbors as God's own people. The Gentile-Christians in Rome reveal how human clinging begins to blind us to the path of life. If our fearful egos can relax and release in faith the false hopes to which our passions clutch, then we will not sacrifice other human beings for our own gain and security.

The German mystic, Meister Eckhart, will ask us to journey still further in our unfolding journey. Eckhart finds in the gospel the gracious invitation to awaken to the abiding truth that not only human beings, but all creation exists because it exists in the Godhead. Life simply as it is is grace. And this grace is nothing other than God's own self. For Eckhart, theology will identify the path of restoration as lying in our waking-up to who we are, to what all creation is – the very words of God.

# CHAPTER 7 – AT-ONE-MENT WITH GOD: SECOND ISAIAH

**Created At-one-ment: Suffering Servant**

The book of Isaiah is really three books in one. The first runs basically from chapter 1 through 39, and is attributed to Isaiah of Amoz (1:1). This First-Isaiah began to prophesy around the year of 739 BCE, in the year of King Uzziah's death. He continued until at least 701, and perhaps as late as 688. For First-Isaiah, Jerusalem (or Zion) was the city God chose as a royal dwelling, and the kings were anointed by God to reign. God was the king of heaven and earth, and the royal descendants of David were God's vice-regents. The problem for First-Isaiah was that Jerusalem had lost its way and now needed to be purified (1:21-28; 29:1-8). The enemy bearing down on Jerusalem was Assyria.

The third book, or Third-Isaiah, includes chapters 56-66. These chapters were written either by Second-Isaiah or one of his disciples. However, the setting has changed. The people have returned to the land of Judah.

Our focus shall be the second book, or Second-Isaiah. When we read Second-Isaiah, chapters 40-55, we come upon an Israel in exile in Babylon. Second-Isaiah shares First-Isaiah's concern for the holiness of God and his vision of God as the great king. However, we find less judgment against the people in these chapters than in First-Isaiah. Second-Isaiah is a prophet of consolation (40:1-2). The people have had their homes destroyed and have been carried away into a foreign land. Now is the time to offer the people hope. God has not forgotten them.

Second-Isaiah seeks to assure the people-in-exile that God is still with them. Despite all their oppression, affliction, suffering, sacrifice, and loss, their God has not abandoned them in Assyria. Of all the verses written by Second-Isaiah, none so embrace and ponder the human and divine tragedy of suffering and loss as the four texts commonly called the 'servant songs' (49:1-6; 50:4-11; 52:13-53:12). Through the words of Second-Isaiah, we discover a faithful nation wrestling mightily with what it means for innocent ones to be slaughtered.

> *Though treated harshly, you bore it humbly*
> *and never opened your mouth.*
> *Like a lamb being led to slaughter,*
> *or a sheep before shearers,*
> *you were silent and never opened your mouth.*
> *Seized by force and condemned, you were taken away;*
> *who would ever have foreseen your destiny?*
> *You were taken from the land of the living,*

> *through the sin of my people,*
> *who deserved punishment.*
> *You were buried with the evildoers*
> *and entombed with the rich,*
> *though you had done no wrong,*
> *and deceit was not found in your mouth.*
> *But YHWH was satisfied to crush you and afflict you;*
> *and put you to grief.*
> (Isaiah 53.7-10a. The Inclusive Hebrew Scriptures)

Though this is one of the most well-known passages in all of the scriptures, we are not even sure of the identity of this 'lamb' that is 'being led to slaughter.' Some scholars argue that the writer is referring to a particular individual. Others contend what we have described here is the suffering of Israel itself. Still others say that the marvel of the passage is that it describes the fate of both individuals and the community. We can think of the 'lamb' as we do 'Jacob' of the Hebrew Scriptures. Sometimes a writer invokes 'Jacob' as the name of Isaac's son and other times the focus is the nation. Similarly, the 'lamb,' better known as the 'suffering servant,' at times may refer to an individual (or individuals), or Israel as a whole, or both.

Of course, Christians see in this suffering servant a description of the passion and death of Jesus. If we turn to chapter 8 of Acts, it is precisely this passage that the Ethiopian is reading and puzzling over when Philip encounters him. The puzzlement of the Ethiopian is quite understandable. Whether we are talking about an individual or a community, the fact of the matter is that this passage in Second-Isaiah describes a human slaughter. What is the faith community of Isaiah, of Philip, of today, to make of this slaughter? The passage raises difficult and troubling questions: Who demands or wants the sacrifice? Who tolerates the sacrifice? Who takes pleasure in the sacrifice? Who is satisfied by the sacrifice? Are we to understand the sacrifice of the innocent victim as something necessary to appease, or satisfy, God?

In none of the four passages of Second-Isaiah that talk about the suffering servant, do we find any hint of guilt. Quite the contrary is true. This servant has done no wrong. She (for the individual could be a woman, as well as a man) has not violated the Torah, offending neither human nor God. She is utterly and thoroughly innocent.

Where, in these songs of innocent suffering, are we to find God present? Some would say that we are to find God in the humility of the servant to suffer willingly and without protest. The servant is being obedient to God, who asks of the servant to endure this torture, public humiliation, and death. The reward of such obedience lies in the power of such innocent suffering to heal, or *atone* for, the lack of innocence of those who not only murder the servant, but of those who stand by to witness. In this reading of Second-

Isaiah, God is the one who not only tolerates such a 'perversion of justice,' but God accepts, and perhaps even demands it, as a suitable sacrifice atoning for the sins of the people. And so we read in Second Isaiah 53:4-6 (NRSV):

> *Surely he has borne our infirmities and carried our diseases;*
> *yet we accounted him stricken,*
> *struck down by God, and afflicted.*
> *But he was wounded for our transgressions,*
> *crushed for our iniquities;*
> *upon him was the punishment that made us whole,*
> *and by his bruises we are healed.*
> *All we like sheep have gone astray;*
> *we have all turned to our own way,*
> *and the LORD has laid on him*
> *the iniquity of us all.*

It is important for us, as readers, to recognize that it is *the witnesses* who proclaim that it is 'the LORD' who has laid on this suffering servant 'the iniquity of us all.' We do not hear from the servant herself, nor do we hear from the Lord. Rather, those who speak on behalf of the servant, and declare to us the meaning of the suffering, are precisely the ones who stand at a distance and watch. They neither raise a voice of protest, nor lift a hand in defense. They stand silent as one of their own is slaughtered. Perhaps they are silent because they do not wish to draw attention to themselves? Maybe their silence is an attempt to hide from the wrath of those who have the power to kill – even one who is 'the messenger who announces peace' (52:7)? Perhaps it is the hope of this nameless and faceless crowd that once this particular sacrifice is completed, the death of the victim will appease the lust of the violators, and 'peace' will once again be theirs?

In the language of today, perhaps what we are hearing in the story of the slaughter of the suffering servant is the mob violence of a community lynching. Who listens to the voice of the victim in the heat of such a moment? Without fail, the dominant voice of the crowd will proclaim the presence of God in its own actions. The victim must die – it is nothing but the will of God. The crowd is the witness that God's will is fulfilled.

Daniel Berrigan, in his poetic book, *Isaiah: Spirit of Courage, Gift of Tears*, offers a very different theology of the suffering servant, and one that deserves our attention. Berrigan hears in the silence of the suffering servant a song crying out for peace and justice. Silence is not resignation to a divinely ordained and demanded fate. Silence is refusal to participate in such ungodly action. There are no words that can make right the human act of slaughtering an innocent victim. The sacrifice of the suffering servant does not atone for human sin, as if any human action could divorce us from the presence of

God. Humanity's inability to see that we are already *at-one* with God, the Creator, is what makes possible this act of supreme violation.

The songs of the suffering servant, as the poetry of her silent ordeal is known, reveal to us, as with the words of Jeremiah, that God does not require human sacrifice. The sufferings and slaughter of the suffering servant do not create a condition where human beings are now at-one with God and each other. From the beginning, God has created us in the divine image. From the beginning, we are at-one with God and each other. Our brokenness is that we fail to see this at-oneness; and in our ignorance, fear, and greed, strike one another down in the name of God.

Second-Isaiah reveals a community struggling to know God as the one on the side of all victims. Whoever this author is, they clearly see the innocence of the victim. But Second-Isaiah also speaks to us of the community's persistent belief that 'it was the will of the LORD to crush him with pain' (Isaiah. 53:10). Thus, there remains tension in the author – and in Israel itself – about the place and role of God in human sacrifice. Somehow this tension will have to be resolved. Berrigan asks us to consider that the resolution is in favor of the victim. It is not human sacrifice God desires, but human mercy and compassion for and solidarity with all victims – for all are at-one with God. When we realize our *at-one-ment* with God and each other, perhaps we will indeed begin to see great things.

# CHAPTER 8 – AT-ONE-MENT WITH EACH OTHER: ROMANS

**Self-Sacrifice, not Sacrifice of Jews**

Paul was not the founder of the Christian community in Rome. He is thus somewhat reticent to offer direction or counsel (at least he says he is in Romans 15:14-29). Rome, imperial and important city that it is, is not, however, the ultimate destination sought by Paul. As he writes his letter, his hope is to visit Spain – what seemed liked the end of the world and civilization in the first century. Paul sought to bring the message of Christ to the end of the earth, and Spain, for all intents and purposes, looked like just that end. Rome lay between and there Paul and Peter were martyred.

Why did Paul attend to Rome, if he had not founded the community of faith? From what scholars can gather – and they are not all in agreement on various parts of the story – Paul wrote his letter to the community in Rome while in Corinth. The year is probably about 56 CE Perhaps one issue both the Corinthian and Roman Christians had in common, at least from Paul's perspective, was how Gentile- and Jewish-Christians were (or were not) relating to one another. In large measure, we can understand Paul's decision to write his letter as a desire, or compulsion of the Spirit, to respond to what he saw unfolding in Rome, which had its similarities with problems he experienced in Corinth and elsewhere.

Gentile and Jewish relations is thus a critical piece of context for how we understand Paul's letter. Krister Stendahl, a Swedish Lutheran biblical scholar, cautions us not to read Paul – contrary to popular opinion – from the perspective of sin and forgiveness. Paul himself, in fact, never even uses the word forgiveness.[39] Nor was Paul preoccupied with individual salvation. If we are to understand Paul, Stendahl encourages us to consider two ways of thinking about God. "One way is to imagine a God who asks, first thing every morning, 'What are the statistics on the saved?' Another is to have a God who asks, first thing, 'Has there been any progress for the kingdom?' These are two distinct theologies. Paul's theology was the latter."[40]

Paul takes his journeys, starts communities of faith, and writes his letters, because he has received a mission from Christ to the Gentiles. And this mission centers on the good news of God – 'I take this liberty because God has given me the grace to be a minister of Christ Jesus among the Gentiles, with the priestly duty of preaching the Good News of God...' (Romans 15:15-16). Paul is drawn into writing a letter to the Romans precisely as an apostle to the Gentiles. He has to respond – it is his mission, his calling.

What is it that has caught his attention? Again, Stendahl urges some caution on our part. Or, at the very least, he invites us to consider some prejudices we may bring to how we read and understand Paul. For Lutherans, Romans is the letter teaching us about *justification of faith* without works of the Law. Calvinists, by contrast, turn to Romans for their doctrine of *predestination*. Roman Catholics, however, find in the letter's second chapter their own doctrine of *natural law*. The great St. Augustine, by actually mistranslating the words of Romans 5:12 as 'in that person,' instead of 'because,' created his doctrine of *original sin*.[41]

What we believe caught Paul's attention is something simpler, yet often more difficult to see and accept. Gentile-Christians were, in a sense, turning against their Jewish sisters and brothers. It may not be proper to speak of anti-semitism at this time in history, but we certainly can talk about anti-Jewish behavior. Paul detects such injustice happening in Rome. He must speak. He must raise the issue. He must offer a corrective – in the name of Christ Jesus, on whose behalf he is on his missionary journey.

Two issues seem to be front and center for Paul throughout his entire missionary work. The first is his own health. Paul suffers from some sort of affliction, about which he is embarrassed, and struggles to come to terms (Galatians 4:13f; 2 Corinthians 10:10, 11:5, 12:7, 12:11). The second issue is Israel. What are Paul, the Romans, and we, to make of the decision of the overwhelming majority of Jews not to accept Christ (as Paul has done), if it is true that God never rescinds a covenant made? How are Jewish-Christians (such as Paul) and Gentile-Christians (who are the overwhelming majority of Roman Christians) to relate to the Jews? How does God continue to relate to the Jews? These are not idle and speculative questions for Paul and his communities, especially Rome.

Strong evidence exists that there was a general climate of anti-Jewish sentiment in Rome. For instance, Rome had expelled Jews from the city because of riots. The Jewish people often lived a precarious existence under Roman rule, especially during the reigns of the Emperors Tiberius (19 CE) and Claudius (49 CE), who each expelled the Jews during their respective reigns. Even though the Christian community in Rome originally had its roots in the synagogue, by the time Paul is writing his letter (around 56 CE, after Claudius had expelled the Jews), the community is overwhelmingly Gentile, and sometimes memories are short – especially when the prevailing values of the dominant culture continually tell another version of history. What we can gather from Romans 11:1, 11, is that 'the Christians in Rome were apparently ready to draw a theological conclusion' about the precarious situation of their Jewish neighbors – namely, Israel had stumbled so as to simply fall flat on its face. Its time and place in God's story were now, so to speak, dead history. Now was the time of the Gentiles. Scholar Neil Elliott concludes that 'Paul wrote Romans to oppose this Gentile-boasting' over Israel, and the corresponding indifference to the plight of real Jews in Rome in the wake' of the expulsion by the emperor Claudius.[42]

Although Roman citizens were reluctant to lash out at other Romans during times of social pressure and economic downturn, they did not show such restraint with respect to the Jews. By venting frustration with Rome through attacking the Jews, citizens, it seems, could avert retribution by the Roman authorities. The dominant culture, in this way, tended to provide citizens cover for their vented frustration – of course, at the expense of the Jews.

Such cover, which distorts the true picture of life and responsibility, drives us to the heart of what Paul calls *hamartia* or sin. Paul is not concerned, as we said earlier, with individual guilt. His focus is the ability of the system so to distort our perceptions, that we end-up thinking that what we are doing is 'ok,' or justified. *Hamartia* has to do with the misuse of power and the affect this misuse has on how we perceive the world and each other. The results are often tragic, because human beings are abused and sacrificed in the name of God and country. 'The tragedy is very clear,' Stendahl says. 'The world is not pretty. But Paul thinks of *hamartia* ... as a kind of cosmic power. *Hamartia* is a power. It is not the sum total of our little sinning – or our big sinning. When you see it as a power game in which we get trapped, or nations get trapped, then it takes on a meaning more tragic than a guilt-ridden individual.' He goes on to say again that the heart of the matter is not guilt. Rather, it is a 'lack of perception. It is a blindness rather than guilt. Human beings could have seen. Hence they are accountable.'[43]

The overall purpose of Romans, we might say, is to help the Gentile-Christians see through their blindness, a blindness caused in part by their willingness to accept the perversion and prejudice of Roman culture. The reality of the situation, says Paul, is that the Jews have *not* stumbled so as simply to fall. The power and mystery of God is that there is grace even in a stumble. The stumble – which we might describe as the unwillingness of the majority of Jews to accept the Christ Paul has accepted – is seen by Paul as a gift to the Gentiles. Paul's mission in Christ has turned to them. But – and this is what is so crucial to Paul – his turn to the Gentiles is *not* a turn from the Jews. Paul has not turned from the Jews, because neither has God turned from them. And so, Paul writes his letter to the Romans, especially 13:1-7, in order 'to advocate for the safety of the Jewish community in Rome.'[44] The Gentile-Christians may not sacrifice their Jewish neighbors on the altar of Roman prejudice.[45]

The Gentile-Christians are deceiving themselves, acting haughtily. They have convinced themselves that they have replaced the Jews in God's heart. Paul reminds the Romans that as Gentiles, they are the ones grafted onto the Jewish tree of life.

> *You might say, 'Branches were broken off so that I could be grafted in.' That is so. But they were broken off for lack of faith. You stand there only through your*

> *faith. So don't become arrogant, but stand in awe.* (Romans 11:19-20. The Inclusive New Testament.)

The Gentiles are the newcomers, and God never discards. This is the truth Paul now sees so clearly. Paul is adamant about God's continued fidelity to the Israelites.

> *Theirs were the adoption as God's children, the glory, the covenants, the Law-giving, the worship and the promises; theirs was the ancestry, and from them came the Messiah – at least, according to human ancestry. Blessed forever be God who is over all! Amen.* (Romans 9:4-5. The Inclusive New Testament.)

Paul continues by insisting that the 'word of God' has not failed (9:6), despite the stumbling. (9:31-33, 11:11). The Gentiles must not deceive themselves by thinking that God has rejected Israel, 'the chosen people' (11:1). Quoting Isaiah, Paul reminds the Romans that 'all Israel will be saved' (11:26), 'for the gifts and the calling of God are irrevocable' (11:29).[46]

The Gentiles, it is true, now find themselves in the place of power and prestige in the Roman community. They are in the position of strength, not weakness. The question Paul poses for them is whether they will know how to act in their strength. Will they act like typical Romans, brandishing their power in a self-centered way, humiliating and dismissing their weaker neighbors, the Jews? If they choose that path, it is the route of 'Death.'

Life, on the other hand, will be known in the willingness to sacrifice everything possible for the sake of helping their sisters and brothers, weakened by Roman prejudice and cruelty. Paul writes:

> *We who are strong have a duty to endure the failings of the weak, without trying to please ourselves. We should be attentive to our neighbors and encourage them to become stronger. For Christ was not self-serving, as it says in scripture: 'The insults of those who insult you have fallen on me.'* (15:1-3. The Inclusive New Testament)

The weakness to which Paul refers here is not that of individual fault or failing. It is the weakness imposed by a society and culture that devalue a group of human beings simply because of who they are – Jew, African, Woman, Serbian, Homosexual, etc. These people are not weak in terms of personal character. They are weak because the social system seeks to rob them of their place, and the dominant culture tries to take away their God-given value. They are declared out of place and unwanted. In other words, they are in exile, something of which Paul, as a Jew, knew only too well.

Will the Gentile-Christians simply go along with Roman prejudice and sacrifice the Jews, or will they be willing to sacrifice their own status to stand in solidarity, just as Christ did on the cross? Neil Elliott summarizes Paul's purpose in Romans very well.

> Paul meant simply to deflect the Roman Christians from the trajectory of anti-Jewish attitudes and ideology along which they were already traveling, a trajectory that would implicate them ever more in the scapegoating of the Jews, already visible in Roman culture – a scapegoating that would become a mainstay of Christian orthodoxy within a generation.[47]

# CHAPTER 9 – AT-ONE-MENT WITH CREATION: MEISTER ECKHART

**Common Ground**

Eckhart was born into lower aristocracy around the year 1260 CE His place of birth, most likely, was Tambach in Saxony. He later (1270's) entered the newly formed Order of Preachers (or Dominicans). The Dominicans sent him on to Paris, a city renowned for its education, where he was promoted to a lecturer in the fall of 1293.

Corruption and turmoil characterized the church and society of the late 13th and 14th centuries. A great debate existed over how theology should be taught and to what extent theologians should make use of some of the rediscovered philosophers, such as Aristotle. One of Eckhart's predecessors, Thomas Aquinas, later canonized a saint, saw his own teaching come under suspicion. After Aquinas' death, church leaders went so far as to have some of his theology condemned and his books burned.

This public humiliation of Aquinas did not deter Eckhart. He continued to hold Aquinas in high esteem, even at the cost of his own reputation. Eckhart's commitment to his friends did not easily wane. For example, he also did not keep his distance from a group of women called the Beguines (laywomen who lived in self-sufficient Christian communities throughout Europe), even though these courageous women were later condemned by the Council of Vienne in 1311-1312. Eckhart knew these pioneering women as partners of his in the mystical journey. Their wisdom and teaching helped feed Eckhart's own spirit and mind. What mattered above all else to Eckhart was the truth. He held 'everything that is true, whether in being or in knowing, in scripture or in nature, proceeds from one source and one root of truth.'[48]

Eckhart became widely known as Meister (German for Master), since he was made a Master in the University. Being Meister Eckhart, however, did not help him escape either the cloud of Roman suspicion or the long hand of its judgment. Pope John XXII appointed two commissions to investigate charges against Eckhart. He died in 1328, while he was en route from his trial. He never heard for himself the verdict. The commissions judged that over twenty of his theological ideas contained either 'the error or stain of heresy,' or were 'evil-sounding and very rash and suspect of heresy.' Two others – which Eckhart had denied ever saying – were also judged as being heretical. And yet, the commissions did not declare Eckhart to be a heretic. Why? Because he had promised to renounce any of the ideas judged to be heretical. Until the end, however, Eckhart denied preaching heresy. He insisted his accusers were unwilling to try and understand his words in their context. Today, Eckhart stands vindicated, even if controversial. Most theologians agree there is nothing heretical in his theology, even if he does challenge some of the basic ways we tend to view God, ourselves, creation and salvation.[49]

Meister Eckhart was born into a world that had erected a wall between the life of the laity and those in religious orders (referred to as 'religious'). He simply rejected such divisions and dared to preach the same word to both lay and religious. His commitment to what we might describe today as the spirituality of all persons seemed to strike terror in the heart of the Roman authorities. When he preached, Eckhart did not moralize. His sermons were invitations because he believed people knew what was best for them, if only they would begin to take the time to look deeply into their hearts and minds.

Eckhart preached to arouse awareness. People were not bad; they were, so to speak, asleep to their own true nature. Other preachers admonished the populace to such devotional practices as meditating on a blood-drenched crucifix or acts of self-inflicted pain. Eckhart believed life offered enough suffering. What we needed to do was to follow the way of Jesus and focus beyond our own self-centered wills. People needed to learn how to transform the suffering life gives them through wise encouragement, not severe asceticism and moral judgment.

> People think God has only become a human being there – in his historical incarnation – but that is not so; for God is here – in this very place – just as much incarnate as in a human being long ago. And this is why he has become a human being: that he might give birth to you as his only begotten Son, and as no less.[50]

You. Me. Everyone and every creature we meet. Each and every one is, for Eckhart, an only begotten child of God. Eckhart was asking the church to see all of creation as having life only insofar as it is in God. Apart from God there is only death. Everything, without exception, is the living presence, or incarnation, of God.

Here we come to at least part of the reason Eckhart preached to both lay and religious – all persons are manifestations of God. Matthew Fox says that for Eckhart 'spirituality is our waking-up – in our consciousness and our work lives and our ways of living – waking up to the divine presence everywhere.'

Because of his theology of creation, Eckhart is drawn to the image of the reign of God envisioned in the gospel of Luke: 'know that the reign of God is near' (Luke 21:31). He celebrates in his preaching that the kingdom of God is within us, and as St. Paul says, that our salvation is nearer to us than we believe (Romans 13:11). Eckhart was able to see what the church authorities could not – 'God is nearer to me than myself . . . He is also near and present for a stone or piece of wood, but they know nothing about this fact.'[51] Eckhart was convinced that it is impossible for us to be far from God. What happens is that we are the ones who can create a false distance where there is none. But, this distance is our creation and not God's.

Eckhart's words, over and over again, seek to heal the fault line separating religious and laity running of the medieval church of the 14th century: the religious lived with the holy and sacred while the laity slugged out life in the dark, profane, and secular world. Meister Eckhart would have none of this. 'God,' he declared, 'is equally near all creatures.'[52] All that exists is sacred, for everything in creation is a word of God.

## COMMON GROUND

As we have seen, for Eckhart creation is united with God from the beginning. But we, as human beings, unlike a stone or a piece of wood, can come to believe and act as if we lived at a distance from God. When Eckhart looked about him in the early 14th century, he saw a church and its piety riddled with this false perception. It shrouded life like a dense fog, blinding people to reality. His preaching was ceaseless fire burning through the haze when he reminded people that every human desire and its fulfillment is to be united with God. "Yes, all things become simply God to you, for in all things you notice and love only God, just as a man stares long at the sun in heaven and sees the sun in whatever he afterward looks at."[53]

Every single person, said Eckhart, is called to the mystical life. The mystical life is nothing other than the journey whereby we discover we are blessed from the beginning by being one with God. To follow the way of Christ is to break through the fog in order to know from our own experience that 'God's ground is my ground, and my ground is God's ground.'

When he preached, Eckhart sought to help people follow this way of Christ. He identified three threads that intertwine like the braids of a Celtic spiral creating a path. As we follow this path we penetrate ever deeper and ever wider into the divine common ground. When we finally break through we taste for ourselves that everything is the presence of the living God. We then begin to care for ourselves, one another, and all creation, from hearts of divine compassion. We attend to Christ whenever Christ draws near, like Martha in Luke's gospel (Luke 10:38-42)

### Thread One: Letting-Go

There is certainly a time and place for prayers of praise and song, lamentations and petitions, in our lives. But, if we are finally to find the ground that is our union with God, Eckhart says each of us must learn to spend time in silence and stillness. This is a time to let go of everything that grabs our attention each day.

Prayer in silence and stillness is time for simplicity. Eckhart asks us to learn to do away with all images and all concepts. We do this in our prayer not because these things are somehow evil or bad, but because they are obstacles.

Creation and all its wonders can be so good that they sidetrack our mind; all our attention becomes absorbed by things of this world rather than the God, or God's ground, from which all things come. This is true of prayer, also. There is a time for the beautiful language of spoken prayer. There is also a time for the beauty of silent listening and waiting in stillness.

So Eckhart invites us to begin our own mystical journey by learning to let go of *everything*. This is the way of centering prayer and then *contemplation*, where the only thing of which we are aware is God's presence. Letting go is the practice whereby we become more than the desires of our individual egos.

Eckhart describes letting go as experiencing a kind of poverty. 'He is a poor person,' he says, 'who wills nothing and knows nothing and has nothing.' He goes on to say 'true poverty of spirit consists in keeping oneself so free of God and of all one's works that if God wants to act in the soul, God himself becomes the place wherein he wants to act – and this God likes to do.'[54] Amazingly enough, Eckhart is promising us that if we persevere in our journey, eventually we will discover for ourselves that in letting go completely, we see that God is completely already with us.

Eckhart speaks of even letting go of God. What he means by this is that the names we have learned to address God get in the way of simply being present to God. We confuse God with our human names and images. Beyond every name we have for God lies the true fullness of God, which Eckhart calls the *Godhead*. The Godhead is God beyond all images and names. The Godhead is our ultimate ground, where there is no language or need for words. Here we rest in the midst of compassion overflowing, with all false divisions burned away, and nothing to prove. Here we know ourselves as God's only begotten child. Here there is only unity. Eckhart tries to describe this by using such words as 'not-God' and 'not-mind.'

> You should love God mindlessly, that is, so that your soul is without mind and free from all mental activities, for as long as your soul is operating like a mind, so long does it have images and representations ... You should love him as he is, a not-God, not-mind, not person, not-image – even more, as he is a pure, clear One, separate from all twoness.[55]

**Thread Two: Birthing**

Once we begin to let go, we experience ourselves being born anew. This rebirth is not a simple being 'born-again.' Eckhart is describing a birthing process that never ends. It is a dawning awareness that 'I and God are one,' because we share the same ground. Unlike many of his contemporaries, Eckhart does not preach that God and I become one through ascetic practices or severe penitence. He says we become aware that we are already one, and we become aware by letting go.

For Eckhart, letting go is how our birthing into a new awareness takes place, and this birthing is just like the birth of Christ. Christ, as the Word of the Trinity, is eternally born in the womb of God. Eckhart's language is remarkably maternal: God is the Mother of the Word, and God is also the Mother of every word. When we each further let go of things we cling to in this world, as if they were god to us, God our Mother births us more fully into the light of divine love.

**Thread Three: Breakthrough**
As a child emerges from the womb of the mother, there is a time in our journey when we finally break through the fog that has blinded us, and we see for the first time that 'God's ground is my ground, and my ground is God's ground.' Eckhart describes this breakthrough as a kind of death – a final letting go of everything. 'In this death the soul loses all her desires, all images, all understandings and all form and is stripped of all her being. . . This spirit is dead and is buried in the Godhead, for the Godhead lives as no other than itself.'[56]

What the soul discovers, Eckhart says, is who she has always been from the beginning but did not know. The only path into this awareness has been the soul's willingness to forsake 'all things, God and creatures.' In whatever the person sees now – a neighbor, a stone, a piece of wood – the person sees God. The fog has been burned away; all that remains is the Godhead. Bernard McGinn insists, 'no mystic in the history of Christianity was more daring and more detailed than Eckhart in the way in which he explored how true union with God' was absolute and total.[57]

## COMPASSION AND JUSTICE
Because our union is with a God who is Compassion and Justice, our breakthrough also entails being born into lives of compassion and justice for one another and all creation. Justice, for Eckhart, is 'a certain rightness' whereby each person receives their 'due.' Since every person and everything is the very presence of God, their due is boundless compassion. Once awake to our divine common ground, we cannot help but care for all God's creation. The great commandment, to love God and one another, is really one gift – the gift of compassion.

Eckhart's mystical way – letting go, birthing, and breakthrough – leads him to view the story of Martha and Mary (Luke 10:38-42) in a remarkably creative and inviting way. For him, compassion and justice were the fruit of the mystical breakthrough. Martha reveals this so clearly when she tells Mary to get up and care for Jesus, not because she is critical of her sister, but because of her love for her. Mary is in danger of being seduced into inaction. Eckhart believes that 'Martha knew Mary better than Mary Martha, for Martha had lived long and well; and living gives the most valuable kind of knowledge.' Mary was in danger of becoming 'stuck' in the pleasure of contemplation. Martha, however, was aware of her ground being God's ground. Eckhart describes her as one of those persons who can 'stand in the midst of things, but not in things.' Because she has discovered her 'splendid ground,'[58] Martha is free to care for Jesus. She invites Mary – and all of us – into the same awareness, where we are totally free to care compassionately for whoever is before us.

### Invitation: Awakening to Our At-one-ment

To be a Christian is to be a theologian in a community of theologians. As Christians, we reflect together on our experiences, endeavoring to see more clearly who and how God is in our midst, as well as who we are and how we are to live in community.

It is clear from our discussions of Second-Isaiah that the Hebrew people were theologians also. In fact, it is accurate to say that each and every person, having been created in the image of God, is invited to be a theologian. A simpler way of saying this is that every one desires, in their heart of hearts, to know and love the One who has given them birth and who calls them home. This One, whom Christians call God, is the beginning and end, the alpha and omega.

One of the essential reasons human beings are gathered by the Spirit is to do theology. When we come together we have eyes beyond our own, and hearts and minds beyond our own, to help us wrestle with our experiences – especially our experiences of brokenness, separation and bondage. It is as if by the sheer fact of being face-to-face with friends, we are reminded that despite appearances, there is a unity already within and among us. The Spirit gathers and re-gathers us, and in so doing, reminds us that we are always already at-one with the living God and each other. But, we forget. Or more accurately, our sight grows dim.

Redemption is about rediscovering sight. Or, we might describe it as re-awakening to the light within all – everyone and everything. In his marvelous book, *The Book of Creation: An Introduction to Celtic Spirituality*, J. Philip Newell describes a Celtic theology of redemption, a description that echoes Meister Eckhart and is helpful to our own discussion:

> In the Celtic tradition redemption is the journey of being reconnected to the light of God within. It is a journey home that takes us through what seems like unknown land....It is not that God has been absent from us but that we have been absent from God, and therefore from the light that is within us and at the center of all life. God's light is the very root of life. Too often in our Western religious traditions we have

been given the impression that sin has had the power to undo what God has woven into the very fabric of being. Redemption in such models of spirituality is about light coming from afar to shine in what is essentially dark. In the Celtic tradition, on the other hand, redemption is about light being liberated from the heart of creation and from the essence of who we are. It has not been overcome by darkness. Rather, the light is held in terrible bondages within us, waiting to be set free.[59]

Where are our own bondages personally, within our families, within our churches, towns, and workplaces? Another way of asking this same question is to consider where we continue to experience ourselves as not being *at-one*. Awakening to our at-one-ment is to have the light of Christ deep within begin to burn away the fog of false separation. Second-Isaiah, Paul, and Meister Eckhart, each in their own way, invite us as a community of faith to reflect and consider together the bondages which hold us down. These bondages try to convince us that we are at odds and a distance from ourselves, one another, and God.

### Awakening to our At-one-ment with God

Second-Isaiah reflects a Hebrew community struggling to see God as the one who is on the side of all victims. The songs of the suffering servant reveal the damage we can do as human beings when we are blind to the light within us. When we lose sight of our at-one-ment with God, we can then use God (who is the Light) to support and justify actions of destruction, actions whose real source is human fear, anger, anxiety. Blind to who we are and who God is we engage in actions that tear at the very fiber of human community. We begin to make the claim, over and over again, and then believe it, that some people (by what they may do or believe) can separate themselves from God. We come to believe, in the words of Newell, that sin has the 'power to undo what God has woven into the very fabric of being.' The songs of the suffering servant are cries of the human heart protesting this human delusion. The suffering servant is a human plea for restored wholeness – a wholeness already within and around us, but to which we become blind.

### Awakening to our At-one-ment with Each Other

Paul is compelled to write a letter to the Romans, a community he had not even helped to found, because of the self-centered behavior of many of the Gentile-Christians. They are under the false impression that God has favorites. Since Israel has not embraced Jesus in the way they have, they act and talk as if the Gentile-Christians have replaced Israel in God's eyes – as if the light of God's loving gaze does not fall equally upon all. Paul seeks to restore a sense of humility, historical perspective and respect. He uses the language, perhaps unfortunately, of the Jews having 'stumbled.' But his goal, nevertheless, seems commendable. Christians are to have a sense of respect and honor for their Jewish neighbors, for they too are God's own people. The Gentile-Christians must not, therefore, behave in such a way as to endanger the safety of their Jewish neighbors in Rome. This 'must not' is not a moral command, but a plea for an awakened heart. An awakened heart could not act otherwise. How would an awakened heart live and act? The Romans need look no further than the selfless act of the crucified one – here is the path of compassionate self-sacrifice. Once the Gentile-Christians in Rome begin to let go of their own egos, they might begin to see that they are at-one with their Jewish neighbors.

The Gentile-Christians in Rome reveal how human clinging begins to blind us to the path of life. What is it that we find ourselves clinging to (perfection, pleasing-others, success, status, knowledge, power, etc.), which, if we were willing to sacrifice, might open our eyes to see more clearly how we are at-one with our family, our congregation, neighbors, co-workers, etc.?

**Awakening to our At-one-ment with Creation**

Meister Eckhart invites us to consider taking a further step in our theology. Not only all people, but all creation, ('wood' and 'stone,' as Eckhart says) exist at all because they exist in the Godhead. Existence itself is nothing but grace. To be alive is the original blessing, with us from the beginning. And this blessing is nothing other, in Eckhart's theology, than God's very own self. Nothing can even exist apart from being in God, the source of all life and all light. Meister Eckhart's theology identifies the path of restoration as lying in our waking-up to who we are, to what all creation is – the very words of God. Just as the Word became flesh, so too do the divine words become flesh. Incarnation is simply another word for creation. Redemption is awakening to the reality that we, and all creation, are nothing other than Christ's own self. It is only to the degree that we are blind to this truth, that we hurt one another. God's ground is our ground and our ground is God's ground.

# ~Exploring At-One-Ment~

## Created At-One-Ment: Suffering Servant of Second Isaiah
### At-One Remembrances

Take a few moments to see if you can recall a time in your life when you experienced a sense of inner peace (a being at-one with your self). What was your experience like?

### Scapegoating

Has there ever been a person/group scapegoated in your town or community (now or sometime in the past)?

### Self-Sacrifice, Not of Jews: Romans Stumblings

Paul believes that the Jews have actually stumbled. How do you perceive this? Might it be possible that no one stumbles or that everyone (Jews, Christian, Muslims, Buddhists) stumbles? What difference, if any, does it make? How might you describe the relationship of Jews, Christians, Muslims, Buddhists, etc. with God? How does your perception impact your congregation's relationships with other religions in your town or city?

## Common Ground: Meister Eckhart
### Compassionate Caring

What gets in your way of caring for others? What do you need to let go of to allow you to care compassionately for others?

## Awakening to Our At-One-Ment with All
### Clinging

The Gentile-Christians in Rome reveal how human clinging begins to blind us to the path of life. What is it that you find yourself clinging to (such as perfection, pleasing-others, success, status, knowledge, power, etc.), which, if you were willing to sacrifice, might open your eyes to see more clearly how you are at-one with members of your family, members of our congregation, neighbors, co-workers, etc.?

# Part IV

# Honoring Humanity

"I consider filiation of God to be reckoned as nothing else than deification, which, in Greek is also called *theosis*."[60]
Nicholas of Cusa

*God is Truth,* and *Truth is God.*
Mohandas Gandhi[61]

The stories of Ezekiel, Corinthians, and Gandhi each speak to how we endeavor to live for the reign of God here and now in very practical ways. The stories embody values that invite us to be "warriors" of transformation.

We will discover that for Ezekiel it is how we treat one another that is of the most utmost concern to God, the *holy* God. God is 'the Human One,' and what matters to God is that 'the human ones' treat one another, care for one another, as *human* beings. The prophet Ezekiel conveys the startling divine message: God is revealed as 'the Human One' because we, as human beings, have not yet learned how to be what we were created to be.

Paul will provide a similar message in his letter to the community at Corinth. In contrast to much of the popular theology of the cross dominant today, we find here that the power of the cross lies in its ability to shake humanity loose from the nightmare through which we rationalize violent retribution. The wisdom of the cross lies in its ability to expose the deathtrap of this so-called redemptive violence. Paul has awakened to the truth that love is redemptive and forgiveness is salvific, healing our brokenness. These enduring truths hang on the cross of Jesus.

Mohandas Gandhi teaches us how to be warriors *of* peace and *for* peace. In Gandhi we see the values of the Christ with their spiritually transcendent meaning and incarnate power. From South Africa to India, Gandhi's life and teaching personify and clarify the power and wisdom of the cross. In the end, the other, like me, is a human one, a friend.

# Chapter 10 – Human Life is Already Divine: Ezekiel

## The Human One: God and Ezekiel

Ezekiel and Jeremiah are the only two prophets who bridge the fall of Jerusalem in 587 BCE They minister both before and after the great catastrophe. In the end, they share a similar humiliating fate – both are buried in foreign soil outside the promised land – Jeremiah in Egypt, and Ezekiel in Babylon (now Iraq). Jeremiah's critical insight into God was the divine pathos. Not so, for Ezekiel. Holiness, or God's unutterable splendor, marks his God.

It is possible to interpret God's holiness as a quality that separates God from creation. As we shall see shortly, however, the word 'separation' would be misleading. It causes us to imagine a gap or distance between God and us. Perhaps a better word to describe the impact of divine holiness would be to say that it *distinguishes* between God and creature. The God of Ezekiel cannot be reduced to or equated with creation. In words that Walter Brueggemann describes as some of 'the most dangerous and stunning texts in the Bible,' the God of Ezekiel proclaims:

> It is not for your sake, O house of Israel, that I am about to act, but for the sake of my holy name which you have profaned... (Ezekiel 36.22, Brueggemann's translation)[62]

The holy God of Ezekiel is a radically free God. God acts to cleanse and free Israel because as a holy being God can do nothing else.

We might ask ourselves, what is it that concerns such a holy God? Elie Wiesel, ironically it seems, says that 'As long as people offended heaven, God, in spite of his anger, was willing to wait. But when they ceased to be human toward one another, He had to intervene and punish them.'[63]

We can put aside for now the question of divine intervention. (For how does a God who is always already present intervene? Such intervention would presuppose that the God in whom we live, move, and have being is sometimes and somehow absent.) What is intriguing about Wiesel's insight is that human interaction would matter to the very holiness of God. God as holy is concerned, deeply concerned, with how human beings treat one another. This may not be the pathos of Jeremiah, but it certainly does not seem to be a holiness detached from human suffering. All of which brings us back to the vision of Ezekiel found in Chapter 1:

> *And above the dome over their heads was something like a throne, in appearance like sapphire; and seated above the likeness of a throne was something that seemed like a human form ('adam). Upward from what appeared like the loins I*

> *saw something like gleaming amber, something that looked like fire enclosed all around; and downward from what looked like the loins I saw something that looked like fire, and there was a splendor all around. Like the bow in a cloud on a rainy day, such was the appearance of the splendor all around. This was the appearance of the likeness of the glory of the Lord. When I saw it, I fell on my face, and I heard the voice of someone speaking. He said to me: O mortal ['son of man'], stand up on your feet, and I will speak with you.* (1:26-2:1 NRSV)

Reflecting on this account, Walter Wink describes it as 'one of the most understated visionary reports ever recounted.' At every turn, Ezekiel qualifies what he sees: 'something like,' or 'in appearance like,' or 'appeared like,' or 'looked like,' or the 'appearance of the likeness.' Ezekiel is at pains to avoid simplistic and misleading language. The vision so surpasses any expectation that the priestly prophet is careful not to reduce God's 'unutterable splendor' to human words.[64]

But, it is this very holy God who, when the decision is freely made to reveal the face of God to Ezekiel, reveals the unutterable splendor as 'something that seemed like a human form' (*'adam*). When the very survival of the Jewish faith hangs in the balance, Wink observes that God reveals the divinity as *'adam*. Or, as Wink translates this Hebrew word, 'the Human One.' Even more, when 'the Human One' addresses Ezekiel, the words spoken are: 'O mortal (or 'son of man').[65] The Human One speaks to the human one.

What might it mean for God to be revealed as 'the Human One' and for Ezekiel to be known and addressed by God as 'the human one'? 'The Human One' is Wink's translation of the Hebrew expression *ben 'adam*, which in Greek is *ho huios tou anthropou*. The more conventional translation of the Hebrew and Greek is 'son of man.' The more correct translation, although it sounds funny to our ears, is 'the son of *the* man.' 'The human being,' or 'the human one' is more inclusive and more accurate. But what does this expression mean?[66]

The expression is used more in Ezekiel than any other book in the scriptures. In fact, no other book even comes close to the ninety-three references found here. The expression, 'the human one,' or 'the human being,' is so central to Ezekiel that it occurs in the opening vision and describes the very face of God when turned to humanity. Much later, Wink notes, the Jesus tradition will draw upon this expression of Ezekiel. Jesus will use the expression more than eighty times and it is *only* Jesus, who uses it. What does the expression, 'the human one,' reveal about God and humanity? We need to return to Ezekiel's vision.

In the year of 593 BCE Israel is captive in Babylon. Marduk, the god of Babylon, for all apparent intents and purposes, seems victorious, dominant and unassailable. Yahweh lies defeated in the dust of the promised land. The priest Ezekiel has had his vision of 'the Human One.' But to put it so simply is to mislead and to misstate. Ezekiel's vision shook the very bedrock upon which Israel's faith was based. This Israelite priest, held captive by the worshipers of Marduk, experiences one of the most profound and moving visions of the holy ever recorded. Its seismic magnitude so shook the rabbis of later centuries that many argued for this book to be censored. Ezekiel, it seems, withheld very little, if any, of what he saw. And what he saw affects so very much, if not all, of our faith.

As Ezekiel waits in Babylon with his people, their faith is in crisis – Jerusalem has been defeated, her people captured and exiled, and the once-maintained unassailable might of Yahweh apparently vanquished. It might seem that Israel's hope would lie in a god refashioned to rival Babylon's Marduk – born, according to the creation myth, in the violent severing of Tiamat. But a god as military-monster is not the vision received by Ezekiel. Quite the opposite – God is revealed as *Human*.

Wink argues that 'the Human One' is not simply a figure of speech. Israel was well acquainted with figures of speech and did not confuse them with reality. Wink has this to say: 'If you had asked Israelites if God was walking in the Garden of Eden in the cool of the day because the noonday heat was disagreeable (Genesis. 3:8), they would likely have dismissed the question as impertinent: Of course not, that is only a figure of speech.'[67]

Ezekiel beholds God as 'the Human One' because this is how God reveals the Godhead. But why would God choose to be known in this way? Perhaps because human beings have not yet learned how to be what they were created to be. In other words, we have not yet acquired the wisdom of what it truly means to be a *human* being. If we were able to live as human beings then we would not abuse, enslave, and slaughter each other – which brings us back to the insight of Elie Wiesel. What mattered to God, the *holy* God, was that the Israelites had ceased being *human* toward one another.

Who is God? God is 'the Human One.' What matters to God? That 'the human ones,' which is to say, human beings who are God's children, treat one another, care for one another, as *human* beings. God asks only that we live as the creatures we have been created to be. Wink puts it rather well. Why does God freely reveal the Godhead as human? 'Perhaps because becoming human is the task that God has set for human beings.'[68]

In no way does this mean that God is *reduced* to being a human being. Ezekiel draws on many other images to describe the indescribable. But it does mean that at this absolutely crucial time in the history of Israel and its faith, God chooses to be known precisely as 'the Human One' and speaks to Ezekiel and through this priest to all of us, as 'the human ones.' Created in the image of God, as Genesis 1:26 reminds us, Ezekiel proclaims that it is the desire and will of God for human beings to become fully ourselves.

Ezekiel's revelation is that deep within us, as our very own selves, is the face of God. As human beings, not as something else, not as something other than who we have been created, God dwells. Israel's problem, our problem, is that we lose touch with our own innermost heart. Through inattention, abuse, fear, anger, and greed, the once tender heart becomes hardened. The holy God, 'the Human One,' appears and speaks to Ezekiel. God is acting and caring for humanity because humanity embodies the very presence of God. If God is to find God's own holiness in creation it will be in the humanity of human beings. God's own holiness is at stake when we fail to treat ourselves, one another, and all creation, with compassion and justice. It is a life and death situation. In the eyes of God, only a transplant will do. Human beings need new hearts – not hearts of angels or of Gods. No, human beings need truly *human* hearts – *hearts of flesh* pumping with the lifeblood of compassion and justice.

> *Thus, the nations will know that I am the Most High, says Our Sovereign God, because in their sight I prove my holiness through you. For I will take you away from among the nations, gather you from all the foreign lands, and bring you back to your own land. I will sprinkle clean water on you and cleanse you from all your impurities; I will cleanse you from all your idols. I will give you a new heart and place a new spirit within you; I will remove the heart of stone and give you a heart of flesh. I will put my Spirit within you and make you live by my statutes, careful to observe my decrees. You will live in the land I gave your ancestors; you will be my people, and I will be Your God.* (Ezekiel 36:23-28, Inclusive Lectionary Texts)

Hearts of flesh – this is God's desire for human beings. Hearts of flesh are holy *as* flesh. It is for this reason that human beings are not to shed the blood of other human beings (see Gen. 9:4-6 and Ez. 33:25). As 'the human ones' each and every one of us is made in the image of 'the Human One.' We do not have to become something else in order to be worthy of life in the eyes of God or each other. Our life has value because it is of the flesh.

Ezekiel's vision goes to the very heart of what it means to be a faithful, religious person. The purpose of human life is not to become divine. Human life, as created by God, in all of its brokenness, ambiguity, shortcomings, etc., is already divine, is already holy, is already sacred. In the words of Wink:

> What the mystics saw, like Ezekiel, was the human face of God, God as humanity needs to know God in order to become what God calls us to be. We become what our desire beholds. So the mystic is one who chooses to seek the God who freely offers us the gift of our own humanity, not as something to be attained, but as pure revelation. God, as it were, a mirror in which we find reflected our own 'heavenly,' that is, potential, face.[69]

# CHAPTER 11 – CROSS AT THE CROSSROADS: CORINTHIANS

## The Cross: Power and Wisdom Corinthians
**Paul and the Corinthians: An Uneasy Relationship**

Around 54 CE, while Paul was in Ephesus, he found it necessary to respond to a letter (which has not survived) from the Corinthians. Paul had founded this community several years earlier and now was somewhat dismayed – as well as defensive and angry, it would appear – to discover divisions and feuds threatening the community's life.

Serious disorders are brought to Paul's attention (1Corinthians 1:11; 5:1; 11:18): rival groups are vying with each other for power and control (1 Corinthians 1:10-17); a scandalous immoral action has occurred and the Corinthians seem indifferent to it (5:1-13); those who are supposedly more enlightened display a certain disdain for others (8:1-11.1); and those less well-off are pushed to the margins of community life (11:17-34). Perhaps what threatens Paul most is that his own authority is being called into question (1:12; 3:1-4.5; 9).

Paul's initial response is 1st Corinthians, which is at times harsh and excessive. After this letter Paul had a disastrous visit with the Corinthians and wrote a grieving 'letter of tears,' which we find today as actually part of 2 Corinthians (2 Corinthians 1:23-24; 7:5-11). There are at least four different and complex theories about how Paul wrote what we now know as 2 Corinthians (between 54 and 56 CE). In 2nd Corinthians, he has vastly changed his approach, perhaps through the influence of Timothy, his companion, and penned one of the most moving letters of the Christian scriptures. There are times where he is ironic and argumentative (chapters. 10-13), but he is also joyful and conciliatory (chapter. 7). All in all, 2 Corinthians is not an easy letter to interpret. But, woven through both of Paul's letters, regardless of mood, is the cross. Again and again he turns to the cross, not only as the source of wisdom to see the Corinthians through their current strife, but as the power to neutralize anger and heal division.

The Corinthians and Paul are on a journey and the cross, so to speak, is their guiding star. The cross has a long history of guiding the human pilgrimage into God. Within a number of the cathedrals of Western Europe there is a labyrinth – if not within the sanctuary itself, then somewhere on the cathedral grounds. A remarkable characteristic of these labyrinths is that at their center most often lies the cross. Originally, labyrinths did not incorporate the cross. Christians, however, embraced the labyrinth, with its wisdom that life is a sacred journey with unforeseen twists and turns, and placed the cross at its heart. The Christian insight was, and remains today, that there is no way into the heart of God, the holy of holies, except through the cross.

## A Messiah Nailed to a Cross

What might it mean to say that there is no way into the heart of God except through the cross? How is it that the cross lies at the heart of the Gospels and even launched the Christian movement? What does the cross say about God? Does God somehow demand Jesus' crucifixion? If we say that the way into the heart of God is only through the cross, does that mean that punishment and blood sacrifice lie at the heart of the way of Jesus? How do we walk the way of the cross today?

Paul's letters to the Corinthians can give us some insight, because it is only in the light of the cross that this Jewish follower of 'the Way' understands and proclaims Jesus. One biblical scholar goes so far as to say that Paul proclaimed a crucified Christ as *the* model of authentic humanity. What kind of humanity is Jesus modeling for us?

Let us look at a couple of opening passages from 1 Corinthians.

> *For while the Jews call for miracles and the Greeks look for wisdom, here we are preaching a Messiah nailed to a cross. To the Jews this is an obstacle they cannot get over, and to the Greeks it is madness — but to those who have been called, whether they are Jews or Greeks, Christ is the power and the wisdom of God. For God's foolishness is wiser than human wisdom, and God's weakness is stronger than human strength.* (1 Cor. 1:22-25. The Inclusive New Testament)

> *As for myself, sisters and brothers, when I came to you I did not come proclaiming God's testimony with any particular eloquence or wisdom. No, I determined that while I was with you I would know nothing but Jesus Christ — Christ crucified.* (1 Cor. 2:1-2. The Inclusive New Testament)

What is it about 'a Messiah nailed to a cross,' as Paul puts it, that is so important that it is the crux of our very salvation? Where are we to find the healing or saving 'power and wisdom of God' in this gruesome act of empire-sanctioned public execution? What can it possibly mean for Paul to say that he knows nothing but 'Jesus Christ – Christ crucified?' These questions run to the very heart of Paul's faith and ours. Paul states without hesitation or qualification that the healing of our brokenness (which is another way to describe salvation) lies in our willingness to trust that the cross reveals the only path to wholeness (which is another way to describe faith). How can this be so?

## Anselm: Jesus Sent by God to Die – Cross Satisfies God's Need for Satisfaction

In *Chapter 7, At-One-Ment with God: Second Isaiah*, we discussed that from the beginning, through the utter graciousness of God, we have been created at-one with God. This is true not only of our relationship with God, but with one another and all creation. This truth about who we are – a people at-one with God — has implications for how we view 'a Messiah nailed to a cross,' and the wisdom of God revealed to us in the crucifixion of Jesus of Nazareth. This truth raises questions about the meaning of the cross, especially as this meaning has been understood in the light of the theology of Anselm. For Anselm, God willed the crucifixion.

Since the twelfth century, almost all of Western Christian theology of the cross has been deeply influenced by the brilliant theology of St. Anselm. Living in a feudal world of medieval Europe, where social order and honor were of paramount importance, Anselm drew upon his culture, as Christians do in every age, to try and make sense of Christ crucified. Richard McBrien, a Roman Catholic theologian who studies the church, describes the theory Anselm created in this way:

> Anselm's theory is to be understood against the background of the Germanic and early medieval feudal system. There is a bond of honor between the feudal lord and vassal. Infringement of the lord's honor is tantamount to an assault upon the whole feudal system. A demand for satisfaction, therefore, is not for sake of appeasing the lord's personal sense of honor but for the sake of restoring order to the 'universe' (feudal system) in which, and therefore against which, the 'sin' was committed. The feudal lord cannot simply overlook the offense, because the order of his whole economic and social world is at stake. So, too, with God.

> For Anselm, the original sin of Adam had offended God – the Great Feudal Lord– and separated humanity from God (ripping apart our at-one-ment). The cross was God's response to this offense and breach of at-one-ment. Using Paul's language, we could say that for Anselm, the power and wisdom of God made manifest in the cross

was that through the crucifixion of Jesus we were once again made at-one with God.[70]

Original sin separated humanity and creation from God. Simple human beings could not repair the breach, because mere mortals can not reach out and touch the divine. Only the death of a divine one – Jesus (because he was both divine and human) – could heal the division caused by Adam and compounded by every human being since. Anselm proposed that Jesus was sent by God to suffer death on the cross for our redemption (which is to say, heal the breach).

Human beings themselves could not restore the order and give God the honor due the divine name, because we are sinful and broken, unable to offer a perfect sacrifice to a perfect lord. God is a perfect Lord who demands a perfect sacrifice. Like a feudal lord, God could not simply overlook our offence. According to Anselm's feudal worldview, things had to be made right again – God's holiness and honor had to be satisfied. For this reason, God became incarnate in Jesus Christ, to heal our sin by offering up the perfect sacrifice of his complete obedience – even obedience to accept God's will that he be unjustly and horrifically crucified by the Romans.

> With Anselm's theology of atonement, the Incarnation's sole purpose was to drive relentlessly to the act of dying... Though he forbade his own monks from joining the Crusades, Anselm's doctrine of the atonement gave support for holy war. Christians were exhorted to imitate Christ's self-offering in the cause of God's justice. When authorities in the church called for vengeance, they did so on God's behalf. As Anselm wrote, "When earthly rulers exercise vengeance justifiably, the one who is really exercising it is the One who established them in authority for this very purpose."
>
> [B]y the eleventh century, the church's rituals had virtually reversed the traditions of Cyril's fourth-century Jerusalem. Instead of mourning the Crucifixion once a year and marking the Resurrection daily, the Resurrection slowly receded in importance."
>
> Anselm's theology and piety crystallized the religious foundation of the Crusades. "Peace by the blood of the Cross.[71]

Jesus alone (who is utterly innocent) was the perfect sacrifice both demanded and accepted by God, thereby wiping the slate clean. Wiping the slate clean – for Anselm, this is the power and wisdom of the crucifixion of which Paul speaks. The crucifixion restores order and makes us once again at-one with God.

## Abelard: How Could Anyone Demand the Shedding of Innocent Blood?

Abelard, one of Anselm's peers, was perhaps the first of countless faithful who have questioned this understanding of the power and wisdom of the cross. Abelard's own words are quite moving:

> Indeed, how cruel and wicked it seems that anyone should demand the blood of an innocent person as the price for anything, or that it should in any way please him that an innocent man should be slain – still less that God should consider the death of his Son so agreeable that by it he should be reconciled to the whole world![72]

Abelard's perception is indeed remarkable, given that he is part of the same medieval feudal culture as Anselm. What is perhaps so tragic in Anselm's theory of atonement is that God can *only* be satisfied by blood-revenge. God, who is love, and whose mercy knows no bounds – even if we were to make our bed in hell (as the psalmist writes) – is reduced by Anselm to a vindictive and petulant parent. God's thirst for satisfaction can only be slated by the killing of his own child. God is no different than any other person or feudal lord. Instead of God's ways not being our ways, God's ways have been reduced to our ways – at least the ways of the bruised ego and its need for social order and honor.

## Power and Wisdom of the Cross:
## Path of Life is in Forgiveness, Not Revenge

But if the power and wisdom of the cross do not lie in its capacity to *make* us one with God, where are they to be found? If God does not demand or will the crucifixion, what else might Paul be referring to when he speaks about the cross's power and wisdom? What might the cross have to say not only to Christians but to all human beings?

One starting place is the words Jesus utters from the cross in the gospel of Luke: 'Abba forgive them. They don't know what they are doing.' (Luke 23:34 The Inclusive New Testament) The crowd had been given a choice. They could have asked Pilate for the release of Jesus Barabbas or Jesus bar Abba. From Mark's gospel we know that Jesus Barabbas was a prisoner 'who was jailed along with the rioters who had committed murder in the uprising' (Mark 14.7). The choice then was quite clear: Barabbas, a child ('bar') of violence – whose parent (or abba) was blood vengeance; or Jesus, a child of mercy – whose parent (or abba) was loving-forgiveness. Barabbas follows the path of endless retribution. Jesus follows the path of endless forgiveness.

The cross looms before humanity at the crossroads. Will we choose the path of death or the path of life? The crowd, John's gospel tells us, chooses Barabbas. They choose to be sons and daughters of violence. They, like the high-priest Caiaphas, think it better that one person die than have the Romans discipline all the Jews. Jesus is the perfect scapegoat, just like every other perfect scapegoat human beings have offered-up thru the ages. And yet, Jesus says, *'Abba forgive them. They don't know what they are doing.'* There is not even a hint from Jesus that his honor is being violated and that, in time, he will demand a satisfying repayment in someone's blood.

The people are convinced that in choosing Barabbas they are choosing life. Oddly enough, like Anselm, they think this sacrifice will satisfy the needs of the oppressive parent – the Roman occupiers – and make things all right again. The crowd seeks a scapegoat, but Jesus does not. He willingly accepts the cross as the consequence of his life committed without reserve to including all within the loving embrace of God. Jesus' table excludes no one – rich, haughty, poor and destitute, women, men, and children. Jesus' company of companions excludes no one – tax collectors, prostitutes, and zealots. Jesus' forgiveness is withheld from no one who accepts it. He is willing to die, not because God has sent him to be crucified, but because he is unwilling not to love whoever is before him, behind him, beside him.

The crowd failed to see that Jesus' inclusive love offered the path of life. The crowd remained wound-up within the nightmare of vengeance. Jesus can only forgive – even from the cross. From the cross, Jesus does not utter words of derision, words of hate, words of judgment, or words of revenge. He utters words of forgiveness. Even more, after his death we have no stories in the gospels of a risen One demanding retribution for his name's sake on the part of the disciples. Jesus shares a meal and invites his friends to continue to do likewise.

Here we begin to see that the power of the cross lies in its ability to shake humanity loose from the nightmare whereby we rationalize retribution and even see God as a God in need of retribution. The wisdom of the cross lies in its ability to expose the deathtrap of redemptive violence.

Jesus offers redemption, not Barabbas. Love is the path of life, not vengeance. God could not have sent Jesus to be crucified because it would contradict who God is: Love Unbound. Any power or principality (human or otherwise), which dares to offer violence as the path of life and of God is exposed by the cross as false. Jesus is not crucified because God wants him to be killed, or God needs him to be killed. Jesus is publicly executed because he will not compromise the love of God, even if it costs him his life.

Love is redemptive. Forgiveness is salvific (or healing). Enemies now are friends. These are the truths that hang on the cross of Jesus. These are the truths embodied in Paul's proclamation of a 'Messiah nailed to a cross.' This is the Jesus who is a model for authentic humanity. They are also truths of which we can all too easily lose sight. The fledgling community of Corinth knows this only too well, which is why Paul writes to remind them of their unity. At times, in his first letter, Paul is extreme in his words. His tone moderates in the beautiful second letter. Whether he is chastising or encouraging, Paul does so with the crucified Christ in mind.

If Corinth is to survive as a *Christian* community, it will only be because they have taken to heart Paul's theology of the cross. They must neutralize – or transform – all obstacles that divide and devalue. Everything must be subjected to the way, the cross, of Jesus (1 Corinthians 15:24- 27a).

# CHAPTER 12 – LOVE WITHOUT BOUNDS: MOHANDAS GANDHI

## *Satyagraha* Warrior

> *Generations to come will scarcely believe that such a one as this ever in flesh and blood walked upon this earth.*
> Albert Einstein[73]

We have said that in the spiritual journey descent invariably precedes ascent. The controlling ego needs to die before the true self, which is always an expression of the larger Self, the Christ, can be born. With the ego firmly in place there is no room for anything to be born. The mystics have accepted this truth and followed it.

In the gospel of Matthew, some of the religious scholars and Pharisees say to Jesus, 'Teacher, we want to see a miraculous sign from you.' They want the light, to be dazzled, at no cost to themselves. Jesus responds, 'It is an evil and unfaithful generation that asks for a sign! The only sign to be given is the sign of Jonah the prophet' (Matthew 12:38, 39. The Inclusive New Testament). The only sign which life offers, or more accurately, which offers life, is the one we actually live – we, ourselves, enter into the belly of darkness and learn to trust. Sooner or later we will be coughed-up on the shores, with our ego left behind and life within and before us.

At the age of 23, Mohandas Gandhi – an educated lawyer dressed in fine clothes – was tossed from a South African train into the belly of apartheid. As he sat through the night, cold, humiliated, desperate, he saw himself faced with a choice: he could take-up violent arms (in the long tradition of zealotry for a just cause); he could give-up and return to India; or, he could stand-up for his rights and courageously face the consequences – whatever they might be.

Gandhi was born in 1869 in Porbandar, India. He was the fourth child of a prominent local politician, who provided a middle-class home, and a devout Hindu mother, given to frequent and extended fasts. Gandhi married Kasturbai when he was 13, a union pre-arranged by the families in traditional fashion. Six years later, he set sail for London to study law. Naive to the ways of the world and ashamed to admit his culturally-arranged marriage, he matriculated as a bachelor, and became a well-dressed Englishman.

> While remaining staunchly Hindu at heart, young Mohandas transformed himself during his years in London into a proper English gentleman. He bought his evening clothes on Bond Street, wore a 'chimney-pot' hat and winged collars whenever he dined out,

and taught himself 'the art' of knotting his black bow tie. 'I wasted ... ten minutes every day before a huge mirror ... arranging my tie and parting my hair.' He paid for private lessons in dancing, French elocution, and violin. He quickly abandoned the violin, though he purchased one, and gave up dancing classes as well, finding it 'impossible to keep time.'[74]

Gandhi was dressing for success. He was molding himself to fit into British society and to rise steadily within its ranks. He had deceived himself as to what the world was like. What he saw when he gazed into the mirror for ten minutes every day was what he wanted desperately to see – an English gent in bloom.

Being thrown from the train, one week after his arrival in South Africa, April of 1893, shattered his mirror, offering him the chance to see through the pretense and discover that it was impossible to keep-up the guise of being someone he was not. Apartheid depended for its survival upon clear-cut boundaries. Although Gandhi spoke English, boasted an education and law degree, and dressed in fine apparel, he could not change the obvious – he was Indian and 'colored.' He was thus unceremoniously tossed from the train because he dared act as if he were a white South African worthy of being seated in first-class.

Gandhi did not strike back violently; nor did he run away a coward. Lying face-down in the dirt he found himself with the perennial options that confront every one of us at some time or another in life: fight or flight, red in tooth and claw or pale-white in hasty escape. Neither course seemed a true option for Gandhi. He stayed in the belly of apartheid for the next 20 years and allowed its unjust and brutal violence to teach him the ways of non-violence (or *ahimsa*), and to chart the course of non-violent action (*satyagraha*).

Nonviolence, said Gandhi,

> is the greatest force at the disposal of humanity. It is mightier than the mightiest weapon of destruction devised by the ingenuity of humanity. Destruction is not the law of humans. Humans live freely by their readiness to die, if need be, at the hands of a brother, never by killing another. Every murder or injury no matter for what cause, committed or inflicted on another, is a crime against humanity.[75]

*Ahimsa* (non-violence) was not a political strategy or tactic for Gandhi. It was a way of life, a way of being with one's self and others in this world. *Ahimsa* is a spirituality flowing from one's faith in God. Gandhi read daily not only from his beloved *Bhagavad Gita*, but also from the Christian Gospels (especially the Sermon on the Mount) and the *Qur'an* (*Koran*). He also studied the writings of Tolstoy, Thoreau, and Emerson. But *ahimsa* was not birthed from thought, but through the crucible of experience.

Gandhi discovered and knew *ahimsa* because it was who he himself came to be – first in South Africa and then in India. The root of violence was the human heart. Beneath violence lay something even deeper: the law of nonviolence. Thirteen years after being tossed to the earth, Gandhi professed a vow to remain faithful to truth, nonviolence, celibacy, poverty, and fearlessness. He would stand up against the South Africans, founding a weekly newspaper (1904), establishing ashrams (communities for growing in the spirituality of nonviolence), leading public disobedience to racist laws (1906), encouraging the burning of registration cards (1908), leading the march from Newcastle to Volksrust (1913 - in protest to the £3 tax imposed on ex-indentured Indians), and negotiating the Indian Relief Act with the South African Government (1914).

The non-passive *ahimsa* of *satyagrahi* (the name for persons committed to the way of *satyagraha*) was clearly not for the faint of heart. 'Non-violence is not a cover for cowardice, but it is the supreme virtue of the brave....Cowardice is wholly inconsistent with nonviolence.... Non-violence presupposes ability to strike.'[76] Although the *satyagrahi* were able to strike, they would not. What distinguished the *satyagrahi* was a willingness to die for a cause rather than kill for it. 'Just as one must learn the art of killing in the training for violence, so one must learn the art of dying in the training for nonviolence.'[77]

The *satyagrahi* were willing to give the ultimate sacrifice. They were not willing to take that sacrifice from another, even an enemy. 'It is *no* nonviolence if we merely love those who love us. It is nonviolence only when we love those who hate us.'[78]

As a realist, Gandhi confronted evil when he found it, whether it is the racist South African registration cards or the unjust English laws forbidding Indians to manufacture their own salt. He mobilized the population so that its mass non-cooperation with evil forced the adversary to change its ways. Gandhi would not sanction violence as a response to violence, for this would only perpetuate its inherently disintegrating force. Violence, for whatever cause, is always based on the falsehood that love is not the law of the universe.

> It is the law of love that rules mankind. Had violence, i.e., hate ruled us, we should have become extinct long ago. And yet the tragedy of it is that the so-called civilized men and nations conduct themselves as if the basis of society was violence.[79]

To speak of love led Gandhi to reflect on God, as well as truth.

> And when you want to find Truth as God, the only inevitable means is love, that is, nonviolence, and since I believe that ultimately the means and ends are convertible terms, I should not hesitate to say that God is Love.[80]

The loving person, who can only be nonviolent if remaining true to their nature, *seeks* out creative ways not to cooperate with evil and injustice. If *satyagrahi* were willing to stand together in nonviolent noncooperation, Gandhi was utterly convinced that no one could withstand their transformative power – not even Hitler.

> Moreover, we should not forget that even evil is sustained through the cooperation, either willing or forced, of good people. Truth alone is self-sustained. In the last resort we can curb the power of the evildoers to do mischief by withdrawing all cooperation from them and completely isolating them.
> This in essence is the principle of nonviolent noncooperation. It follows, therefore, that it must have its roots in love. Its object should not be to punish the opponents or to inflict injury upon them. Even while noncooperating with them, we must make them feel that in us they have a *friend*, and we should try to reach their heart by rendering them humanitarian service whenever possible.[81]

We cannot help but hear echoes of the Christian gospels and the reign of God in Gandhi's way of *ahimsa*. The person of Jesus figures centrally in Gandhi's *ahimsa*. Gandhi insisted that 'all great religions of the world' are 'God-given,' realizing that there could be no lasting peace 'unless we learn not merely to tolerate but even respect the other faiths as our own.'[82] And yet, when Gandhi looked out upon the sea of Christianity he saw contradiction. 'Christ came into this world to preach and spread the gospel of love and peace, but what his followers have brought about is tyranny and misery. Christians, who were taught the maxim of 'Love thy neighbor as thyself,' are divided among themselves.'[83]

Even if Christianity swayed from its gospel of love and peace, Gandhi had no misgivings about Jesus. 'Jesus expressed, as no other could, the spirit and will of God. It is in this sense that I see him and recognize him as the Son of God....I believe that he belongs not solely to Christianity, but to the entire world, to all races and people.'[84] For Gandhi, 'Jesus was the most active resister known perhaps to history. His was nonviolence par excellence.'[85]

Gandhi had no hesitation about embracing Jesus and his teaching embodied in the Sermon on the Mount. He also had no qualms about reading from the *Qur'an* for its wisdom. Gandhi went where the Truth led him – regardless.

I would say with those who say 'God is Love,' God is Love. But deep down in me, I used to say that though God may be Love, God is Truth above all. If it is possible for the human tongue to give the fullest description of God, I have come to the conclusion that God is Truth. Two years ago, I went a step further and said that Truth is God. You will see the fine distinction between the two statements, 'God is Truth,' and 'Truth is God.'[86]

Follow the Truth and it will always lead to God, who is love, whose way is nonviolence. This is the Truth at the heart of all creation, a Truth which reveals the lie contained in any and all violence. Violence violates God, because it rejects the love which is the Truth of God's very being. As Gandhi spent increasing time in silence, devoting a day a week to silence later in his life, he came to know this Truth intimately. What is the aim of life? 'It is to know the self. This realization of the self, or self-knowledge, is not possible until one has achieved unity with all living beings, until one has become one with God. To accomplish such a unity implies deliberate sharing of the suffering of others and the eradication of such suffering.'[87]

In this we hear a distinct echo of Jesus. The only sign we have is to go deep within the belly of the whale. This journey does not take us away from others. On the contrary, the more we come to experience who we truly are – one with God in love – the more we are drawn to eradicate the suffering of others. Such love, lived in eradicating the suffering of the world, is simply another word for the reign of God. 'My experience,' said Gandhi, 'tells me that the Kingdom of God is within us, and that we can realize it not by saying, 'Lord, Lord,' but by doing God's will and God's work. If therefore we wait for the Kingdom to come as something coming from outside, we shall be sadly mistaken. Try to identify yourselves with the poor by actually helping them.'[88]

*Ahimsa* is effective because an 'ocean of compassion' is the law of life. God's reign is the reign of God because its life-spirit is nonviolence. Jesus testified to God's nonviolent reign, bearing the ultimate sacrifice – his violent crucifixion. Gandhi observed that 'The ministry of Jesus lasted only for three brief years. His teaching was misunderstood even during his own time, and today's Christianity is a denial of his central teaching, 'Love your enemy.'" Islam fared no better in Gandhi's eyes. 'Six centuries rolled by and Islam appeared on the scene. Many Muslims will not even allow me to say that Islam, as the word implies, is unadulterated peace. My reading of the Koran has convinced me that the basis of Islam is not violence.' Gandhi came to a striking conclusion: 'I am convinced that both these great faiths will live only to the extent that their followers imbibe the central teaching of nonviolence. But it is not a thing to be grasped through the intellect, it must sink into our hearts.'[89]

When Gandhi married Kasturbai, he first envisioned himself more as her lord and master than a friend and partner. He believed that Kasturbai was 'born to do her husband's behest, rather than a helpmate, a comrade, and a partner in the husband's joys and sorrows.' The way of violence had penetrated deep into his heart. But if *ahimsa* is a way of life, not a political strategy, then it must be allowed to reorder all of our relationships. Gandhi was thus a champion of women in India, a commitment born from a realization in his marriage – 'I am no longer a blind, infatuated husband. I am no more my wife's teacher. *We are tried friends*, the one no longer regarding the other as the object of lust.'[90]

The similarity of Gandhi's *ahimsa* with Johannine theology is striking. In John's gospel, Jesus no longer calls us servants; we are friends. Jesus has revealed all to us. And what has he revealed? God is love. And there is no greater expression of love than to lay down one's life for one's friends. And who are our friends? In Gandhi's eyes, *everyone*. Love has absolutely no bounds. Enemy is an empty word, a false word.

Gandhi is saying that if we do as Jesus bids us, loving our enemies (Luke 6:27), then they cease to be our enemies. Living from the divine wellspring of love, we find ourselves unable to name an enemy. Gandhi never shot back at the South Africans or the British. 'There is no such thing as shooting out of love.'[91]

Gandhi spent over six years in prison. His vision only grew clearer. On August 15, 1947, India won its independence. The bullets then flew between Hindu and Muslim, as India and Pakistan went their separate ways. Hoping to stop the warring and move the people to unity and peace, on September 1 Gandhi declared a fast unto death. As he approached death, the violence stopped.

Gandhi was keenly aware that there were many of his own Hindu tradition who vehemently disagreed with his embrace of the Muslim and Christian. *For them Truth was not God, rather God was their version of the truth.* So many of his Indian sisters and brothers had not been transformed by *ahimsa*, but had used it as a political tool only. Now, they reverted to guns and violence with their Muslim neighbors. Gandhi sensed that one of the religious fanatics might well kill him.

> On January 29, he said to a friend, 'If someone were to end my life by putting a bullet through me, and I met his bullet without a groan and breathed my last taking God's name, then alone would I have made good my claim.' Gandhi felt that he had failed to convince India that nonviolence was the only way to independence. The partition of the country, the massacres, the riots, the deep hatreds, and the world war left him sad and depressed. Still, he continued his public work of disarmament and planned to travel to Pakistan. On

January 30 1948, at 5:10 p.m., as he walked through the garden to his evening prayer service, Gandhi was shot and killed. He fell to the ground calling out God's name.[92]

**Invitation: Honoring Our Humanity**

Each one of us as theologian draws upon the scriptures as a resource for our work, our life, our ministry. When we turn to the scriptures, what we are trying to do is draw from their stories pictures of three different worlds: the world behind the scriptures, the world of the scriptures, and the world the scriptures envision.

This third world – the world the scriptures envision – is another way of speaking about the reign of God. As followers of the way of Jesus we live for the reign of God that has been born in our midst, yet is still being born in and about us. What do the stories of Ezekiel, Corinthians, and Gandhi have to say to us as we endeavor to live for the reign of God here and now? How does the Spirit work through these stories to transform our friendships, families, churches, civic organizations, cities and nations? What values do they invite us to embrace and, yes, even be warriors for?

In *The Human One: God and Ezekiel*, we discovered that how we treat one another is of the most utmost concern to God, the *holy* God. Who is God? – God is 'the Human One.' What matters to God? – that 'the human ones' treat one another, care for one another, as *human* beings. God is revealed as 'the Human One' because we, as human beings, have not yet learned how to be what we were created to be. We are to treat one another in ways that are reflections of the Human One, and, in doing so, we become closer to our true selves as God created us.

We discovered a similar message in *The Cross: Power & Wisdom – Corinthians*. The power of the cross lies in its ability to shake humanity loose from the nightmare through which we rationalize violent retribution – within our families, neighborhoods, schools, workplaces, churches and among nations. The wisdom of the cross lies in its ability to expose the deathtrap of this so-called redemptive violence – especially when it is done in the name of justice or national security and our *holy* God is invoked for legitimation. Any power or principality that dares to offer violence as the path of life and of God is exposed by the cross as false. Love is redemptive, returning us to the way of Jesus. Forgiveness is salvific, healing our brokenness. Enemies are friends, with boundary lines dissolved. These are the enduring truths that hang on the cross of Jesus.

*Mohandas Gandhi: Satyagraha Warrior* brought us into the company of a holy and tenacious fighter. But Gandhi was a fighter the likes of which the West had not seen for a very long time – a warrior *of* peace and *for* peace. Gandhi, refusing to cooperate with violence, was a *satyagraha* warrior on behalf of 'the human ones' in South Africa and India. He knew quite well the power and wisdom of the cross, suffering in the end the crucifixion of the bullet. The path of *ahimsa* was the path of working hand-in-hand with 'the human ones' about him to help restore their God-given humanity. The path of *ahimsa* awakened its followers to the truth that restoration of one's human dignity could never, ever, come at the expense of another human one's dignity – even if the other was an unjust and brutal oppressor. In the end, the other, like me, is a human one. We are the same. Or, in the teaching of Jesus, supposed enemies are in reality friends.

Gandhi walked humbly with his people, which is to say that he walked among and beside them. He led by example – incarnating in his daily life the power of love and forgiveness. He knew that the true path to redemptive peace lay within tenacious loving kindness for all. We could say that, for Gandhi, humanity was always already holy, but we all too often failed to see and appreciate this truth.

Not unlike Ezekiel, Gandhi's very heart seemed to beat to the rhythm of a holy God stirred to action by the inhumanity of humans. But this is not a holy God being incited to a righteous obliteration of the unholy – especially as revealed in the cross of Jesus. God is moved to invite human beings to discover the sacredness of their very God-given humanity. We could say this differently: What we begin to realize is that religion is about the binding together again of human beings in relationships of love, freedom, and creativity. Ezekiel, Paul and Gandhi all help us to remember that at the heart of honoring and worshiping the *holy* God is the honoring of one another's humanity. Nothing matters more in the reign of God.

The prophet Micah (8th Century BCE) perfectly summarizes the prophetic teaching on *true* religion.

> *He has told you, O mortal, what is good;*
> *and what does the LORD require of you*
> *but to do justice, and to love kindness,*
> *and to walk humbly with your God?*
> (Micah 6:8, NRSV)

Here we have a vision of a world in which a 'human one' is someone who learns how to practice justice and kindness, while walking with feet planted firmly on the ground (humility). When we bring together the vision of Micah with the theology of 'the Human One,' the power and wisdom of the cross, and the witness of Gandhi, we discover anew God's call to us to face human suffering and degradation in our own communities. True religion is embodied in our willingness and effort to recognize, recover and restore the full humanity of our neighbors.

# ~Exploring Our Humanity~

## The Human One: God and Ezekiel
### Visions of God
Think of a time when you experienced a crisis in your life where you were aware of God's presence in the midst of it. What did God look like for you during this crisis? How did this divine presence affect your heart?

### Broken Human Life as Already Holy
We have said that Ezekiel's vision goes to the very heart of what it means to be a faithful, religious person. What if the purpose of human life is not to become divine by becoming someone different? What if human life, as created by God, in all of its brokenness, ambiguity, shortcomings, etc., is already divine, is already holy, is already sacred?

### Forms of Religion
Richard Rohr, a Franciscan and director of the Center for Action and Contemplation, has this to say: 'There are two utterly different forms of religion: one believes that God will love me *if* I change; the other believes that God loves me so that I *can* change. The first is the most common; the second follows upon an experience of personal Indwelling and personal love.' How does Rohr's observation relate not only to Ezekiel's vision, but your own experience of religion and God?

## The Cross – Power and Wisdom: Corinthians
### Eucharistic Prayers and the Crucifixion of Jesus
Read through the selections from the three Eucharistic prayers below.

> *Eucharistic Prayer 1 (BCP, 334)*
> All glory be to thee, Almighty God, our heavenly Father, for that thou, of thy tender mercy, didst give thine only Son Jesus Christ to suffer death upon the cross for our redemption; who made there, by his one oblation of himself once offered, a full, perfect, and sufficient sacrifice, oblation, and satisfaction, for the sins of the whole world; and did institute, and in his holy Gospel command us to continue, a perpetual memory of that his precious death and sacrifice, until his coming again.

> *Eucharistic Prayer A (BCP, 362)*
> Holy and gracious Father: In your infinite love you made us for yourself; and, when we had fallen into sin and become subject to evil and death, you, in your mercy, sent Jesus Christ, your only and

eternal Son, to share our human nature, to live and die as one of us, to reconcile us to you, the God and Father of all. He stretched out his arms upon the cross, and offered himself in obedience to your will, a perfect sacrifice for the whole world.

*Eucharistic Prayer 3 (Enriching Our Worship, 63)*
Glory and honor are yours, Creator of all,
your Word has never been silent;
you called a people to yourself, as a light to the nations,
you delivered them from bondage
and led them to a land of promise.
Of your grace, you gave Jesus
to be human, to share our life,
to proclaim the coming of your holy reign
and give himself for us, a fragrant offering.
Through Jesus Christ our Redeemer,
you have freed us from sin,
brought us into your life,
reconciled us to you,
and restored us to the glory you intend for us.

Comparing these three different Eucharistic prayers, what are the reasons (theologies) given for Jesus' life and death? Which theology(ies) resonate most deeply with your own experience of God and the cross? Why do you believe Jesus of Nazareth was crucified?

# Part V

# From Domination to Wholeness

"God's works are so secured by an all-encompassing plenitude, that no created thing is imperfect. It lacks nothing in its nature, possessing in itself the fullness of all perfection and utility. And so all things which came forth through Wisdom, remain in her like a most pure and elegant adornment and they shine with the most splendid radiance of their individual essence."[93]

Hildegard of Bingen

*My Lord, I do not ask you for anything else in life but that You kiss me with the kiss of your mouth, and that you do so in such a way that although I may want to withdraw from this friendship and union, my will may always, Lord of my life, be subject to Your will and not depart from it…*
Teresa of Avila[94]

We now turn to the three very different worlds of Hosea, Colossians, and Teresa of Avila. And yet, despite their real differences, we will ask ourselves if there might not well be a common thread running through it all – the Spirit of God in our midst, continually inviting us, in the face of so much domination and oppression, to discover and restore redeeming wholeness.

Hosea is a remarkable prophet; because despite Israel's failure as a faithful covenantal partner, his final words will speak of renewal, not destruction. Although Hosea knows the traditional story line well, he invites us into the awareness that it has been human beings, in our fear, anger, and greed, who have created a God of wrath to fulfill our own desires. Our traditional story has all too often hidden the all-compassionate One behind stories of vengeance and retribution. Hosea enables us to retell the story in a new, liberating, and expansive way -- a way that offers wholeness. We begin to recognize that God is 'big' enough to embrace all of us.

And yet, we find ourselves restricting the gracious reach of God, in the very name of God. Colossians illustrates this restrictive theology at work. The author of Colossians, contrary to Pauline baptismal theology, will narrow the divine embrace by arguing for 'an ethically softened or humanized notion of domination and rule' as how we are to 'live in the Lord.'

The author of Colossians offers a fine example of creative theology, but fails to consistently perceive the restoration of wholeness as the will of God and envisions the reign of God such that there is room for subordination of wives, ownership of children, and the domination of slaves. Colossians raises pivotal questions for the faith community: Are we gathered by the Spirit into communities where domination rules? Or is it true that 'There is no longer Jew or Greek, there is no longer slave or free, there is no longer male and female; for all of you are one in Christ Jesus?' (Galatians. 3:28). Which story will be ours?

For Teresa of Avila the form the story takes is not a speculative matter. Like Hosea before her, Teresa will survey her surroundings and through prayer and conversation awaken to a God who does not desire her subjugation. She is the property of no one.

Because Teresa acknowledges that God is indeed in her, she wakes up to the beauty and worth of her own interior life. Her interior awakening flows into social justice, as we would say, initiating reform of convent life that reflects the transformation she herself has undergone. She envisions a world in which the liberating grace of God reigns among us, making us whole.

# CHAPTER 13 – BLINDNESS AS HUMANITY'S ISSUE: HOSEA

### Renewal, not Destruction

As the Irish poet William Butler Yeats surveyed the lands of war-ravaged Europe in the second decade of the 1900's, he beheld a world being torn apart. All was thrown out of balance. Human equilibrium was gone. And so he began his poem, *The Second Coming*, with these words:

> TURNING and turning in the widening gyre
> the falcon cannot hear the falconer;
> things fall apart; the center cannot hold;
> mere anarchy is loosed upon the world,
> the blood-dimmed tide is loosed, and everywhere
> the ceremony of innocence is drowned;
> the best lack all convictions, while the worst
> are full of passionate intensity.[95]

In the 8th century BCE, Hosea knew only too well the results of 'mere anarchy' being 'loosed upon the world.' The 'blood-dimmed tide' of Assyria was steadily rising and covering the earth. In the face of this assault, 'the best,' or supposed best, of Israel lacked all convictions, while 'the worst' – well, simply take a look at what we find in II Kings 15- 17, summarized by the scholar James Limburg:

> Jeroboam's son Zechariah ruled only six months and was assassinated by Shallum. Shallum ruled for a month, only to be assassinated by Menahem (745-736) who ... became a vassal of Assyria. Menahem's son Pekahiah was in office for two years (737-736) before being assassinated by Pekah....In 732 Pekah was assassinated by Hoshea, who first submitted to Assyria but then rebelled (II Kings 17:3-4). Hoshea was then imprisoned and thus presided over the downfall of the nation and the deportation of the inhabitants in 722. B.C.[96]

Political stability was gone. Not only was there political anarchy, but a reading of Hosea makes it quite clear to us that religion was in crisis as well (4.4-6). Priests and prophets, the supposed best, had failed in their responsibilities. 'There is no faithfulness or loyalty, and no knowledge of God in the land,' laments Hosea. As a result, 'Swearing, lying, murder, and stealing and adultery break out; bloodshed follows bloodshed.' What is left? A land that mourns 'and all who live in it languish: together with the wild animals and the birds of the air, even the fish of the sea are perishing' (4:1-3).

In his poem, Yeats continues by saying in the next verse, 'Surely some revelation is at hand.' And so it is with Hosea. The stability, or status quo, which Israel once knew and took for granted, is gone. The nation's equilibrium has been lost. Israel has fallen and is in chaos, so many of its people are either slain or taken into Assyrian captivity. Surely *some* revelation, *some* guidance, from God must be forthcoming.

Revelation is at hand in the prophetic life and words of Hosea. This so-called minor prophet from the northern kingdom of Israel, along with Amos and Micah (as well as Isaiah, a major prophet), speaks out loudly and clearly. But, *in the end* (not initially), what Hosea has to say catches the faithful of Israel (and us) by surprise. For they hear a very new word punctuating the violent and deadening cacophony.

### Accusation/Judgment/Destruction: Amos and Hosea

The final stanza of Yeats' *The Second Coming* does speak a word, however, very much like the one we *would* expect to hear from a prophet living in the time of Hosea.

> Surely some revelation is at hand;
> surely the Second Coming is at hand.
> The Second Coming! Hardly are those words out
> when a vast image out of Spiritus Mundi
> troubles my sight: somewhere in sands of the desert
> a shape with lion body and the head of a man,
> a gaze blank and pitiless as the sun,
> is moving its slow thighs, while all about it
> reel shadows of the indignant desert birds.
> The darkness drops again; but now I know
> that twenty centuries of stony sleep
> were vexed to nightmare by a rocking cradle,
> and what rough beast, its hour come round at last,
> slouches towards Bethlehem to be born?[97]

Although it is true enough that Hosea would not speak of 'The Second Coming,' we might well expect him quite naturally to speak words of 'darkness' dropping again upon idolatrous Israel. Accusation, judgment and destruction would seem to be what is due this nation. The only real question for the prophet might be, 'And what rough beast, its hour come round at last, Slouches towards Bethlehem (or Israel, in this case) to be born?'

In order to better understand the new word that will be spoken by Hosea, it is helpful to turn first to Amos. Amos, who preceded Hosea by about 40 years, knew all too well and had spoken all too eloquently about the rough beast of divine justice. Amos, writes Abraham Heschel, 'had proclaimed the righteousness of God, His *iron will* to let justice prevail.'98 *Injustice* is what Amos saw plainly within Israel, where the wealthy lay upon beds of ivory while the poor had no food.

> *Listen to this word, you rich cows of Bashan*
> *Living in the mountain of Samaria:*
> *You defraud the poor, steal from the needy,*
> *and call out, 'Bring me another drink!'*
> (Amos 4:1 The Inclusive Hebrew Scriptures)

Over and over and over again, Amos painfully describes the degrading ways in which the people are violating one another, abusing and humiliating the most fragile and poor of society. For this violation of the covenant, Israel would know the iron will of divine justice. The God known by Amos (and Israel) passionately strikes out leaving only a remnant (Amos 9:9-15). This is a God who cannot but help bear witness to those who continually trample on 'the poor, exhorting inhumane taxes on their grain,' and who persecute 'the righteous,' take bribes, and 'who deny justice to the needy at the city gate!' (Amos 5:10, 11, 12).

The God seen and proclaimed by Amos to Israel is 'the selfless and exalted being whose sensibilities and concern for justice are pained by the sinful transgressions of Israel.'99 This pained God responds to the suffering of those trampled by greed and power, by striking back, and striking back hard! The rough beast of Assyria will avenge the downtrodden.

> *The Sovereign YHWH swears this in holiness:*
> *The days are coming*
> *when you will be dragged out in baskets,*
> *every last one of you in fish baskets.*
> *You will be taken out of the city*
> *through the nearest breach in the wall,*
> *to be flung onto the nearest dung heap.*
> *– It is YHWH who speaks. (Amos 4:2-3)*
> *You who wish for the Day of YHWH to come –*
> *why do you want it?*
> *What will the Day of YHWH mean to you?*
> *It will be a day of darkness, not light!* (Amos 5:18-19)

> *For now I will issue orders*
> *and shake out the House of Israel among all the nations,*
> *as grain would be sifted with a screen*
> *to make sure not a single pebble gets through.*
> *All the sinners among my people*

> *will perish by the sword —*
> *all who brag, 'No misfortune will ever touch us,*
> *or even come anywhere near us!'*
> (Amos 9:9-10. The Inclusive Hebrew Scriptures)

As we read Amos, we encounter an iron will of God capable of saving a remnant, but passionately driven to destroy the sinners. The unjust are not redeemable. They can only die.

Even though idolatry, and not injustice, is the sin caught in the sights of Hosea, the anticipated divine reaction would at first seem to echo and reinforce the inevitable crushing blow of the divine iron will shouted forth by Amos. In each of the three sections that compose the book of Hosea (1-3, 4:1-11:11, and 11:12-14:9), we encounter the familiar cry of accusation, judgment, and promise of destruction.

In the first section, Hosea imagines Israel's relationship with God to be that of an unfaithful spouse. God's patience is all but spent. 'Plead with your mother,' Hosea cries out, referring to Israel, that 'she put away her whoring.' But the cause seems lost.

> *Therefore I will hedge up her way with thorns; and I will build a wall against her, so that she cannot find her paths.*
>
> *She shall pursue her lovers, but not overtake them; and she shall seek them, but shall not find them.*
>
> *Then she shall say, 'I will go and return to my first husband, for it was better with me then than now.'*
>
> *She did not know that it was I who gave her the grain, the wine, and the oil, and who lavished upon her silver and gold that they used for Baal.*
>
> *Therefore I will take back my grain in its time, and my wine in its season; and I will take away my wool and my flax, which were to cover her nakedness.*
>
> *Now I will uncover her shame in the sight of her lovers, and no one shall rescue her out of my hand.*
>
> *I will put an end to all her mirth, her festivals, her new moons, her sabbaths, and all her appointed festivals.*
>
> *I will lay waste her vines and her fig trees, of which she said, 'These are my pay, which my lovers have given me.' I will make them a forest, and the wild animals shall devour them.*
>
> *I will punish her for the festival days of the Baals, when she offered incense to them and decked herself with her ring and jewelry, and went after her lovers, and forgot me, says the LORD.* (Hosea 2.6-13, NRSV)

God is a furious spouse, threatening to deliver Israel over to wild animals – let them devour Israel lying naked and without protection. Israel has lost its very religious and moral compass. To whom does it offer its heart's love? To whoever comes along? To whoever captures a passing fancy? Israel no longer seems even to remember what truly matters in life, nor who it is that has loved it so dearly.

Amos decries the people's lack of justice. Hosea turns his gaze inward and sees a people who no longer trust in the presence and power of God. They have sought salvation in the power of their own warriors. In the words of Jewish scholar Abraham Heschel, 'Hosea attacks the absence of inwardness.'[100] They are not lost in the desert, their hearts have *become* deserts – arid and without love. No hope seems possible, and the future portends nothing but gruesome death and destruction.

> *When Ephraim spoke, there was trembling; he was exalted in Israel; but he incurred guilt through Baal and died. And now they keep on sinning and make a cast image for themselves, idols of silver made according to their understanding, all of them the work of artisans. 'Sacrifice to these,' they say. People are kissing calves! Therefore they shall be like the morning mist or like the dew that goes away early, like chaff that swirls from the threshing floor or like smoke from a window. Yet I have been the LORD your God ever since the land of Egypt; you know no God but me, and besides me there is no savior. It was I who fed you in the wilderness, in the land of drought. When I fed them, they were satisfied; they were satisfied, and their heart was proud; therefore they forgot me. So I will become like a lion to them, like a leopard I will lurk beside the way. I will fall upon them like a bear robbed of her cubs, and will tear open the covering of their heart; there I will devour them like a lion, as a wild animal would mangle them. I will destroy you, O Israel; who can help you? Where now is your king, that he may save you? . . . Compassion is hidden from my eyes. Although he may flourish among rushes, the east wind shall come, a blast from the LORD, rising from the wilderness; and his fountain shall dry up, his spring shall be parched. It shall strip his treasury of every precious thing. Samaria shall bear her guilt, because she has rebelled against her God; they shall fall by the sword, their little ones shall be dashed in pieces, and their pregnant women ripped open.* (Hosea 13:1-10a, 14b-16. NRSV)

If these were the last words spoken by God, Hosea and Israel would have remained firmly held in the grasp of a divine justice exercised as vengeance. Nothing very new here. We have encountered this face of the divine in history in the prophet Amos. Nothing much, if any, of holy tenderness and mercy. It is important for us to be very clear. Israel *has* failed miserably to remain faithful to the covenant – abusing the poor, trusting in its own brutal power, and seeking recourse in the formalities of ritual and sacrifice. The heart of its faith seems to have wasted away into the arid desert it once passed through. So, it would seem, the people must pay, receiving the heavy and crushing end of the divine iron rod of angry justice. Otherwise they will never learn.

### Renewal, Not Destruction: Hosea's New Word

But — these are *not* the last words spoken by God. In each of the three sections of Hosea, the prophetic words do not end in destruction but continue. A new last word punctuates mightily and irreversibly the relationship between God and Israel. We hear in Hosea:

> *How can I abandon you, Ephraim? How can I hand you over, Israel? My heart is aching within me; I am burning with compassion.* (11:8. The Inclusive Hebrew Scriptures)

Heschel movingly describes these new words: 'Amos had proclaimed the righteousness of God, His iron will to let justice prevail. Hosea came to spell out the astonishing fact of God's *love* for man.'[101] Even more, says Heschel, 'A new factor not found in Amos is the sense of *tenderness and mercy*. Hosea is able to express as no other prophet the love of God for Israel in its varied forms.'[102] And then Heschel arrives at the heart of the new last words:

> From the perspective of the fundamental disposition of love, it is understandable that *healing and reconciliation, not harm and destruction*, finally prevail.[103]

To understand how this can be, we need to remember that the scriptures are texts that were toiled over, works of great effort and labor. The people of the scriptures and the authors and editors of the various books are struggling to see ever more clearly who this God is in whom they believe. And who are they as the people of this God? The conversation among themselves and with God never ends. As the history of the people evolves and new experiences give rise to new insights, new stories are written to capture, celebrate, and pass on these insights. There are times when these insights shatter and reassemble the faith of the people into a new form. Such times punctuate the history of Israel and Christianity. The book of Hosea is just such a new punctuation in Israel's life.

Oftentimes, we tend to imagine life evolving in a fairly smooth progression. Many scientists even speak of the evolution of life in terms of gradual development from extraordinarily simple microorganisms to amazingly intricate and complex forms of life such as human beings. But the fossil record reveals a very different picture, one in which there are quite long periods of relative equilibrium, with very little change in life forms, interrupted or punctuated by bursts of enormous creativity producing new species. Scientists Stephen Jay Gould and Niles Eldredge have offered a nuanced theory of evolution to account for this dynamic, which they call 'punctuated equilibrium.'

We seem to be encountering a similar phenomenon here in the history of Israel. The stories told of who God is and how God interacts with the people seem to remain fairly consistent and stable for a while. And then, something happens. Maybe it comes from the desire for a home and children such as with Abraham and Sarah. Maybe it comes from the experience of degrading slavery, and the longing for freedom, as with Moses and Miriam. Maybe it comes from discovering the importance of fidelity and companionship as with Ruth and Naomi. Or, maybe it comes from realizing we are not in control as with Job and Jonah. There is an experience that the story as it has been told thus far is no longer able to include and tell in a convincing way. So, a new word is spoken, and the story is forever changed, and the story has a new power to transform those who now hear it.

Hosea's words graciously stamp a new punctuation on Israel's story of faith. Where the promise of destruction seemed imminent, a new hope abruptly breaks through. As the first section of Hosea draws to a close, the final form of the text, Walter Brueggemann tells us, 'speaks a final word to Israel of well-being and restoration.'[104] And so to our utter surprise the promise of vengeance is replaced by a God wooing tenderly in love.

> *'After that, however, I will woo her; I will lead her into the desert, speaking tenderly to her heart. There I will return her vineyards, and change a valley of trouble into a door of hope. There she will sing as she did when she was young – as she did at the time when she came out of Egypt. On that day,' says YHWH, 'you will call me Ishi – 'My Spouse,' and will no longer call me Ba'ali – 'My Superior.' For I will take away the names of the Ba'als from her lips and she will no longer pray to those names. On that day will I make a covenant for them with the beasts of the field and with the birds of air, and with the creeping things that move about the earth. I will smash the bow and sword and abolish war from the land, so that all may sleep in safety. I will bind myself to you forever – yes, I will swear myself to you in rightness and justice, in tender love and in deep compassion. I will swear myself to you in love and faithfulness, and then you will truly know YHWH.* (Hosea 2: 16-22 The Inclusive Hebrew Scriptures)

But Hosea is not finished. In the next section we come across one of 'the most remarkable oracles in the entire prophetic literature.' Brueggemann points out for us that unlike the tender words we encounter in Hosea 14 (which we will read shortly), God's resolve to heal Israel does not come after devastation. 'Here the devastation is averted. The ground for averted devastation moreover is YHYH's own sense of YHWH. YHWH is not 'a man' to react in anger; YHWH, rather, is 'God.' More than that, YHWH is 'the Holy One in Israel.'[105] Hosea, and through him, Israel, is discovering that for God to be God means that the Holy One is *not* captivated by emotions as the human ego is.

> *How can I abandon you, Ephraim? How can I hand you over, Israel? How can I make you like Admah? How can I treat you like Zeboiim? My heart is aching within me; I am burning with compassion! No, I can't do it! I cannot act on my righteous anger! I will not turn around and destroy Ephraim! For I am God – no mere mortal – the Holy One who walks among you'* (Hosea 11:8-9. The Inclusive Hebrew Scriptures)

How will the Holy One come to this people, this idolatrous nation? Three chapters later Hosea writes:

> *I will heal their rebelliousness and love them freely, for my anger against them has subsided. I will be as the morning dew for Israel and they will bloom like the lily. Their roots will spread like the cedars of Lebanon. Their branches will stretch forth. They will be as beautiful as the olive tree and their fragrance like the Lebanon cedar. People will once again find comfort in their shade. They will be as abundant as the grain. They will be as fruitful as a grapevine and they will be as renowned as the wine of Lebanon.* (Hosea 14.4-7. The Inclusive Hebrew Scriptures)

**Whose Inner Struggle?**

Most commentaries seem to interpret these poetic passages of wooing, tenderness, and healing love, coming as they do on the heels of harsh words of vengeance and iron justice, in an almost literal way. *God*, they say, is the one who is struggling. 'These verses passionately describe a struggle, as it were, within the heart of God...'[106] Heschel tells us that it is 'Hosea who flashes a glimpse into *the inner life of God* as He ponders His relationship to Israel.'[107]

But could it be, and isn't it of the utmost importance that it be, that the struggle is actually taking place *within Israel and Hosea*? Could it not be they who are projecting *the human struggle* onto God? If God as God has been, is, and always will be love, perhaps what we have been punctuating in our history in the book of Hosea is a profoundly new awareness of who God actually is. What if the central issue is *not* God struggling to become a compassionate Holy One capable of reining in the divine passions, but humanity struggling with its own blindness to the Divine Reality? If blindness has been, as it always will be, humanity's issue, might it not well be the case that God is not the one struggling to be true to the divine self, or even to discover what that divine self is? No. We, as human beings, in and through the lives of Israel and Hosea, are striving to see beyond our own ego, our own projections of fear, anger, and need for revenge, and glimpse a truer face of the divine in history.

# Chapter 14 – What Kind of Clothes: Colossians

**Clothed with a New Self**

It was a well accepted practice in ancient times for a relatively unknown figure, who was a disciple of a much better known and respected author, to write a letter pseudonymously -- which is to say, the relatively unknown writer attributes the letter to the better known master. Such a practice was not perceived as being dishonest. It was an honorable custom, or tradition, seen as paying respect and homage to the known author.

The very brief letter to the Colossians (four short chapters in all), as the great majority of scholars now agree, is a pseudonymously written letter. We don't know for certain who wrote the letter, but we do know that the author was a disciple of Paul. Most likely, this disciple addressed the Colossians sometime after Paul's death, perhaps during the mid-60's CE.

This disciple was not shy about making changes in Paul's theology. In fact, the writer made some changes in very significant areas, all the while attributing such theological ideas to Paul. For instance, Colossians claims that believers have already been raised with Christ (2:12 and 3:1). Paul, on the other hand, was clear in his own letters that although believers have died with Christ, they have not yet been raised. There are other examples of divergence as well. Paul is fond of drawing upon the metaphor of the 'body' to describe how followers of the way of Jesus are to relate to one another – 'for as in one body we have many members' (Romans. 12:4; see also 1 Corinthians. 12:12-27). Colossians extends the image, thereby changing it into a hierarchical metaphor, where Christ becomes 'the head of the body, the church' (Colossians. 1:18). Colossians also advocates a theology in which in Christ there is 'forgiveness of sin' (1:14, 2:13, 3:13), rather than *freedom* from sin as Paul writes in his own letters (Romans. 8:21).

The author of Colossians is not hesitant to change some of Paul's most critical theological ideas – ideas relating to death and resurrection, the church as the body, and freedom from sin. Nowhere is this willingness more apparent than in chapters 3 and 4, where the author speaks about the new life in Christ.

> *So if you have been raised with Christ, seek the things that are above, where Christ is seated at the right hand of God. Set your minds on things that are above, not on things that are on earth, for you have died, and your life is hidden with Christ in God. When Christ who is your life is revealed, then you also will be revealed with him in glory.* (Colossians 3:1-4 NRSV)

> *Put to death, therefore, whatever in you is earthly....Do not lie to one another, seeing that you have stripped off the old self with its practices and **have clothed***

> *yourselves with the new self*, which is being **renewed** in knowledge according to the image of its creator. In that **renewal** there is no longer Greek and Jew, circumcised and uncircumcised, barbarian, Scythian, slave and free; but Christ is all and in all! (Colossians 3:5, 3:9-11. NRSV, emphasis added)

Exactly what kind of clothes is the author of Colossians asking us to wear? When we look closely, we discover that the author is drawing upon Galatians 3:27-28 (NRSV).

> As many of you as were baptized into Christ have clothed yourselves with Christ. There is no longer Jew or Greek, there is no longer slave or free, there is no longer male and female; for all of you are one in Christ Jesus.

But, there are some very significant changes. Perhaps these changes are appropriate. We will look and see. How, though, *do* we see? In other words, how are we to decide whether or not the author of Colossians is being faithful to Paul? And, even more, if the two disagree, why should we accept one letter over the other? What might be our criteria? Such are the inevitable questions of theological interpretation of scripture, or in the technical language of theology, hermeneutics.

## What Does the Author See?

The letter to the Colossians is sometimes described as being an advocate of an excessive, or enthusiastic, realized eschatology. This simply means that for the author, as well as the community at Colossae, we have not only been 'buried with Christ in baptism,' but we '*were* also raised with him through faith in the power of God, who raised him from the dead' (2:12 NRSV). The resurrection has already happened – it has already been realized, here and now, in baptism.

You might think that such a perspective would lead the author of Colossians to emphasize all the more the importance of life in this earthly world, since *it is in this earthly existence* that we have experienced the resurrection. Not so. The author exhorts the Colossians to set their 'minds on things that are above, not on things that are on earth' (3:2). They are to 'put to death...whatever in you is earthly: fornication, impurity, passion, evil desire, and greed (which is idolatry).'

These earthly ways are the path to death. 'On account of these the wrath of God is coming on those who are disobedient' (3:5, 6). The clothes the faithful put on in baptism – the clothes of those *already* raised to life in Christ – come not from the earth, but from 'above' (3:1). Whereas, it would seem, things earthly are wrought through and through with evil passions, things heavenly are untainted.

> *As God's chosen ones, holy and beloved, clothe yourselves with compassion, kindness, humility, meekness, and patience. Bear with one another and, if anyone has a complaint against another, forgive each other; just as the Lord has forgiven you, so you also must forgive. Above all, clothe yourselves with love, which binds everything together in perfect harmony. And let the peace of Christ rule in your hearts, to which indeed you were called in the one body. And be thankful.*
> (Colossians 3:12-15. NRSV)

What does it look like for a Colossian to wear the garment of this heavenly compassion, kindness, humility, meekness, and patience? Where does the author look for examples? Certainly not from the earthly realm since it is nothing but destructive passions and desires. We encounter a great surprise here because in the final verses of chapter 3 the author offers a set of rules for the Christian household that do not originate in any of Paul's writings or the gospels. Instead, and surprisingly, the author turns to the Greco-Roman culture of the ancient world. Some of the most controversial passages of the Christian scriptures are found in Colossians. They draw from these very *earthly* traditions, standards which are to govern the behavior of those already risen in Christ. The author also claims for them a heavenly status as being 'in the Lord.'

> *Wives, be subject to your husbands, as is fitting the Lord.*
> (3:18. NRSV)
>
> *Children, obey your parents in everything, for this is your acceptable duty in the Lord.* (3:20. NRSV)
>
> *Slaves, obey your earthly masters in everything, not only while being watched and in order to please them, but wholeheartedly, fearing the Lord.* (3:22. NRSV)

We see here the author describing three sets of relationships: wives and husbands, children and parents, slaves and masters. The relationships are basically between those who live in the role of servants and those who dominate as a kind of earthly lord.

| Servant roles | Dominators/Lords |
| --- | --- |
| wives | husbands |
| children | parents |
| slaves | masters |

Husbands, parents (oddly enough, this also includes wives who are the property of husbands, much like a servant) and masters require subjection and obedience of their servants. Sociologists would describe these pairs of relationships in terms of domination hierarchy. It is quite clear from our studies of ancient history that Greco-Roman culture in all of its social relationships – wives and husbands, children and parents, slaves and masters, citizens and rulers – was based upon domination hierarchy where friendship between the different groups was not truly possible. Women, children, and slaves were the *property of their lords*, not their friends and companions.

And yet, the author of Colossians is claiming that to be clothed in Christ is to live in such a way that women, children, and slaves are to meekly submit to their dominators as 'in the Lord'. We seem to be very far indeed from the true *renewal* of life spoken of in 3:11. And contrast this with the baptismal hymn Paul sang in Galatians 3:28 which claims that in Christ 'there is no longer Jew or Greek, there is no longer slave or free, there is no longer male and female; for all of you are one in Christ Jesus.' In Colossians, not only are members of the community not one, but the cultural divisions are accepted as normative, and the faithful are urged to wear them in the name of the Lord.

Paul's vision of baptism as a burial of the divisions that falsely separate God's children from one another is turned on its head by the author of Colossians. The very baptismal hymn itself is altered in ways that over the following 19 centuries allow it to be readily used at different times to sanction subordination of women, corporal punishment of children, and grotesque slavery.

Christian scripture scholar Elizabeth Schüssler Fiorenza points out that what concerns the author of Colossians is not so much the behavior of wives but that of slaves. She believes this is true, in part, because of the expansive way in which the author treats this third pair of relationships.

> *Slaves, obey your earthly masters in everything, not only while being watched and in order to please them, but wholeheartedly, fearing the Lord. Whatever your task, put yourselves into it, as done for the Lord and not for your masters, since you know that from the Lord you will receive the inheritance as your reward; you serve the Lord Christ. For the wrongdoer will be paid back for whatever wrong has been done, and there is no partiality. Masters, treat your slaves justly and fairly, for you know that you also have a Master in heaven.* (Colossians 3:22-4:1. NRSV)

Completely absent from this passage is any hint of the Johannine wisdom in which Jesus says, 'I do not call you servants any longer, because the servant does not know what the master is doing; but I have called you friends, because I have made known to you everything that I have heard from my father' (John 15:15 NRSV). We are regarded not as friends of Jesus, but as servants and slaves of God-the-Master. We have not so much the renewal of relationship, abolishing all forms of dehumanizing domination, as we do the reinforcement of human servitude and the claim that such servitude is God's will.

Schüssler Fiorenza explains what is going on here in this way:

> The expansion of the [household] code's third pair, slave-master, indicates that the obedience and acceptance of servitude by Christian slaves are of utmost concern. Colossians asks slaves to fulfill their task with single-mindedness of heart and dedication 'as serving the Lord and not men' (3:23). It not only promises eschatological reward for such behavior but also threatens eschatological punishment for misbehavior (3:24f). The injunction to masters, in turn, is very short and has no Christian component except the reminder that they, too, have a master in heaven. Slave behavior is likened here to the Christian service of the Lord, while the 'masters' are likened to the 'Master' in heaven.[108]

Whereas Paul, in Galatians and Romans and Corinthians, speaks of God's real compassion and desire to transform the actual suffering of human beings, this is no longer the case in Colossians. The author 'spiritualizes' the baptismal covenant. The 'renewal' pertains not to things earthly but only to things of the spirit or heavenly. Whereas Galatians is a clarion call to transform things earthly so that they embody God's heavenly will, Colossians demands submission to earthly injustice, for what matters is the heavenly reward.

The author of Colossians would seem right to be enthusiastic about the presence of Christ here and now. We can hear in the letter distant echoes of Luke's proclamation that the reign of God is at hand. God is always already with us, and the resurrection – as does baptism – confirms this reality. But what about the author's perception of *how* we are to perceive Christ as being present with us here and now – such as in the call for slaves to obey their masters and wives to be subject to their husbands?

To use more contemporary language, the author of Colossians does not seem to distinguish between systems built by the ego and systems infused and transformed by Christ. The author is right to look at Greco-Roman culture, just as today we are right to look at our many cultures, for clues as how to care for one another and creation. All things that exist live, move, and have their very being in God. God is the creator of all, earth as well as heaven. Jews and Christians have always borrowed codes of conduct from their cultures. *But* – and this is a very important caveat – we have borrowed appropriately *only* when we do so in the light of the God of the Exodus and baptism. In other words, we borrow and then *transform* whatever it is we borrow in the name of the God who is with us to set us free from all forms of degradation, servitude, and slavery.

Marriage and parenthood are a part of Greco-Roman, as well as Jewish, culture. The author of Colossians is perfectly right to affirm these forms of human relationship. But the God of Jesus of Nazareth, and the risen Christ of Paul, seeks to transform these and all relationships so that no longer are there masters and servants but now only friends in Christ.

The author of Colossians is not only adaptive of Paul's teaching but also extends it in quite new ways. The scriptures are full of such dynamic and creative application – which is why we have four gospels in the canon and not just one. Created in the image and likeness of a creative God, it is also our *responsibility* to seek *new* ways to express God's passionate desire to restore all creation to relationships of characterized by love and liberty – relationships where people are free to express their love creatively. These kinds of relationships restore people to wholeness. This kind of wholeness is indeed a garment that resurrects the human spirit and renews us to live again despite all suffering.

As theologians, we need to ask whether the author of Colossians is able to perceive this restoring of wholeness as the will of God. Might there be a blindness (for what reason?) to the truth that there is no room within this wholeness for subordination of wives, ownership of children, and the domination of slaves? If it is the case for the author of Colossians that to 'live in the Lord' is to accept 'an ethically softened or humanized notion of domination and rule',[109] how are we to deal with this text in light of Paul's theological imperative that all such domination and rule is clearly submersed and drowned in the waters of baptism?

# CHAPTER 15 – LEAVEN OF FREEDOM: TERESA OF AVILA

## Betrothed to Christ, Set Free to Reform

> God leads souls by many paths and ways.
> I want to speak now of the way He led my soul.
> There is no reason why we should
> expect everyone else to travel by our own road,
> and we should not attempt to point them
> to the spiritual path when perhaps we do not know what it is.
> Teresa of Avila[110]

We find these words of Teresa of Avila in both her earliest book – her *Autobiography* – as well as her later and greatest work, *The Interior Castle*. They reveal a mystic, a prioress, and a teacher whose early years give very little hint of a woman later set free as an egalitarian reformer.

### 16th Century Spain: A World of Dominating Hierarchies

It is fair to say that Teresa was born in Avila because of the abuse, if not persecution, her grandfather, Juan Sanchez, and her father had endured in Toledo – embarrassing information suppressed by earlier biographers which only became public in the 1940s. Juan Sanchez, a *converso*, a person who 'converted' to Christianity from Judaism,

> had been a wealthy *converso* merchant and tax farmer in Toledo. In 1485 the Inquisition of Toledo prosecuted him as a *judaizante*, a secret practitioner of Jewish customs. He was found guilty and sentenced to walk along with his children in penitential processions to Toledo's churches on seven consecutive Fridays.[111]

After this public humiliation, Juan Sanchez moved his family to Avila where he began the slow task of rebuilding his family's honor. He established a 'rich shop of woolens and silks' and eventually was granted such status as a gentleman that he was exempt from taxes. But in truth, everyone still knew that Juan Sanchez was a *converso* and never could be fully accepted as one of them – Christian from birth.

To be a *converso* was to be always second-class and held with some suspicion because a *converso* family often mixed together Jewish ritual practices with Christian belief usually under the cover of the family home and away from the watchful public eye. Such suspicion could be harmless enough until the political winds changed, as they were to do during Teresa's life, with the purifying fervor of the Inquisition. To be of *converso* heritage was also to have one's honor held in question. The matter of honor features heavily throughout Teresa's writings, and a close reading of Teresa's later writing reveals the continued influence of Jewish mysticism in her life.

In 1528 when Teresa was just 13, her mother, Dona Beatriz, died. One of 12 children, Teresa was left without womanly guidance, for her eldest sister married not long after the mother's death. Considered an unusually beautiful woman, Teresa found friendship in female cousins who reinforced in her the importance of this beauty for asserting and maintaining her honor. When a male cousin became enamored with Teresa, her father caught wind of the relationship and moved to avert an honor-shattering predicament by placing her in the convent of Nuestra Senora de Gracia (Our Lady of Grace). This Augustinian convent was not an ascetic prison as it received the daughters of the well-to-do. The daily life was quite strict, however, and after eighteen months, Teresa left, but she did leave changed.

About five years later, at the age of 20, she decided on her own to enter a convent, but this time she chose one whose rule of life was much more relaxed: the Carmelite house of la Encarnacion (the Incarnation), one of the biggest convents in Avila and a house for the city's upper classes. Many of Teresa's relatives and friends were already members of this convent. 'Most of the nuns descended from the 'honored and principled men of the city.' While entering the religious life, they remained women of privilege.'[112]

Such privilege took quite practical forms. 'For example, whereas women of more limited economic means slept together in a common dormitory, the wealthy lived in their own quarters, enjoying both relative comfort and privacy. Many elite nuns had their own servants, or even slaves.' La Encarnacion reproduced 'in microcosm' the conditions of Avila society, perpetuating 'the issues of class, caste, and 'honor.''[113]

Teresa, not a woman of limited economic means, resided in her private two-story quarters with several relatives, free to come and go. She spent hours in conversation and gossip about the daily affairs of Avila society. Attractive, witty, and popular, Teresa was a nun who benefited from her family's wealthy merchant status. She was a woman of honor (or privilege) in an institution that gave elevated status (or honor) to the more wealthy.

**Teresa's Personal Transformation**

Deirdre Green, a Teresian scholar, summarizes Teresa's view on marriage: She was, she says, 'afraid of marriage' which she saw as little more than being a slave to one's husband. A wife, she says, must follow her husband's every whim, appearing happy *if* her husband is happy and sad *if* he is sad, regardless of how she may actually feel. 'See what slavery you have escaped from, sisters!' A natural 'leader,' courageous, adventurous, intelligent, a little headstrong, Teresa could not bring herself to take on a role of total submission.[114]

For Teresa, marriage would have meant entering into a life of illusion, where how *she* felt inside would not have mattered. She would have had to live a life of 'as if.' At least partially motivated to enter the convent in order to escape a life of married slavery, she gradually discovered that another form of slavery continued to dominate her life.

The class structure and honor culture of 16th century Spain permeated every nook and cranny of convent life. The prayer life of the convent existed, in large part, to satisfy the prayer requests of wealthy patrons who had died. Sisters might well be in prayer rotations 24 hours a day, 7 days a week – prayers paid by the wealthy for the souls of the faithful departed. This prayer-income was a primary source of revenue, keeping the convent financially solvent and tied to the city's elite.

In 1538 Teresa almost died. In fact, her relatives thought her paralyzed body was dead. She awoke in the midst of being prepared for burial. Her recovery was excruciatingly slow, and she never fully recovered her health, battling various illnesses until her death from cancer. Being near death was for Teresa a call to wake-up, but she did not awaken all at once. With many ups and downs and twists and turns, the next twenty years embark Teresa on a gradual awakening without one single momentous conversion experience. She is transformed by the grace of God from someone obsessed with maintaining worldly privilege (or honor) and status to someone set free to courageously engage in reform in the face of tremendous and potentially lethal opposition.

Teresa's journey into freedom began with her fall into sickness. That sickness gave her soul new eyes, so for the next twenty years she explored what she called 'mental' prayer, or contemplative prayer, much to the chagrin of spiritual advisors who knew only the way of spoken prayer.

Frail, yet determined, Teresa in her mid-twenties experienced her first divine revelations. The initial impact is that she began to see her times of gossip 'with the eyes of the soul' and found them no longer attractive. As the days, weeks, months, seasons, and years passed, she grew increasingly dissatisfied with her way of life, but her attachment to the 'things of the world,' such as honor, possessions, family, kept hold of her heart.

For fifteen years she stayed faithful to her way of 'mental' prayer. Then, somewhere around her 40th year she began to experience a profound and new transformation:

> [Teresa] began to have frequent and powerful spiritual experiences, hearing voices, seeing visions, and even achieving a coveted mystical Union with God. She came to recognize the connection between behavior and prayer and the reception of divine favors. 'Now then,

when I began to avoid occasions [of sin] and to devote myself to prayer, the Lord . . . started to grant me favors.'[115]

Her heart began to find pleasure and peace in service and care rather than honor and status. The transformation was rooted utterly in her life of 'mental' prayer. The so-called experts she sought out for guidance concluded she suffered from demonic delusions. Fortunately for her, Teresa found kindred souls in the Jesuits.

These Jesuit friends and guides encouraged Teresa, and she came to trust without reserve that God was the origin of her mystical experiences. For Teresa, her mental prayer was 'nothing else than an intimate sharing between friends.'[116] The image of friendship here is crucial. She was becoming friends with very influential religious reformers. Like Teresa, these men and women had been transformed by the intimate presence of God in their lives. They felt called to a mission to change the world about them. Transformation in Christ was not a private affair: it called the heart out into the world. The basis of her friendships was no longer a common social status. Union with God was what united friends in their common mission.

## Teresa's Transformation of the Church:
## Reforming the Carmelites

In 1560 Teresa received a new vision with very practical consequences. 'I was thinking about what I could do for God, and I thought that the first thing was to follow the call to the religious life, which His Majesty had given me, by keeping my rule as perfectly as I could.'[117]

Teresa felt commanded by God to found a new monastery – one in which she and her sisters would keep the rule as 'perfectly' as they could. Since much of the imperfection of the Carmelites lay in its tethering to the honor system (the privileged) of Spanish culture, Teresa boldly cut through this debilitating financial tether. She insisted that her houses 'rely entirely on the fruits of their own labor and on God to move people to donate alms for their survival.'[118]

Teresa was creating economic independence for the nuns and it did not go unnoticed. She had to contend with the challenge of angry townsfolk, who saw their traditional role of influence being diminished. She also had to convince potential sellers that her convents would not become poorhouses, unable to sustain themselves, and a debt the seller could not recoup. Teresa prevailed, and the reformed Carmelite houses she established were founded in poverty, depending solely on the sisters' labor and alms. Economic freedom was thus partially won.

This economic freedom supported and nurtured a new egalitarian culture within the convents. Jodi Bilinkoff describes this new culture:

'[The sister] who is from nobler lineage should be the one to speak least about her father. All the sisters must be equals.' At San Jose [one of Teresa's convents], Teresa abolished all distinctions based on social rank.[119]

Her egalitarian reform struck at the heart of Spanish society and convent life. Birth and blood were no longer important. For a woman of *converso* heritage this reform was particularly liberating. Teresa was saying there was no need to look *back* in order to discover one's source of value. Value was to be found here and now in union with God. This egalitarian message did not go unheard by the *conversos*. Between 1567 and 1582, they supported and became members of Teresa's convents of Discalced (wearing sandals, not shoes) Carmelites.

Teresa was pioneering a new form of spirituality, especially among women. It is true that she influenced, and was influenced by, her many male friends, one of whom was John of the Cross. But Teresa's convents offered the women of her age something truly new – the ability not only to trust one's own experience of God but also to speak humbly, yet forthrightly, about this experience in public before the learned men of the day.

She initiated her reforms during the Spanish Inquisition, an accusatory and dangerous crusade that imprisoned her friend John of the Cross, along with many others, and sentenced many to their deaths.

This was a time when women were not taught to read in the power-languages of the church: Latin and Greek. The experts were the male theologians, well-trained but often with little experience of spirituality. Teresa, politically very astute, proved more than able to respond to their inquiries.

The Papal Nuncio, Felipe Sega, described as 'one of the most powerful Churchmen of Teresa's time,' offered this account of her life:

> A restless, disobedient, stubborn, gad-about female who, under the guise of piety, has invented false doctrines, left the enclosure of her convent against the orders of the Council of Trent and her own superiors, and has gone around teaching like a Professor, contrary to the exhortations of St. Paul who said that women were not to teach.[120]

Teresa would not be dismissed. She trusted in herself. She trusted in her union with God. So, she spoke of the way of contemplative prayer and she acted to reform the life of the church consistent with her own transformed life.

A modern reader might be taken aback by Teresa's self-deprecating language. How can such language be consistent with a woman convinced of her own worth? Deirdre Green explains Teresa's tactics in this way. 'Teresa's apparently negative and self-deprecatory allusions to being a woman often turn out to be simply a ruthlessly realistic acknowledgment of the limitations under which women in sixteenth-century Spain were forced to operate.'

Teresa's writing and reforming efforts placed her life at stake during the Inquisition. She survived, which is a testimony to the creative and transformative power of her contemplative spiritual life. Rooted in the experience of her radical openness to the presence of God, she laid before the oppressive church and society an alternative vision of Jesus' view of women:

> Nor did you, Lord, when you walked in the world, despise women; rather, you always, with great compassion, helped them. And you found as much love and more faith in them than you did in men. Among them was your most blessed mother. . . .Is it not enough, Lord, that the world has intimidated us. . .so that we may not do anything worthwhile for you in public or dare speak some truths that we lament over in secret, without your also failing to hear so just a petition? I do not believe, Lord, that this could be true of your goodness and justice, for you are a just judge and not like those of the world. Since the world's judges are sons of Adam and all of them are men, there is no virtue in women that they do not hold suspect. Yes, indeed, the day will come, my king, when everyone will be known for what he is. . .these are times in which it would be wrong to undervalue virtuous and strong souls, even though they are women.[121]

Except for the first sentence, this entire passage of Teresa was not included in the second editing of the *Way of Perfection*. Even today it is often omitted from Spanish editions of Teresa's writings.[122]

It is perhaps impossible to determine how self-aware Teresa was in drawing upon sources of Jewish mysticism in her writings, but Jewish mystical imagery does pervade her work. The central image of the *Interior Castle* is a 'beautiful crystal or diamond castle, symbolizing the soul, with seven mansions . . . each with many chambers.'[123] These are images rooted deeply in the *Jewish Kabbalah mysticism* of 16th century Spain.

For Teresa, the soul could experience a spiritual marriage, or betrothal, with God in the inner castle. This betrothal imagery might sound peculiar or inappropriately sexual to modern ears, but for someone steeped in the Jewish spirituality of the Song of Songs, this language was able to convey a sense of bare intimacy of the soul with God. *Conceptions of the Love of God* is Teresa's brave commentary on the Song of Songs. Brave, because it invited the scrutinizing eye of the Inquisition – an unconventional woman of Jewish heritage writing about the spiritual life in terms of intimate sexuality.

My Lord, I do not ask you for anything else in life but that You kiss me with the kiss of your mouth, and that you do so in such a way that although I may want to withdraw from this friendship and union, my will may always, Lord of my life, be subject to Your will and not depart from it; that there will be nothing to impede me from being able to say: 'My God and my Glory, indeed Your breasts are better and more delightful than wine.'[24]

## A 'Doctor' and a Saint -- with Blindness

This 'gad-about female' who went 'around teaching like a Professor' was canonized 40 years after her death, and in 1970 Paul VI added her name along with that of Catherine of Siena to the list of those considered 'Doctors of the Church.' These are theologians distinctly recognized for their 'eminence in theology and holiness.'

Teresa is not a saint because she was without fault. She had a glaring blindness when it came to the Protestant reformers. Indeed, much of her energy directed toward the establishment of convents stems from her desire to combat the inroads of the Reformers. She also shared her culture's prejudice against the 'infidels' of Islam.

She was a child of her age, yet she called her age, her church, and her society into a new way of life. She was courageous enough to trust her own experiences; she was wise enough to forge friendships with other reformers who not only supported her work but challenged and corrected her as well. She established 17 convents of the Discalced Carmelites, places that offered a vision of community free from the shackles of honor and lineage, where women might come to *trust* their experiences of union with God – leaven of freedom for the rest of the church and the world.

# Invitation: Envisioning the Reign of God – From Domination to Wholeness

As theologians, we distinguish three distinct yet interrelated worlds as we tell, retell, and reform our defining stories as a people of God:
- ➤ The world behind the tradition/story
- ➤ The world of the tradition/story
- ➤ The world the tradition/story envisions

Our focus now is this last world – the world the tradition/story envisions – because it, above all else, is the world we are endeavoring to live into here and now in the present. As Christians, the world the tradition/story envisions is, simply put, our response, in word and deed, to living out the reign of God in our midst.

We have been discovering and discussing the worlds *behind* and *of* Hosea, Colossians, and Teresa of Avila. We ask now whether we have before us simply more than a collection of different worlds and their stories. Might there be a common thread running through it all? Might this thread be the Spirit of God in our midst, continually inviting us, in the face of so much domination and oppression, to discover and restore redeeming wholeness? It is this thread, this Spirit of God, which weaves the many, many different stories into a common history – a history of a people moving from the slavery of domination to the liberation of wholeness.

**Renewal, not Destruction: Hosea**

Despite all expectations to the contrary, Hosea's prophesy does not end in words of destruction for Israel. Israel has failed to be a faithful covenant partner – abusing the poor, trusting in its own brutal power, and seeking recourse in the formalities of ritual and sacrifice. The traditional theology would speak of God's mighty and righteous divine justice bearing down on Israel.

Hosea knows the traditional story line well. But it no longer has the power to make sense of what Israel is experiencing. Hosea's faith has offered him a glimpse of a different face of God. Hosea struggles for ways to give expression to this new vision in which 'healing and reconciliation, not harm and destruction, finally prevail.'

Hosea's words change the trajectory of the story in a very profound way. His words graciously stamp a new punctuation on Israel's story of faith. He 'speaks a final word to Israel of wellbeing and restoration.' And so to our utter surprise the promise of vengeance is replaced by a God wooing tenderly in love. What makes God YHWH, Brueggemann tells us, is that 'YHWH is not 'a man' to react in anger; YHWH, rather, is 'God.'"[125] Hosea, and through him, Israel, is discovering that for God to be God means that the Holy One is not captivated by emotions as the human ego is. God cannot be reduced to the human need for revenge and bloodshed – no matter how great the injustice.

Hosea invites us into the awareness that it has been human beings, in our fear, anger, and greed, who have created a God of wrath to fulfill our own desires. God does not dominate, nor is God dominated by and enslaved by the emotions of fear, anger, and greed. God is YHWH because God is always a God of healing and reconciliation. We, as human beings, have gotten it wrong. Our traditional story has all too often hidden this all-compassionate One behind stories of vengeance and retribution. Through Hosea, we are able to retell the story in a new, liberating, and expansive way -- a way which offers wholeness. God, we begin to recognize, is 'big' enough to embrace all of us.

## Clothed with a New Self: Colossians

However, again and again we find ourselves restricting the gracious reach of God, and we do this in the very name of God. We need look no further than the book of Colossians to see this restrictive theology at work. We discovered that the author of Colossians would have us believe that 'an ethically softened or humanized notion of domination and rule' is how we are to 'live in the Lord.' Paul, on the other hand, declares that all such domination and rule is clearly submersed and drowned in the waters of baptism.

And so, we did not criticize the author of Colossians for being creative with, as well as adaptive of, Paul's teaching. We have become keenly aware that the scriptures are full of such dynamic and creative application. Created in the image and likeness of a creative God, it is our *responsibility* to seek *new* ways to express God's passionate desire to restore all creation to relationships characterized by love and liberty – relationships where people are free to express their love creatively. These kinds of relationships restore people to wholeness. This kind of wholeness is indeed a garment that resurrects the human spirit and renews us to live again despite all suffering.

The author of Colossians fails to consistently perceive this restoration of wholeness as the will of God and envisions the reign of God such that there is room for subordination of wives, ownership of children, and the domination of slaves. The tensions and conflict we discover in the worlds envisioned by Colossians requires of us, as theologians, to judge which vision of the reign of God is true. Exactly what kind of clothes are we to wear, to use the biblical language? Does the Spirit gather us together in communities where there remains room for domination? Or, are we called to be a whole people in which, as the letter to the Galatians reminds us, 'There is no longer Jew or Greek, there is no longer slave or free, there is no longer male and female; for all of you are one in Christ Jesus?' (Galatians. 3:28). Which form will the story as we retell it, take?

## Betrothed to Christ and Set Free to Reform: Teresa of Avila

Which form will the story take as we retell it? This is not an idle question as Teresa of Avila's life reveals. Almost 1500 years after Colossians was written, Teresa finds herself called by God, her betrothed, to confront the church about its oppression of women. Teresa is not content to be a critic. Her life is not simply about deconstruction, or taking things apart. She envisions a new way of life rooted in the way of Jesus. As with Hosea, Teresa looks about her, and through prayer and conversation, discovers a God who does not desire her subjugation. She, as a human being, is the property of no one. God helps Teresa wake up to the beauty and worth of her own interior life – her faith, her hopes, her failure, her intellect, her creativity.

Teresa initiates a reform of convent life that reflects the transformation she herself has undergone. Her convents will be a place for women, many of whom are *conversos,* to discover that they too are creative children of God; they too are leaders and reformers of the church. Teresa is wise enough to know that her reform, God's reform, is not the crusade of a lone woman. It is the spiritual movement of the women of God who are full members of the church of God. Teresa is envisioning a world in which the liberating grace of God reigns among us, making us whole. One final time we quote Teresa's prophetic words:

> Nor did you, Lord, when you walked in the world, despise women; rather, you always, with great compassion, helped them. And you found as much love and more faith in them than you did in men. Among them was your most blessed mother. . . .Is it not enough, Lord, that the world has intimidated us. . .so that we may not do anything worthwhile for you in public or dare speak some truths that we lament over in secret, without your also failing to hear so just a petition? I do not believe, Lord, that this could be true of your goodness and justice, for you are a just judge and not like those of the world. Since the world's judges are sons of Adam and all of them are men, there is no virtue in women that they do not hold suspect. Yes, indeed, the day will come, my king, when everyone will be known for what he is. . .these are times in which it would be wrong to undervalue virtuous and strong souls, even though they are women.

## A Theology of Liberation:
## From Domination to Wholeness: How Shall We Live?

Hosea and Teresa, each in their own way, invite us to consider how we will live together as people of God. As theologians, Hosea and Teresa reflect upon their traditions and the stories they hold to discover how God may be at work now in their lives. Their discoveries lead to new words that retell and reform the stories. In the face of brokenness, the prophet speaks a word of healing; in the face of Inquisitorial persecution the mystic speaks one of equality. Both words invite the communities to become redemptively whole.

We are all theologians --- be we prophets, mystics, parents, teachers, custodians – and therefore we are all leaders. As theologians, we ask our communities to face head-on whatever form of domination threatens, and then invite them into a more gracious embracing way of life. Theologians, as Teresa reminds us, speak of what they have experienced and know in their own lives. They invite because they already know that transforming power of the ever-present God. Theologians, as leaders, are midwives of redeeming wholeness.

# ~Exploring Domination and Wholeness~

## Renewal, not Destruction: Hosea
### Whose Struggle?
What if the central issue is *not* God struggling to become a compassionate Holy One capable of reining in the divine passions, but humanity struggling with its own blindness to the Divine Reality?

- ➢ What would this sense of struggle mean for your theology, and for your understanding of the scriptures as the word of God?
- ➢ How does Hosea's punctuation of the Hebrew faith relate, if it does, to the decisive events which punctuate your life journey drawn in your timeline?
- ➢ How have your decisive events affected your personal faith story? Who changed? You? God?

## Clothed with a New Self: Colossians
### Baptism – Clothed with a New Self
The baptismal garment originally signified being clothed with a new self. Followers of Jesus entered into a new common life, which dismantled the social privilege enjoyed by some, thereby giving all the same stature before God (beloved) and each other (friends in Christ).

- ➢ How does your experience of baptism continue to clothe you with a new self today?
- ➢ Have you lost any sense of being washed free of the trappings of domination and set free for lives of mutual respect? If so, how?

## Grounded in God
We have distinguished three ways Christians tend to understand God's relationship with the scriptures. Some see the scriptures as 'Dictated by God.' Some see them as 'Inspired by God.' Others would speak of the scriptures as 'Grounded in God.' According to this last view, the scriptures are written by human beings created in the image and likeness of God. Human persons were not passive vessels but actively and willingly drew upon their God-given gifts to write what they felt called by the Spirit to write. Scripture itself is a text-in-travail, where human ignorance, prejudice, anger, greed – that is, human brokenness – is part of the stories. Passages of scripture at times conflict, images of God and community evolve and change, and there are errors to be found. Yet, *in it all*, God is present and inviting the community into fullness of

life. The scriptures are not meant for teaching geology, biology, astronomy, etc.

> ➤ Drawing upon the theology of the scriptures as being 'Grounded in God,' how might you understand the conflict between the theology of Colossians and that of Paul?
> ➤ Scripture is composed of texts written in travail and contains passages condoning slavery, male dominance, and ownership of children by parents. If these passages are mistaken about the true will of God due to human blindness, how might God *still* be present in *all* of it even in the error? In other words, is God even able to use human error as a way of revealing the path of life?
> ➤ How does grappling with these questions represent an experience of death...of resurrection...in your own faith journey?

## Betrothed to Christ, Set Free to Reform: Teresa of Avila
### The World the Tradition/Story Envisions

How does your vision of the reign of God invite you to critique the abuse of power by church leaders and civil leaders?

Teresa sent forth her sisters to found new convents. How are you sent forth today? When do you go forth? For whom do you go forth? What vision of the way of Jesus do you carry?

Teresa created convents where women could learn, pray, and develop leadership skills. Who are those today, in your own cultures, who need a place to gather safely and be fed in mind and spirit, as well as body? How do you respond?

### Wise as Serpents and Gentle as Doves

How might we, like Teresa, be 'wise as serpents and gentle as doves,' as we work to survive and transform oppressive institutions in our lives?

> ➤ As you have worked to survive and transform oppressive institutions in your life, what compromises have you found yourself making (such as Teresa's self-deprecatory statements in the face of the deadly Inquisition)?
> ➤ As you have worked to survive and transform oppressive institutions in your life, what have you hidden of yourself for the sake of your own 'mission' (such as Teresa's own *converso* heritage)?

## Envisioning the Reign of God: From Domination to Wholeness
### A Theology of Embrace

Remember that you are a theologian in a community of theologians. As such, identify several examples of domination which you have experienced individually or as a member of a group. Explore the following questions:

➢ How has the experience affected your willingness to be compassionate? Are you more or less gracious to others as a result of the experience?

➢ How has the experience changed how you read the scriptures? How has it changed what you look for from tradition to sustain your faith?

➢ What would it mean to have the ministry of theologian lifted up, identified and supported in your congregation?

# PART VI

## A COMPASSIONATE WHOLE

"He gave us divinity, we gave him humanity."
"Our body was Your clothing, Your Spirit was our Robe." [126]
St. Ephrem the Syrian

> *I saw that [God] is to us everything which is good and comforting for our help.*
> *He is our clothing, who wraps and enfolds us for love,*
> *embraces us and shelters us,*
> *surrounds us for his love;*
> *which is so tender that he may never desert us.*
> Julian of Norwich[127]

Our ability to acknowledge that God permeates and sustains all creation makes a fundamental difference to our self-identity and how we view the world. This means that how we perceive ourselves and our world matters a great deal. It makes a practical difference in our lives if we recognize God as our ground. We suffer because we build lives on the shifting sands of false perceptions. When our prophetic world-view is obsessed with judgment, we are unable to experience the healing gift of restoration. When we are driven as Christians to obtain status and power, there is little room in our soul to receive the wisdom, love and friendship of others. When our theology of God is such that God is ever-poised in anger to strike us down, then no image of Christ as mother in the end can calm our deepest fears of annihilation.

Through our explorations of Micah, Paul, and Julian of Norwich we will hear voices leading us to the acknowledgement that creation *is* a compassionate whole. Compassion, not judgment, is the deepest character of the sacred and creation.

We will draw upon *Spiral Dynamics*, with its theory of human development that maps the complexity of evolving human beings, to help us delve into Micah, Paul, and Julian. One of the challenges we face as human beings is that as persons and as cultures we perceive reality not as it is, but as we are. God invites us to awaken so that we might be able to receive God as God is. Spiral Dynamics can sharpen our self- and cultural-perception.

God speaks to us through the wise and holy voices of Micah, Paul, and Julian of Norwich. Their experiences of God cannot be contained by the dominant world-views of their times. On the contrary, here are prophetic voices affirming the God of boundless compassion who embraces all creation. The result is a significant development within the tradition to a fuller awakening of the human spirit. 'Who do you say that I am?'

Micah will exemplify for us the importance highlighted by *Spiral Dynamics* of distinguishing world-views. Micah consistently struggles to proclaim a God who is present and responsive to a people's unjust suffering. His world view has what we will describe as authoritarian, warrior, and egalitarian characteristics. Micah illustrates for us that although God is not changing, we, as human beings are being transformed, and so is our theology (our evolving perception and articulation of who God is).

Personal and collective transformation often slowly unfold. Several hundred years after Micah we find that Paul and the Philippians are also struggling with authoritarian and warrior world-views. Now the icons are Christ and Caesar. The question for the Philippians has become whether their life and piety will still be controlled by an egocentric concern with status. Or will they receive the holy wisdom offered by Paul. Living almost 2000 years before the Enlightenment, Paul births an egalitarian vision of community: there is no longer Jew nor Greek, slave nor free, male and female.

Julian of Norwich (to draw upon the language of *Spiral Dynamics*) awakens to the Second Tier universality of God's compassion. We can only marvel when Julian speaks forthrightly of the motherhood of Christ, transcending Anselm of Canterbury's feminine images that are misshapen by anxiety over damnation and retribution. Fear warps his theology of Christ. As Julian transcends Anselm she changes the entire conversation. Love is now the 'word summing up the message' of Julian's revelations: 'All will be well.'

Julian will challenge the dominant world-view, by deepening the profound words of Paul that we live and move and have our being in Christ. Because God is our mother we have not only been 'knit' together within God, we continue to live within the divine embrace.

For Julian to awaken to the truth of at-one-ment, means her realization that the human vocation shared by each and every human being is the awakening to the truth that we are 'Christ': beings anointed with the Spirit of God. All is enclosed in God and God's love for creation is boundless; all are saved.

# Chapter 16 – The Authority to "Call Out": Micah

## From Judgment to Restoration
### Judgment and Salvation: Who is God?

The book of Micah is one of the twelve *minor prophets'* writings in the Hebrew Scriptures. Micah was from Moreshet, a village in the rural, agrarian area southeast of Jerusalem, during a time of crisis similar to the setting of the prophet Isaiah. The name 'Micah' actually means 'Who is as Yahweh?' The question is posed near the end of the book, verse 18 of chapter 7. The reply is resoundingly clear: there is none like YHWH. Walter Brueggemann suggests that we understand Micah as a book of meditative praise focused on Yahweh's character as it has been experienced during critical moments in the life of Israel.[128]

Who does the book of Micah envision YHWH to be? There are two very different kinds of speeches in Micah: judgment speeches (chapters 1-3, 6; 7:1-7) and salvation speeches (chapters 4-5; 7:8-20). Most scholars attribute the judgment speeches to the prophet Micah himself, during the period in which both Samaria and Jerusalem were threatened by the imperial expansion of the Assyrian empire (1.6-9). Micah delivered these harsh speeches – at times quite graphic and gruesome in detail – to an elite group of rulers who were corrupt and complacent.

> *I said, 'Now listen, you leaders of the House of Jacob,*
> > *rulers of the House of Israel,*
> *you should know how to judge rightly,*
> > *yet you still hate good and love evil;*
> *you skin my people,*
> > *stripping them to the bone.*
> *You devour the flesh of my people,*
> > *flay their skin and crush their bones,*
> *then chop them up for the kettle,*
> > *more meat for your stewpot.*
> *Someday you'll cry out to YHWH,*
> > *but God will not answer you.*
> *God will look the other way*
> > *because of all the crimes you've committed.'*
>
> (Micah 3:1-4. The Inclusive Hebrew Scriptures)

The crimes of the ruling elite of Samaria and Jerusalem – rulers, judges, priests, and prophets – are heinous. They are *devouring* the 'flesh of my people.' Micah declares, 'God will not answer you. God will look the other way.' Why?

'Because of the all the crimes you've committed.' The rulers have gone too far. They may cry out, but there will be no answer in their own time of need – just as *they* did not answer the pleas for life from their own people. All they can expect is condemnatory judgment.

Later, when the people are in exile, the words of condemning judgment are no more. In their stead, we read of salvation (as we encountered in Second-Isaiah). The words of God now speak of restoration and express such themes as 'life among the nations' (5:7), 'divine forgiveness' (7:18), 'return to Judah' (4:6), and 'the restoration of Jerusalem' (4:8, 7:11).

> *'On that Day,' says YHWH,*
> *'I will gather in the lame of the flock,*
> *and retrieve the sheep who had strayed –*
> *the people whom I afflicted. (Micah 4:6)*

> *'And you, watchtower of the flock,*
> *citadel of the people of Zion,*
> *your former sovereignty will be restored,*
> *the dominion of beloved Jerusalem.' (Micah 4:8)*

> *What god can compare to you?*
> *You take away guilt,*
> *you forgive the sins of the remnant of your people.*
> *You don't let your anger rage forever,*
> *for you delight in mercy and steadfast love.*
> (Micah 7:18. The Inclusive Hebrew Scriptures)

These salvation speeches were written not only by a different hand(s), but in a very different historical context. The issue is no longer the corruption of the ruling elites, but a defeated and weary people in exile. It is as if we are reading speeches from two different prophets with two very different visions of YHWH.

What are we to do with these two contrasting visions of YHWH's character side by side in the same book? The *Access Bible* says this: 'Therefore it may be best to understand [the salvation speeches] of Micah as supplements added in the sixth century by those who preserved Micah's prophesy, in order to link Micah's message to a new era.' We are to read Micah 'as an anthology of short speeches rather than as a unified narrative.'[129]

But to say that the salvation speeches were added later does not answer our basic question: *who is Yahweh?* The editors responsible for the final form of the book of Micah, Brueggemann tells us, did not feel the need to sort out the tension between two very different visions of God.[130] Biblical scholars are able to help us understand fairly clearly what the text is saying. We need further help, however, which takes us beyond the field of biblical studies, to ask what truth the text has for us today. *We need a theological framework to help us determine the truth of the matter of YHWH's character.* What kind of God *is* God? Does it simply depend on the circumstances? Does God choose to listen or not? Does God sometimes destroy or not?

## An Integral Approach and *Spiral Dynamics*

In *Part I, An Integral Theology as Transformative*, we discussed an integral approach to the self. We identified four quadrants that help us comprehend what it means to be a human being who is incarnate Spirit. As theologians, we could choose to study the book of Micah from any one of these four quadrants, each offering a distinct perspective on the prophet.

Our question concerns the character of YHWH in the book of Micah. Character is a matter of personal, spiritual identity. Character reveals a person's values and priorities. On the one hand, character is a deeply individual matter. On the other hand, character develops in the context of a group or community.

From an integral perspective, character concerns two of the quadrants: the internal or subjective knowledge which lies at the heart of Quadrant 1, 'Who am I?' and the interpersonal and cultural knowledge of Quadrant 3, 'Who are we?' Within these two quadrants there are many possible disciplines and methods for theology to draw upon. *Spiral Dynamics* is one resource that uses both of these quadrants and can help us gain a clearer sense of the book of Micah and the issue of YHWH's character.

*Spiral Dynamics* is a theory of human development that maps the complexity of evolving human beings – individually and culturally. Don Beck is one of *Spiral Dynamics'* principal proponents and he brings a wealth of practical experience. He has applied *Spiral Dynamics* in diverse cultural settings and with profound results. He played a role in the peaceful creation of a democratic South Africa, making over sixty-three trips to the country between 1981 and 1999.[131]

To draw upon *Spiral Dynamics* as *a* framework for understanding the question of YHWH's character in Micah, we first need to lay out the stages of the Spiral.

## Spiral Dynamics: A Developmental Framework[132]

*Spiral Dynamics* recognizes that human beings are not static creatures. We are dynamic and evolving as is all of creation. When living conditions get bad enough, human beings develop new ways of thinking, perceiving, and relating to deal with the conditions. How are we able to do this?

> Spiral Dynamics is based on the assumption that we have *adaptive* intelligences, 'complex, adaptive, contextual

intelligences,' which develop in response to our life circumstances and challenges—what Spiral Dynamics calls *Life Conditions*. What we're always focusing on are the causative dynamics created by the Life Conditions and then the kinds of coping mechanisms and collective intelligences that are forged in response to those conditions. These collective intelligences are what we call *memes* (mēm: 'A self-replicating element of culture, passed on by imitation' Oxford English Dictionary).

....Each successive meme contains a more expansive horizon, a more complex organizing principle, with newly calibrated priorities, mindsets, and specific bottom lines. It's a way of solving problems. It's a way of assigning priorities to what's most important and why, formed in response to the Life Conditions. And just like a biological DNA code, which is a code that replicates itself throughout the body, a meme code is a bio-psycho-social-spiritual DNA-type script, a blueprint that spreads throughout a culture, and plays out in all areas of cultural expression, forming survival codes, myths of origin, artistic forms, lifestyles, and senses of community.[133]

**Meme: A World-View**

As our Life Conditions change and the current way of living loses its effectiveness, an amazing thing happens. We adapt. New intelligences awake, which are more suitable for the changed Life Conditions. Meme is the technical term *Spiral Dynamics* has coined for each new adaptive intelligence. Persons and cultures evolve through the awakening of new memes. Meme may be thought of in terms of a 'world-view.' A world-view is not abstract; it is not simply a mental idea. A world-view is much more comprehensive. A world-view is how we take-in and experience life. It is simply how things naturally are for us. We don't question it until it is no longer effective for us. World-views do not awaken in us in a haphazard manner. They emerge in an order, according to a deep pattern in the evolution of human consciousness.

*Spiral Dynamics* has identified eight different world-views, or eight distinct levels of psychological and cultural existence, or value systems (see the color image of the Spiral in Figure A). Not only does an individual have a world-view, but so does a culture, and the same principles or levels of existence apply as much to a single person as to an entire society. A world-view is therefore the cultural glue of a group.

Each distinct world-view builds upon the one or ones that precede it. When a new world-view awakens in you or me, or in a culture, it embraces the previous world-view but enables the person or culture to do new things incapable of even being considered before. The new world-view thus embraces and transcends what has gone before. The new world-view enables a person to respond in a more comprehensive and suitable way.

The first six world-views share a basic characteristic and collectively form what *Spiral Dynamics* calls the First Tier. The last two world-views are distinguished from the first six, and form the beginning of the Second Tier. There is a quantum leap between the First and Second Tier world-views. Each of the First Tier world-views remains certain that *its* view of life is all there is. All six world-views of the First Tier share a common concern for survival or existence. The implication is that the world, or life, has a lethal dimension to it. The primary benefit of this concern is that it attempts to ensure the survival of the individual or culture, insofar as this is possible. But conflict and war between the various world-views is perpetual. With the awakening into the Second Tier, humanity crosses over into a whole new way of life, characterized by an awareness of and a commitment to unity, integration, and wholeness. A person becomes aware for the first time that each world-view has integrity and a contribution it can to make.

*Spiral Dynamics* uses a simple color-based code in order to move beyond the dualistic cultural stereotypes of black and white, or good and bad. The six colors used for the First Tier are: **BEIGE, PURPLE, RED, BLUE, ORANGE,** and **GREEN.** The Second Tier uses **YELLOW** and **TURQUOISE.** (**CORAL** is a possible next level emerging on the evolving Spiral.) We will look at each in turn, bearing in mind that we are of necessity working with very general descriptions, which overlook much nuance. Given that, *Spiral Dynamics* may help us see with new eyes and understand afresh.

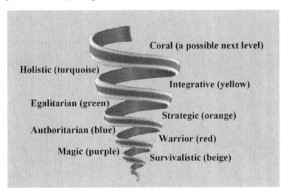

Figure A

# The First Tier of Spiral Dynamics
## The SURVIVALISTIC/INSTINCTIVE (BEIGE) World-View

From the **SURVIVALISTIC** world-view, life is mostly about *individuals* scratching out survival from day to day. At the dawn of humanity, 100,000 years ago, *homo sapiens* had to discover a way to survive amidst many other animals competing for existence. The **INSTINCTIVE** world-view is focuses primarily on survival, just as with any other animal.

Survival pressures mean that people do not have much time to be introspective. Energy is directed to the acquisition of food and water, warmth, sex, and safety. The group serves a utilitarian purpose: *individuals* band together as a means to perpetuate life. **BEIGE** is the most primitive world-view, but that does not mean ignorant or dumb. The human senses are developed to a keen level. They need to be, otherwise one will be killed.

> Oh, one can find pieces of BEIGE in street people who are basically hunter-gatherers, who get what they eat where they find it. You can certainly see it in the horrible conditions of extreme poverty in Somalia or Ethiopia [Detroit or Applachia], where it's a hand-to-mouth existence. And also, it's evident in newborn infants…[134]

### The MAGICAL/ANIMISTIC (PURPLE) World-View

Over the next 50,000 years the species had secured a niche. Family groups expanded. A new challenge arose: keep the spirits happy and the *tribe's* kin warm and safe.

> PURPLE is animistic, tribalistic, and mystical. …Suddenly a clan, which is loosely structured, solidifies into a tribe of, say, four to five hundred people, so that the previous clan can now survive in the midst of competition with other clans. So one of the Life Conditions changes that led to the shift from BEIGE to PURPLE had to do with territoriality and access to resources.
>
> This was the first sense of the metaphysical. In the BEIGE mind, events seem to be scattered, each one unto itself, without much predictability. But, for example, in Africa, if the moon is full and the cow dies, the PURPLE mind connects the two events, one causing the other. So the awakening of the metaphysical system, together with the capacity to work more firmly in a team arrangement, occurred in the transition from the Dawn People (BEIGE) to the [MAGICAL] People (PURPLE), precipitated by the changing Life Conditions that occurred during the Ice Age, about fifty thousand years ago.[135]

### The IMPULSIVE/WARRIOR (RED) World-View

Roughly 10,000 years ago, the impulsive and egocentric **WARRIOR** world-view awakened. We come upon *individuals* who live by the basic imperative of 'be what you are and do what you want, regardless.'[136] This is the dangerous world of 'red in tooth and claw,' immortalized in poem by Alfred Lord Tennyson.

The allegiance to chief, elders, and clan is replaced by persons who have broken free from any domination or constraint and whose focus of attention and energy is directed toward pleasing the self. **RED** is the world-view of impulsive warriors and conquerors. They stand tall, expect attention, demand respect, and call the shots. The **WARRIOR** world-view needs dragons to slay, and if there are none around, it can and does create them. Although there is no sense of guilt or remorse, to 'lose face' is unacceptable.

## The AUTHORITARIAN (BLUE) World-View

5,000 years ago the conquering states of impulsive warrior kings gave way to the rise of the more purposeful and **AUTHORITARIAN** world-view. Humanity's need for law and order gained ascendancy and human beings were ready to sacrifice individual ego desires for a greater good.

Self-sacrifice to the transcendent Cause or Truth or righteous pathway became more important than endless, chaotic, bloody battles of conquest. For the **AUTHORITARIAN** world-view, the transcendent Cause or Truth becomes a source of human order. Organized religion emerges for the first time in human history. The whim of human might is replaced by a code of conduct based on eternal and absolute principles. Present satisfaction is no longer as important as a guaranteed future reward. The focus of attention and energy are applied to laws, regulations, and discipline, all of which build character and strong moral fiber. Guilt becomes a principle tool for curbing impulsive behavior and assuring compliance with the group norm.

## The STRATEGIC/ACHIEVIST (ORANGE) World-View

The plagues of the middle-ages shook loose the trust or faith which many had placed unhesitatingly in the religious system. All the prayers and rituals seemed impotent in the face of such apocalyptic loss of life. Entire towns and cities were left virtually desolate. Into this breach of faith arose the **STRATEGIC/ACHIEVIST** world-view, coinciding fairly closely with the emergence of the Enlightenment.

The **STRATEGIC** world-view rejects the restrictions of the **AUTHORITARIAN** world-view's control of human inquiry and freedom. The theme of **ORANGE** is 'Act in your own *self*-interest and play the game to win.' The orientation is now toward *personal* achievement. *STRATEGIC reasoning replaces moral law*. Rather than enforcing a system in which everyone has their proper 'God-given' place, change and advancement are seen as inherent within the very scheme of things.

*Progress is the motto* and the key strategy is to learn what makes nature tick and apply these lessons. The scientific method is the 'holy grail.' There is no hesitation about dominating and manipulating the resources of earth, for their value is strictly utilitarian. The key to prosperity is strategic thinking, technological innovation, and competitive edge.

The cutting-edge of the **STRATEGIC** world-view is its conviction in changeability, rather than **AUTHORITARIAN** fatalistic determinism. Modern science and the industrial revolution are both children of **ORANGE**. So are ecological crisis and the reduction of the human person to a cog in the economic wheel.

> ...some fascinating things happened in the European brain that seemed to occur for the first time in the 1700s—the mathematical sense, the sense of cadence, the linear sense that made possible written music, that made possible quantification and measurement. These classical left brain capacities uniquely developed in the Western brain in the ORANGE system.[137]

### The EGALITARIAN (GREEN) World-View

About 150 years ago a world-view emerged of 'seek peace within the inner self and explore, with others, the caring dimensions of community.'[138] This **GREEN** world-view is all about *community and egalitarianism*. The human spirit seeks to free itself from captivity to greed, dogma and divisiveness. Rather than dominate and exploit the resources of the earth, human beings are moved to share resources and provide opportunities equally for all and search for spirituality.

The **EGALITARIAN** world-view transcends both **AUTHORITARIAN** and **STRATEGIC** world-views, reaching out to include those who have been left behind by both dogmatic religion and blind economics. There is an impatience to this world-view. Unlike the **AUTHORITARIAN** world-view which sacrifices in order to obtain a heavenly reward, the **EGALITARIAN** world-view's sacrifice is focused on the present. Sacrifice *now* so that one can obtain a reward *now*.

> At its peak, **GREEN** is communitarian, egalitarian, and consensual. Without **ORANGE** we wouldn't have **GREEN**, because in **ORANGE** the inner being was bypassed and ignored. Our science left us numb, without heart and soul, and with only the outer manifestations of success. The 'good life' was measured only in materialistic terms. We discover that we have become alienated from ourselves, as well as from others.[139]

Although the **EGALITARIAN** world-view is the most developed of the First Tier world-views, it still remains unable to truly appreciate the world-views that precede and set the stage for its very own awakening. In the name of absolute equality, **GREEN** even tears apart what has made possible its own emergence in history.

> Only those people who have been successful in **ORANGE**—who have good bank accounts, who have some guarantee of survival, who don't have the wolf at the door—will begin to think **GREEN**. But unfortunately, when **GREEN** starts launching these attacks on the **BLUE** and **ORANGE** meme levels—the nuns with rulers and the fat cats in corporate suites—it's like a person who climbs to the top of a house and then throws down the ladder that got him up there.[140]

## Second Tier – The Ability to Experience the Wholeness of Life

We need to recognize the enormous awakening within human beings represented in the 100,000 year evolution from a species utterly obsessed with survival and existence to the investment of time and energy in the formation of egalitarian communities. Much of humanity has negotiated through periods of incessant warfare (**WARRIOR**), the emergence of the world's religions (**AUTHORITARIAN**), as well as the enlightenment and the scientific revolution (**STRATEGIC**).

And yet, each First Tier world-view remains convinced that its view of the world is the *only* valid perspective. Even though each successive world-view depends for its existence on those that have preceded it, each acts as if survival depends upon discrediting, deconstructing, or destroying the previous world-views – a primary reason why we continue to be at war.

The Second Tier – made-up of the **INTEGRATIVE (YELLOW)** world-view and the **HOLISTIC (TURQUOISE)** world-view – is a quantum leap from the First Tier. The Second Tier no longer views the world dualistically, i.e., my world-view vs. the inferior others. Within the Second Tier, all life is experienced as of a whole and interconnected. Spirit infuses and sustains all that is. Since Spirit permeates all existence, on the most fundamental level of reality there is no boundary.

The Second Tier prizes such qualities as 'flexibility, spontaneity, and functionality.' Individuals 'experience wholeness of existence through mind and spirit.' We need no longer choose between the individual and the collective, because the self is 'both distinct and a blended part of a larger, compassionate whole.' Everything that exists is interconnected and change is a given fact of evolving life.

*A different theology characterizes this Second Tier*, that of 'Evolutionary Panentheism.' God is always already present in all that is; because that is the only way anything could ever even exist. God is the ground of being of each and every life. All life is sacred, every world-view, no matter how incomplete, is valued for the contribution it makes to evolving life. We could say that the reign of God is always already present, but it is not static. The reign of God is dynamic and growing, evolving, as the Divine Spirit invites all of creation into an awareness that all of life is a compassionate whole, reflective of and embodying divine compassion.

**Micah and the Character of YHWH**

Who does the book of Micah envision YHWH to be? What is YHWH's character? The book itself is a kind of extended prophetic reflection on this basic religious question. The words of the prophet and his later editors are not consistent. The initial harsh speeches of judgment are followed by the hopeful speeches of salvation. The final editors of the book, Brueggemann tells us, did not feel the need to sort out the tension between these two very different visions of God. An integral theology does feel the need to sort out this tension.

Who is God? Is God changing? Or are *human beings* evolving in such a way that our ability to perceive God is changing, broadening and deepening? Biblical studies and its tools are *incapable* of enabling us to reach an answer about YHWH's character. We need additional assistance to help us determine what *truth* the text has for us today (as well as yesterday). What kind of God is God?

In and through the book of Micah, Israel is struggling to see more clearly the character of YHWH for what it is. The catch, however, is that we always see and receive reality as *we* are. This holds true for Micah, his later editors, Israel, and you and me. Whatever stage of development we are in (**BEIGE, PURPLE, RED, BLUE, ORANGE, GREEN, YELLOW,** or **TURQUOISE**) is the lens through which we perceive reality. Reality may be offering much, much more than we are able to receive. At what stage of development were Micah and his editors?

*Spiral Dynamics*:
**YHWH through a Predominately BLUE World-View**

The Hebrew tribes in their earliest years believed in many gods, as did their neighbors. YHWH becomes a God above all gods because YHWH has the *power to conquer* all the other gods. Jealousy, rage and retaliation are never far from the divine heart of a **WARRIOR** YHWH. YHWH would have been perceived primarily as a **WARRIOR** deity during this period because the character of the Hebrew tribes' leaders was at the **WARRIOR** world-view stage of human development.

There came a time in Israel's history, however, when continual war and conquest became less and less desirable and tenable. Micah embodies, in part, Israel's growing recognition of the limits of a **WARRIOR** world-view. There is more to life than an individual powerful ego asserted against the world. A sense of common good and purpose can bring order and meaning to human life. Self-sacrifice can become the ideal. What the corrupt leaders of Israel have failed to grasp is that human beings exist for more than the pursuit of personal wealth, power, and pleasure.

*Micah has seen past the egocentricity of the WARRIOR world-view.* 'Now listen, you leaders of the House of Jacob, rulers of the House of Israel, you should know how to judge rightly, yet you still hate good and love evil; you skin my people.' Micah is claiming that his religious insight is not unique to him alone. The rulers and the populace should be able to grasp the sense of 'how to judge rightly.' Micah is calling the people to a bigger and more ordered world-view. This **AUTHORITARIAN** world-view is the primary evolutionary context of the book of Micah. To paraphrase from *Spiral Dynamics*:

> In the **AUTHORITARIAN** system, people gladly accept authoritarianism and self-sacrifice for the common good.
>
> When the **AUTHORITARIAN** world-view first develops, it has to handle the **WARRIOR**. And that's why in the Old Testament you have such punitive measures as 'an eye for an eye and a tooth for a tooth.' If there is a heavy **WARRIOR** component, then you have, in religious systems and legal systems, the very heavy punitive form of the **AUTHORITARIAN** world-view. It's designed to address the threat of the **WARRIOR**, so as long as the **WARRIOR** threat is there, the punitive expression of the **AUTHORITARIAN** world-view will continue to exist. But as the **AUTHORITARIAN** world-view moves away from having to contain the violence in the WARRIOR world-view, it goes on its life cycle toward its own healthier version, taking the form of more institutionalized systems, in which righteousness, discipline, accountability, stability, perseverance, and order prevail.

The book of Micah is a manifestation of the **AUTHORITARIAN** world-view. YHWH transcends the ego-centric needs of the rulers of Israel. These impulsive rulers are devouring the flesh of God's people. They are capable of knowing better. Micah has 'called them out' by raising their awareness.

A new religious sense of what is good is unfolding within the community of Israel. And yet, this new religious sense is itself a mixture. Evolutionarily speaking, we interpret the **AUTHORITARIAN** world-view salvation speeches as a religious insight which invites the people beyond the God of the **WARRIOR** world-view judgment speeches. Ironically, Micah's own perception of YHWH remains tethered in part to the **WARRIOR** world-view. Even as Micah calls out to the rulers of Israel, he himself remains limited by a vision of God subject to impulsive retribution and violence.

*This does not imply, necessarily, that the WARRIOR judgment speeches are wrong*, but that they represent only the limited words of judgment and retribution that the prophet and the people were capable of hearing (whatever God was saying). Micah is struggling to proclaim a God who is present and responsive to a people's unjust suffering. He sees that God opposes such crime against humanity. But he himself remains in large part a child of the **WARRIOR** world-view. He can only imagine a divinity who responds to violence with more violence.

The prevailing culture of Israel at this time remains within the impulsive **WARRIOR** and **AUTHORITARIAN** world-views, but the salvation speeches reveal a people developing an ability to hear words of judgment with restoration, beyond violent justice. In the work of the editors of Micah we witness more advanced levels of development emerging. We hear words bearing characteristics of the **EGALITARIAN** world-view, and even aspects of the **INTEGRATIVE** and **HOLISTIC** Second Tier: *universal* mercy and compassion begin to be glimpsed as the very *character* of God.

# CHAPTER 17 – THE WAY OF SELF-EMPTYING: PHILIPPIANS

## An Empty Lordship, A Loss of Status

We cannot deny the reality of a human history full of immeasurable suffering and destructive division. Yet an integral theology proclaims that the ceaselessly creating, loving, and liberating eternal Spirit is never absent – an insight grounded in the unshakable and undeniable experience of mystics. God is already in this place and every place but all too often we are unable to see God's presence. This partial blindness holds true not only for individuals, but for communities as well.

There are certain milestones throughout salvation history that mark significant developments in the clarity of our theological perception – what once seemed reasonable, or seemed possible, changes dramatically. We have noted some of these changes throughout the stories of Jeremiah, Second Isaiah, Ezekiel, Corinthians, Hosea, Colossians, and Micah.

Now we come to Philippians and its startling words:

> *Christ, though in the image of God,*
> *didn't deem equality with God*
> *something to be clung to –*
> *but instead became completely empty*
> *and took on the image of oppressed humankind:*
> *born into the human condition,*
> *found in the likeness of a human being.*
> *Jesus was thus humbled –*
> *obediently accepting death, even death on a cross!*
> *Because of this, God highly exalted Christ*
> *and gave to Jesus the name above every other name,*
> *so that at the name of Jesus every knee must bend*
> *in the heavens, on the earth and under the earth,*
> *and every tongue proclaim to the glory of God:*
> *Jesus Christ reigns supreme!*
> (Philippians 2:6-11. The Inclusive New Testament)

This Philippian hymn sings of a new God, sings forth a new vision of who the eternal God has always been: *a God empty and without status*. Paul most likely wrote to the Philippians from prison. He may have been in Rome, Caesarea, Ephesus, or Corinth. The exact date for the letter is not certain, but lies somewhere between 50-60 CE. We don't know if Paul wrote this hymn, although John Dominic Crossan believes it may well be his. We do know that it proclaims a vision of Christ and possibly of God that drains the power from the dominant imperial theology of the Roman Empire.

As we explore the God who is empty and without status, three of the questions that arise and guide our inquiry are: How did Paul come to see Christ in this new way? What is new in Paul's theology expressed here? What are the implications for our understanding of the very character of God?

## The Limits of a WARRIOR (RED) and AUTHORITARIAN (BLUE) Divinity

In the language of *Spiral Dynamics*, human beings, individually and collectively, evolve through the stages of development, or world-views. The world-view describes how we perceive reality and understand ourselves. Each world-view represents a distinct level of human development, with each successive world-view incorporating its predecessors and making possible a broader and deeper vision of the world and understanding of one's own self.

Religion, as we know it, emerged about 2500 years ago. The dominant world-view up to that point in history had been the **WARRIOR** world-view. The **RED**'s impulsive, individual, egocentric vision of self and the world had been ruling much of humanity for about 7500 years. Everyone looks out for themselves, and the warrior exemplifies this best of all: always conquering, and never conquered. In a society built around clan loyalty, the warrior is chief, who leads the clan into battle against all foes. If there are no dragons, they are created. War is the glue holding life together. The success stories, the legends retold around the fire, speak of the power and feats of the warriors.

YHWH is in many ways a **WARRIOR** deity. YHWH is LORD because of the ability to conquer, crush, and destroy the other gods. YHWH is not like Baal, or the gods of Egypt or Assyria. YHWH is a jealous God who alone is Lord of lords. And yet there is something new about this God of Israel. God's ways are not our ways (Jeremiah). God is also known in the suffering servant (Second Isaiah). The Human One reveals the face of God (Ezekiel). Renewal not destruction, mark the ways of this God (Hosea), who seeks to restore, not judge, humanity (Micah).

In the language of *Spiral Dynamics*, organized religion on a widespread and institutional scale emerges out of the **AUTHORITARIAN** world-view. Life is neither simply nor primarily about me getting whatever I want, by whatever means. 'Life has meaning, direction, and purpose with predetermined outcomes.' Again and again the prophets call Israel back to be faithful partners of the covenant. The covenant gives Israel its sense of meaning, direction, and purpose: YHWH. There is more to YHWH now than simply the **WARRIOR**. Sacrifice and community, renewal and restoration, suffering and compassion, are not the qualities of life valued and championed by **RED** warriors or deities. YHWH is Lord of life – not the kings of Egypt, Syria,

Babylon or Greece. Despite appearances to the contrary – slavery, exile, corrupt Israelite kings – YHWH is proclaimed as Lord and Ruler, King of kings, and Lord of lords.

## The Power of Rome: The 'Form of God'

A primary prism through which we understand society is that of 'class.' We talk of the different economic classes, class warfare, and the struggle of the lower classes to rise and succeed. The ancient world however, and Rome in particular, was not structured around that concept of class. *Power was a matter of patronage.* Everyone was in debt, in the sense of being in the service to and under the protection of, a more powerful patron.

> [S]ociety resembled a mass of little pyramids of influence, each headed by a major family ---- or one giant pyramid headed by an autocrat --- not the three-decker sandwich of upper, middle, and lower classes familiar to us from industrial society. The client of a power wielder thus becomes a powerful man and himself in turn attracts clients...It is quite different from the three-layer sandwich of a class society....Patronage virtually precludes independent political relations for those patronized.[141]

Like every ancient society, there was a Roman imperial theology to justify that social structure. This theology was a part of the air that Rome, its citizens, and its conquered peoples, breathed in, whether interacting in a public space or a private house, or engaging in a sacrificial ritual or a social meal. Caesar was lord and king because he was at the top of the pyramid, with all of society below, dependent upon his power for their existence. It was only because of his power, might and glory that he, and only he, had the ability to sustain all his clients – the Roman Empire. The further removed one was from Caesar, the less claim one had to life itself. One's value was not intrinsic, but derived from what one received from Caesar. In addition, one did not climb their way up the social hierarchy – one's position was simply a given. The duty of everyone as client was to satisfy the next higher ranking patron.

In the language of *Spiral Dynamics*, Roman imperial theology was a mixture of **WARRIOR** and **AUTHORITARIAN** world-views. Caesar was a mighty warrior and conquering hero, which is all quite **RED**. But Roman imperial theology and morality also spoke eloquently of social duty, responsibility, and sacrifice – qualities of **BLUE**. Rome represented a major advance in human evolution. The Roman Empire could only have come into existence because human beings were willing to sacrifice individual desire for a greater whole. Much of Western law is traced back to the philosophers of Rome, such as Cicero, Gaius, Ulpian, and many others. Waterways, roadways, economics, and political theory: the Romans were pioneers in all of these areas in ways that continue to impact us today.

And yet, for all of its glory, Rome's exercise of power cast a shadow of suffering over the ancient world. Roman imperial theology remained shackled to an honor-based social system in which 'status' governed every aspect of life. One's status depended upon the number of clients held in patronage and status was a zero-sum quality, that is, there was a finite and fixed amount of status to go around. For Caesar to have so much status meant that others had less. Caesar embodied and revealed for all to see the very 'form of God.'

## Philippi: Division from Economic Suffering

Piety, war, victory, and peace formed the Roman rhythm of life throughout the expanding empire. A disruption of any step in the sequence would threaten to throw everything into chaos. Disruption was seen as seditious, and Rome took such threats quite seriously, as its practice of mass crucifixions testifies. Paul's letter to the Philippians was such a disruption, a direct confrontation to the piety of Roman imperial theology and its understanding of the 'form of God' embodied in Caesar.

The Roman Empire in the 1st century CE was far flung. Rome had expanded by conquering other kingdoms, which meant that many of the people ruled by Caesar were not Roman citizens. As a kingdom and its cities were defeated, land and property were given over to Roman soldiers (an example of patrons granting favors to their clients).

Until quite recently, many scholars assumed that Philippi was inhabited principally by former Roman soldiers and was a fairly well-to-do colony. (For an example of this, see the *Access Bible's* introduction to Philippians.) Scripture scholar Peter Oakes has developed a very different picture. Philippi, he says, was a city in which the 'majority of the population of the town were probably not Romans and not citizens' but 'Greek,' because 'many were ethnically Greek and their predominant language would have been Greek.' Oakes divides the population roughly in this way:

    37% service groups (craft workers)
    20% slaves
    20% colonist farmers (10% owning; 10% renting)
    20% poor
     3% elite[142]

The city of Philippi was situated in the midst of high quality land that would have been farmed. Mines, which at one time had been a source of wealth, would have long been exhausted. The overwhelming majority of people, 97%, were of lesser status, situated well below a small but very powerful elite. You would have met slaves every day, but they were not a majority of the population.

What about the Church? The typical picture described by scholars looks something like this.

> In contrast to other places, the [Christian] community is probably composed not of the proletariat but mainly of members of the middle class . . . The veterans settled in Philippi are not slaves but free people, who mainly own their land . . . A church that is financially so well placed can give Paul material support.[143]

Oakes describes a very different Church, one in which there were 'mainly Greek non-citizens living in one of the most strongly Roman colonies in the eastern Empire.' *What this means is that because most of the residents were not Roman citizens they enjoyed less status and power than the ruling Roman minority.* The numbers look something like this.

43% service community (craft-workers)
25% poor
16% slaves
15% farmers
1% elite landowners[144]

The members of the Church at Philippi were *struggling* to make a living. They were suffering economically 'at the hands of fellow-townspeople.' The struggle had reached the point where the Church-community was beginning to be torn apart and divided against itself.

### Suffering and Division among the Philippian Christians

Some have proposed that the Christians were suffering spiritually either because a heretical group was sowing strife with its different understanding of the gospel, or Jewish opponents were attacking their way of faith. But the origin of the Philippian suffering did *not* lie in *theological* disagreement. Paul focuses on the themes of suffering and unity in response to divisive threats posed by the economic hardship experienced by members of the church.

What did Paul perceive as so threatening that he wrote a letter with a theology of Christ and God that challenged the underpinnings of Roman imperial theology?

# 'To Suffer for Christ' (1:28)

The five groups of people in the Philippian church (service community, the poor, slaves, farmers, elite landowners) each underwent a distinct form of suffering. Oakes offers an extensive description of the craft-workers or service community.

If we consider a family of Greek craft-workers, all of whom are Christians, what would 'suffering in Christ' be likely to involve for them? Let us imagine that our family are bakers and consist of a married couple called Simias and Ianthe, three children, an elderly grandmother and a slave-girl. They make and sell bread from a one-room bakery and shop. They live in the bakery and in a low mezzanine room above it. When trade is good, they just make ends meet. They sell half their bread as a regular order to three elite families. The rest is sold from their shop to a mixture of customers from the town and the countryside. Simias has for many years been a member of a burial club. A number of members are also bakers and these contacts provide our baker with access to extra oven-space which he needs whenever he receives an order which is larger than usual.

What could 'suffering for Christ' mean for this family? The most obvious possibility is that problems might arise over the burial club [with its Roman Imperial Theology and practices]. Simias might stop paying his subscription or the club might hold a celebratory meal, at the grave of a former member, which Simias was expected to attend but did not. The result of such unfriendly behavior by Simias was likely to do damage to his relationships with some other members of the club. Some could be regular customers who might change where they bought bread. More seriously, the other bakers might deny him access to oven-space when he needed it. Since our family of bakers were living at subsistence level already, any such economic suffering would be very serious. Although an organization such as a burial club did not perform major social functions, disruption of relationships with other members could cause substantial suffering.

Problems could also arise at the shop. Ianthe has removed the shrine to the god that was popular among Greek bakers. This had been quite visible from the shop counter and, although most customers did not notice its absence, some did and started to spread word that Simias and Ianthe were dishonoring the gods. This was particularly unpopular among the other bakers. Extra oven-space became impossible to find and our bakers had to change their supplier of flour. They ended up paying 10 percent more than they had previously. This, again, was a severe problem.

Things became worse as word went round that the family were members of a strange, subversive, Jewish organization. Some people challenged Simias and Ianthe over this and they responded by

> seeking to persuade them to join the organization and join in the dishonoring of the gods. The daughter of one of the other bakers was actually persuaded. Her father came round in a rage, along with three friends. They beat up Simias and started breaking up the shop. Neighbors, worried that a fire might start, ran to the magistrates. Simias and the other baker were taken off to answer for the disturbance. The magistrates had seen one or two of these troublesome Christians before. Simias received a further beating and a night in prison. Simias was unable to work for a week. This was a particular problem because the usual neighborly extra pairs of hands for such an emergency were unavailable. However, Ianthe and the rest of the family coped with the work. In fact, the workload proved unexpectedly light because, two days after Simias' night in prison, one of the three elite families who were their main customers stopped their order. Simias and Ianthe lived in terror of the other two doing the same....
>
> The crucial form of suffering for the bakers was economic. Broken relationships, broken reputations and broken heads would all be serious forms of suffering in themselves. However, for a family on a subsistence income, the most serious aspect of each of these would be the long-term economic effect that it produced.[145]

Each of the groups would have had their own personal stories of hardship to tell. To be a Christian was not and could not be a private matter in the ancient world. Such suffering required these early Christians to establish new relationships among themselves. Those relationships crossed over the boundaries of status and patronage that held their Roman society together. The more well-to-do in the Church would need to reach out and provide economic assistance to people such as Simias and Ianthe, risking loss of status, privilege and power. Non-Christians would see that crossing over, feel its threat to the social order, and the repercussions would ripple outward.

Economic aid might also be needed for a very long time, threatening impoverishment of everyone in the church. The fear of losing status must have tempted some to not provide economic assistance, and even to disassociate themselves from those suffering public humiliation. A third danger would have been 'the immense weight that Roman society placed on law and order . . . In Roman society, if someone was regarded as a troublemaker then there was a moral imperative for others not to associate with him.'[146]

## Philippians as a Call for Unity: An Empty Lordship

Paul saw the failure to provide mutual assistance and the retreat from association with fellow Christians as a threat to the heart of the gospel. Economic suffering was undermining the very unity of the church.

The Philippians were afraid. They lived in a world utterly defined by the patronage system, which meant that life and livelihood depended upon having status. To lose one's status was to forfeit not only one's own life, but the lives of those who were dependent upon you. The entire hierarchical structure of life could be undone by the loss of status. The Philippians were caught. They could not survive as a community as long as members clung to their status – sisters and brothers needed economic help now. But if status were sacrificed, they could not survive among the non-Christian inhabitants of Philippi. They would be ostracized, beaten, perhaps killed.

Paul proclaims a startling word of strange hope into this world of gathering despair. The Philippians can only be saved by remaining united. Christ, not Caesar, has to be their model for living and caring for one another. In a world dominated by status and patronage, what is so startling and strange about Paul's words of hope is not that he proclaims Christ as their model, but the kind of model that Paul envisions Christ to be. Let us look again at the heart of Paul's vision found in chapter 2, verses 6-11 (The Inclusive New Testament).

> *Christ, though in the image of God,*
> *didn't deem equality with God*
> *something to be clung to –*
> *but instead became completely empty*
> *and took on the image of oppressed humankind:*
> *born into the human condition,*
> *found in the likeness of a human being.*
> *Jesus was thus humbled –*
> *obediently accepting death, even death on a cross!*
> *Because of this, God highly exalted Christ*
> *and gave to Jesus the name above every other name,*
> *so that at the name of Jesus every knee must bend*
> *in the heavens, on the earth and under the earth,*
> *and every tongue proclaim to the glory of God:*
> *Jesus Christ reigns supreme!*

The image of the divine that dominates the Philippians' theology holds them captive – Christ made in the image of Caesar, made in the image of the **WARRIOR**. Christ is more divine and powerful than Caesar, to put it crudely, because Christ has more status than Caesar. To be like Christ is to be someone of status and power. Whether it be Christ or Caesar, the Philippians are still controlled by the **WARRIOR** world-view's concern with status. They are paralyzed by their deathly fear of losing it.

What the Philippians are unable to see is that to be willing to let it all go, is the only path of life. Paul, who has lost his status in the ancient world – dropping from Pharisee to Christian – and is now imprisoned, knows what it means to be publicly humiliated, threatened with death, and to lose prestige and power. As long as the Philippians cling to *status as their savior* they will be lost, with no way out. Christ is the key. Christ clings to nothing. Jesus is willing to accept death out of his compassion for others. In Paul's eyes, 'Christ was seen as undergoing a loss of status greater than any that Philippians might risk by offering economic help.'

If concern for status continues to govern the relationships among the Philippian Christians, they will not come to one another's aid. Mutual help will only become possible if the current hierarchy that divides and causes so much unnecessary suffering crumbles. The Philippian Christians cannot exist as a typical Roman community where patronage divides and rules relationships. Their only path to wholeness will be as sisters and brothers in Christ (as we know from Galatians).

In Christ, Paul writes, there is no clinging. Christ accepts the lowest possible status imaginable, becoming empty of all claims to divine equality, and being one of us. There could be no greater drop in status imaginable. And why does Christ do this? Out of deep and abiding compassion. If we turn to 1 Corinthians 1-4, where Paul speaks of God's power or wisdom as being that which the world calls weakness or stupidity, we begin to get a better understanding of Paul's theology.

There is power and wisdom, *divine* power and *divine* wisdom, in the apparently foolish action of losing one's status and caring for a vulnerable other. Christians follow the way of Jesus when they establish relationships of mutual care where they experience a new found freedom: freedom from the fear of losing status, privilege, position, power.

**Empty Christ reveals an Empty God**

As Christians, we speak of Christ as the *imago dei* (or image of God). To say that Jesus is Christ is to experience and see in Jesus the divine face. This is not to say that God is not seen in the faces of other figures of history. But for Christians, Jesus reveals the way by revealing who God is.

Jesus, Paul tells us from his own experience, is the one who totally emptied himself. In today's language we would say Jesus let go of egoic desires to be lord of life. He let go of the need to reign in power over himself and others. The Greek word for this is *kenosis*, which means self-emptying. As one who is self-empty, Jesus has a heart whose compassion is boundless because it is completely attentive and receptive to the person before him. To let go is to be in a position to receive. To be empty is to surrender to life. To be kenotic is to be without fear – there is nothing to lose because one desires to hold onto nothing.

*The God of Jesus is no Caesar of the universe.* We are not ruled by the power of a kingly god jealous about status. Paul glimpses a very different God revealed in Jesus.

> A God whose gracious presence as free gift (Paul's *charis*) is the beating heart of the universe and does not need to threaten, to intervene, to punish, or to control. A God whose presence is justice and life, but whose absence is injustice and death...[147]

Surrender is the message Paul is speaking to the Philippians and to us. Surrender and receive the life that only God can give. Status will not, can not, bring life. Marcus Borg offers a marvelous description of 'the way' of Jesus. Although Borg is referring to John's gospel, his words capture Paul's theology as well.

> But 'the way' that John speaks of is not about believing doctrines about Jesus. Rather, 'the way' is what we see incarnate in Jesus: the path of death and resurrection as the way to rebirth in God. According to John, this is the only way – and, as I shall soon suggest, it is 'the way' spoken of by all the major religions of the world. Dying and rising is the way. Thus Jesus is 'the Way' – the way become flesh. Rather than being the unique revelation of a way known only in him, his life and death are the incarnation of a universal way known in all of the enduring religions.[148]

## Self-Emptying: The Decisive Authority of the Universe

Borg's description of 'the way' returns us to the startling nature of Paul's letter. Surrounded by the **WARRIOR** and **AUTHORITARIAN** world-views of the Roman Empire and its imperial theology based on egocentric status and patronage, Paul experiences a Christ of emptiness and boundless compassion. Paul knows a Christ in which there is no longer Jew nor Greek, slave nor free, male and female. Christ lives in Paul so thoroughly that the hierarchical boundaries of his society dissolve. Mutual respect and compassion become possible. The fear of losing status is transformed into the courage to care for others even in the face of death. In the language of *Spiral Dynamics*, Paul embodies the more expansive Second Tier world-view; a world-view that does not negate the contributions of the **WARRIOR** and **AUTHORITARIAN** world-views, but embraces and transcends them. In Paul is a glimpse of universal compassion.

The way of Jesus reveals the invitation of God to all of humanity. All of humanity is capable of discovering this invitation. We close with the words of

Borg, describing the way of self-emptying as the heart of Christianity, which is also the heart of the world.

> This process is at the heart not only of Christianity, but of the other enduring religions of the world. The image of following 'the way' is common in Judaism, and 'the way' involves a new heart, a new self-centered in God. One of the meanings of the word 'Islam' is 'surrender': to surrender one's life to God by radically centering in God. And Muhammad is reported to have said, 'Die before you die.' Die spiritually before you die physically; die metaphorically (and really) before you die literally. At the heart of the Buddhist path is 'letting go' --- the same internal path as dying to an old way of being and being born into a new. According to the *Tao te Ching*, a foundational text for both Taoism and Zen Buddhism, Lao Tzu said: 'If you want to become full, let yourself be empty; if you want to be reborn, let yourself die.'[149]

# CHAPTER 18 – ENCLOSED IN A LOVING GOD: JULIAN OF NORWICH

## The Motherhood of Christ: All Will Be Well

> *He [Jesus] put Himself between us and His Father*
> *who was threatening to strike us,*
> *as a Mother full of pity puts herself between*
> *the stern angry father who is going to strike it.*
> Anselm of Canterbury[150]

> \*\*\*

> *For as the body is clad in the cloth,*
> *and the flesh in the skin,*
> *and the bones in the flesh,*
> *and the heart in the trunk,*
> *so are we, soul and body,*
> *clad and enclosed in the goodness of God.*
> *Yes, and more closely, for all these vanish and waste away;*
> *the goodness of God is always complete and closer to us,*
> *beyond any comparison*

> *The deep wisdom of the trinity is our mother,*
> *in whom we are closed.*

> *So Jesus Christ, who opposes good to evil, is our true mother.*
> *We have our being from him,*
> *where the foundation of motherhood begins,*
> *with all the sweet protection of love which endlessly follows.*
> *As truly as God is our Father, so truly is God our Mother...*
> Julian of Norwich[151]

## *Spiral Dynamics*:
## Julian's Ability to Experience the Wholeness of Life

Within First Tier development distinguished by *Spiral Dynamics*, we can understand almost the entirety of human history as one long battle: light against darkness, good against evil, heaven against hell, righteous against sinner, Christian against infidel, spirit against body, God against satan. God's very *character* is defined as the one who stands against the threat of evil, oftentimes personified as satan. In religious terms, there is always a holy war, of some kind, going on in the First Tier: good and evil – my side and your side – are at odds and cannot be reconciled within dualism.

Julian of Norwich, like those before her, and each one of us, was born into this warring world of First Tier duality. And yet, unlike almost all of her contemporaries, she was not held captive by the warring world-view, but experienced an alternative world and taught a startling *new* vision. That vision invites Christianity into the Second Tier, where there is the ability to 'experience wholeness of existence through mind and spirit.' The world-view of Julian offers a way through the incessant war. Duality is resolved because she is able to affirm what is distinct while incorporating the warring sides into a 'blended part of a larger, compassionate whole.' For Julian, everything that exists is interconnected. In contemporary language we would say that Spirit is seen to permeate all of existence, so that on the most fundamental level of reality there is no boundary. Theologically, we may describe this world-view as panentheistic – God is always completely, but never exhaustively, present in each and every creature. God is utterly present in all that is, but all that is never fully captures the divine.

How did Julian of Norwich arrive at this uncommon vision that unites all of creation in Christ? Let's start where she began, with a dualistic world-view wherein an omnipotent and threatening God stood ever poised to strike out against creation.

### A Culture with an Angry God

We opened above with a quote from St. Anselm:

> He [Jesus] put Himself between us and His Father who was threatening to strike us, as a mother full of pity puts herself between the stern angry father who is going to strike *it*.

We begin with Anselm because his theology expresses so well the dominant world-view of the age. Creation is a place of corrupting temptation. Human reason becomes compromised by the desires of the body. The home of God is apart from us in heaven. God is known here as a 'stern angry father who is going to strike.' Fear, not in the Hebrew sense of awe, is the only rational human response. As sinners, human beings can have no hope. The Father stands eternally poised to lash out in the name of divine justice. Humanity's only hope lies in Jesus, sent to stand between God and us. More accurately, Jesus, as our mother, places himself between us and God, protecting her brood from the irate Father.

The scholar Ritamary Bradley says, '[Anselm's] picture is directly contrary to Julian's portrayal of a God in whom there is no wrath.'[152] Again and again Julian speaks of creation and humanity as God's home. Julian's world-view distinguishes her from the other English medieval mystics such as Richard Rolle, Walter Hinton, and the author of the *Cloud of Unknowing*.

> Each of them devoted pages to spelling out the evils of the world, the need for strict custody of the senses to ward off temptation....The absence of such warnings is glaring in Julian's text.[153]

Julian claims that humanity, contrary to the vision of Anselm, 'was meant to be God's city and dwelling place.' [154]

## God & Sin: Julian's Dilemma

We know next to nothing about Julian's early life. The consensus is that she 'probably adopted the name 'Julian' after the patron saint of the church where she established her anchorhold.'[155] The best evidence is that she was about thirty years old when she received her visions (May 1373). She was so ill that she was given the last rites. However, Julian recovered and wrote her *Showings*, which exists in two versions. There is the Short Text, which was composed first, and then the Long Text, written 15 years or so later. In the time between these texts, Julian prayed, reflected, and struggled, especially with this dilemma:

> Ah, good Lord, how could all things be well, because of the great harm which has come through sin to your creatures? And here I wished...for some plainer explanation through which I might be at ease about this matter.[156]

Julian was perplexed by a dilemma that never occurred to Anselm: 'Why [does God] *not* see us 'blameworthy' for our sin.'[157] The church taught that as human beings we are to be blamed for our sin. Caught in the sinful wake of Adam, we choose against God. In this choosing is the reason for the fall and blame in Genesis. Left corrupted by sin, human beings are justly condemned by God to hell. Sin and blame had always gone together. Yet in her visions Julian experienced a God in whom there was no blame.

Julian was fully aware of the church's teaching and desired to remain faithful. And yet her own *Showings* revealed to her, in language so simple and direct, that 'All will be well'[158]. How could it be true that some – many, if not most – are condemned to hell because of their sin, in and through Adam, and 'all will be well'? '*All* will be *well*' implies for Julian that all will be *saved*, not just some. Julian's *Showings* thus involved a teaching that was apparently very unorthodox, at the least, and for some, heretical.

Julian struggled mightily with this dilemma and prayed for a 'plainer explanation' of her vision. The 'plainer explanation' Julian receives is in the form of a parable, 'the lord and the servant.' The meaning of the parable, at first, is about as clear as a mud. Julian doesn't even include it in her first composition of the *Showings*, or the Short Text. For the next 15 to 20 years she wrestles with the meaning of this parable, for within it lies the resolution of her dilemma, and the way out of the warring dualism of her age.

## Parable of the Lord and the Servant

The teaching of the church, as Julian understands it, is that human beings are blameworthy for their sin. Anselm of Canterbury's theology typifies the dominant church teaching. He offers an example in his *Cur Deus Homo? (Why Did God Become Human?)*, which is striking in its contrast with Julian's parable:

> Perhaps if his inability has no cause in himself, he can be partially excused. But if there is any guilt in that inability, it neither lightens the sin nor excuses him when he fails to pay his debt. Suppose that a man enjoins some task on his servant, and charges him not to throw himself into a pit which he points out to him, out of which he cannot possibly escape. But that servant despises the command and the warning of the master and, of his own free will, throws himself into the pit that has been shown him, so that he is unable to carry out his assigned task. Do you think that his inability is worth anything as an excuse for not performing the assigned task?[159]

It would seem that at first Julian assumes this teaching to be the only possible world-view theology may offer. Yet, this daughter of the church receives a very different vision, which shatters this dominant world-view taught by Anselm and most of the church. In Chapter 51 of the Long Text, we can sense immediately how very different her relationship with God is from Anselm's relationship with God.

> And then our *courteous* Lord answered very mysteriously, by revealing a wonderful example of a lord who has a servant, and gave me sight for the understanding of them both....I saw two persons in bodily likeness, that is to say a lord and a servant; and with that God gave me spiritual understanding. The lord sits in state, *in rest and in peace*. The servant stands before his lord, respectfully, ready to do his lord's will. The lord looks on his servant very lovingly and sweetly and mildly. He sends him to a certain place to do his will. Not only does the servant go, but he dashes off and runs at great speed, *loving to do his lord's will*. And soon he falls into a dell [a pit] and is greatly injured; and then he groans and moans and tosses about and writhes, but he cannot rise or help himself in any way. And of all this, the greatest hurt which I saw him in was lack of consolation, for he *could not turn*

> *his face to look* on his loving lord, who was very close to him, *in whom is all consolation*; but like a man who was for the time extremely feeble and foolish, he paid heed to his feelings and his continuing distress....I was amazed that this servant could so meekly suffer all this woe; and I looked carefully to know if I could detect any fault in him, or if the lord would impute to him any kind of blame; and truly none was seen, for the only cause of his falling was *his good will and his great desire*. And in spirit he was as prompt and as good as he was when he stood before his lord, ready to do his will. And all this time his loving lord looks on him most tenderly...*with great compassion* and pity. [160]

Whereas Anselm saw a servant who 'despises the command and the warning of the master and, of his own free will, throws himself into the pit that has been shown him, so that he is unable to carry out his assigned task,' Julian sees a wholly different picture. Julian spent at least 15 years struggling to discern the 'plainer' meaning of this parable. If the servant was Adam it made no sense to Julian that he was without blame. The parable was saying that the servant fell, but not because of ill will.

Within the world of the parable, Julian encounters a servant whose only fault is that he cares too much. She studies the servant very carefully 'to know if I could detect any fault in him, or if the lord would impute to him any kind of blame; and truly none was seen, for the only cause of his falling was his good will and his great desire.' We fall because we care too much? We stumble out of haste to do the will of God? Within the world-view of Anselm, none of this makes any sense whatsoever.

Julian is faced with a new question. How *could* the lord ever hold such a *willing* servant blameworthy? Julian sees that God does not. 'And all this time his loving lord looks on him most tenderly...with great compassion and pity.' The greatest hurt Julian can detect has nothing at all to do with divine judgment and wrath. Quite the contrary, we find that Julian's heart is clearly moved by what she sees transpiring. 'And of all this, the greatest hurt which I saw him in was lack of consolation, for he could not turn his face to look on his loving lord, who was very close to him, in whom is all consolation.' God is there, present to console, never absent, but the fallen servant, with head turned and unable to move, cannot behold the divine compassion. Blindness to the ever-present compassion of God: this is the source of greatest pain.

For 15 years Julian was pulled in both directions of this dualism: a sinful, blameworthy Adam, versus 'All will be well' because God is compassionate. This dualism, separating Adam (humanity) from God, made perfect sense within the world-view of Anselm. Julian recognized that it was impossible for all to be well if we were all blameworthy.

The dilemma finally resolved as Julian awakened to the surprising truth that the servant in the parable is *both* Adam and Christ. There *never* has been a time that creation has been without Christ. 'When Adam fell, God's Son fell'.[161] Historically, Adam came before Christ, but from the perspective of God, reality is different. God 'made us all at once. And in our making he knit us and united us to himself, by which union we are kept as clean and as noble as we were made'.[162]

In stunning fashion, the parable is revealing that in and through Christ God embraces *all* that is. There is no duality in Julian's world-view, because in the end she 'realized that 'Love' was the word summing up the message of her revelations.'

> What, do you wish to know your Lord's meaning in this thing? Know it well, love was his meaning. Who reveals it to you? Love. What did he reveal to you? Love. Why does he reveal it to you? For love. Remain in this, and you will know more of the same. But you will never know different, without end.[163]

We live because Christ lives in us – as was true of Adam – and Christ desires only to do the will of God. We hurt one another and turn from God, but never from our deepest center, because that center is Christ and God never abandons Christ just as Christ never abandons God. 'Peace and love are always in us, living and working,' sings out Julian, 'but we are not always in peace and in love.'[164]

**The Motherhood of Christ**

Anselm envisioned Christ as a mother who acts to protect us from the wrath of God. Christ acts like a mother bear placing herself between her cubs and a lethal threat. For Anselm, the incarnation was necessary to save humanity from the impending divine judgment.

The compassionate God of Julian poses no threat. Jesus does not protect us from God, because we need no protection. Why, then, do we have the incarnation? 'For Julian, unlike Anselm, the motive of the Incarnation is not the necessity of atoning for sin. Rather, it is the desire of Christ 'to become our mother in all things,' including those which divine creativity could only accomplish in created beings.'[165]

Anselm, as well as Julian, speaks of the motherhood of Christ. But motherhood for Julian is not about protection. Humanity and creation are not at war with God. They are not separated by a chasm of sin. Julian proposes a wholly different kind of motherhood, reminiscent of that portrayed in the Book of Wisdom (7), Sirach (15) and Isaiah. Why is love the answer for Julian? How can peace and love be always alive in us? What is there within us that eternally moves God to look upon us with the most tender compassion?

The answer for Julian lies in the motherhood of God and Christ. The divine motherhood is the theological soul of the parable of the lord and the servant.

Julian's motherhood metaphor reveals not only 'the intimacy which God in the Trinity establishes with creatures,' it also portrays 'the closeness of Christ to humanity.' Motherhood characterizes the entire Trinity for Julian, but it is especially appropriate in her eyes for Christ. And in the motherhood of Christ 'lies the answer to the question explained in the lord and servant parable: why God does not see us 'blameworthy' for our sin. Her answer has been, of course, that God sees us in our union with Christ, specifically in the 'godly will' by which we never cease to will the good.'

Julian's world-view completely dismantles the assumptions of the dominant world-view. Human beings are sinful, but the 'godly will' in us does 'never cease to will the good.' Our deepest self, for Julian, is none other than Christ. All creation is 'knit' and united in Christ. When God sees us, God is looking at our truest self, our soul, which is Christ. We are creatures anointed with the very Spirit of God, which is the very meaning of Christ.

The only path open to the lord is to love the servant; a God of compassion can only love us. This does not imply that God isn't free. Julian perceives God's *character* in a way quite unlike that of Anselm and in a manner which his dualistic world-view cannot contain. God who is love is free when loving. Since human beings in their truest selves are nothing other than Christ, or the presence of God's own self in creation, all God *can do* is love us.

## Second Tier World-View
### All Will Be Well

> *I saw that [God] is to us everything which is good and comforting for our help.*
> *He is our clothing, who* wraps *and* enfolds *us for love,*
> embraces *us and* shelters *us,* surrounds *us for his love;*
> *which is* so tender that he may never desert us.
> Julian of Norwich[166]

Julian can envision that 'all will be well' because the motherhood of God wraps, enfolds, embraces, shelters, surrounds, and never deserts us. Julian sees that God 'has made everything totally good.'[167] What then are we to make of sin? Julian has said that 'Peace and love are always in us, living and working, but we are not always in peace and in love.' How is it that 'all will be well' when we are not always living in peace and love? Sin cannot be our truest self, or the core of our soul, if Christ is always already present there. Sin cannot be some 'thing' that takes away our basic goodness. Nothing has the power to destroy the presence of Christ, which is the very presence of God in creation.

If we return to the parable we can discover Julian's theology of sin. Looking upon the servant, Julian says that 'the greatest hurt which I saw him in was lack of consolation, for *he could not turn his face to look* on his loving lord, who was very close to him.' The servant 'could not turn his face to look.' He was unable to *see* the loving lord embracing and sheltering him, a lord who would never desert him. Sin, for Julian, is a *blindness* of the soul. Blindness causes the servant to fall.

> I understood in this way. Man is changeable in this life, and falls into sin through naiveté and ignorance. He is weak and foolish in himself, and also his will is overpowered in the time when he is assailed and in sorrow and woe. And the cause is blindness, because he does not see God; for if he saw God continually, he would have no harmful feelings nor any kind of prompting, no sorrowing which is conducive to sin.[168]

It is the very presence of Christ within us that can never be separated from God. Christ within, as our very truest self, can will only what is good. In Julian's world-view, sin is our blindness to our truest Christ-self. Human suffering stems from our blindness, not our badness. Badness implies the world-view of Anselm and the dualism of the dominant theology. Julian's world-view is that 'the created universe is fundamentally good and reveals God.'[169] We are blind to our own Christ-rooted goodness. As a result, pain is never a punishment from God. It is our blindness that causes us to make such a claim. 'But in God there can be no anger, as I see it,' proclaims Julian.[170]

The ramifications of Julian's world-view are astounding at times. Her theology is one of love and friendship, echoing the gospel of John.

> For it was a great marvel, constantly shown to the soul in all the revelations, and the soul was contemplating with great diligence that our *Lord God cannot in his own judgment forgive, because he cannot be angry* – that would be impossible. For this was revealed, that our life is all founded and rooted in love, and without love we cannot live....we are endlessly united to him in love, it is the most impossible thing which could be that God might be angry, for anger and friendship are two contraries; for he dispels and destroys our wrath and makes us meek and mild – we must necessarily believe that he is always one in love, meek and mild, which is contrary to wrath. For I saw most truly that where our Lord appears, peace is received and wrath has no place; for I saw no kind of wrath in God, neither briefly nor for long. For truly, as I see it, if God could be angry for any time, we should neither have life nor place nor being....For though we may feel in ourselves anger, contention and strife, still we are all mercifully

> enclosed in God's mildness and in his meekness, in his benignity and in his accessibility.[171]

'Mercifully enclosed in God's mildness,' creation is eternally embraced in the loving motherhood of Christ. Julian's vision of divine motherhood, according to the scholar, Joan Nuth, 'expresses the very essence…of Christ's activity towards humanity, summarizing the whole doctrine of salvation.'[172] 'The deep wisdom of the trinity,' Julian now realizes, 'is our mother in whom we are closed.'

If we are closed or embraced by God there is no way anyone *ever* could be lost. Julian's world-view leads her to affirm that in the end all are saved and none are lost. How this is so, she doesn't know, but with God all things are possible. As our true mother, 'Mother Jesus, he alone bears us for joy and for endless life'.[173] Julian is adamant about the salvation of all. Let us listen once more to her words. 'And in our creating he joined and united us to himself, and through this union we are kept as pure and as noble as we were created'.[174]

> And for the great endless love that God has for all mankind, he makes no distinction in love between the blessed soul of Christ and the least soul that will be saved.…Greatly ought we to rejoice that God dwells in our soul; and more greatly ought we to rejoice that our soul dwells in God. Our soul is created to be God's dwelling place, and the dwelling of our soul is God, who is uncreated.…And I saw no difference between God and our substance.…We are enclosed in the Father, and we are enclosed in the Son, and we are enclosed in the Holy Spirit. And the Father is enclosed in us, the Son is enclosed in us, and the Holy Spirit is enclosed in us, almighty, all wisdom and all goodness, One God, one Lord.[175]

In the end, Julian's world-view assures us that all are saved because all is enclosed in God whose love for creation is endless. Christ is the heart and soul of every creature of creation. Christ is the wellspring of each and every life.

Julian's panentheistic world-view is a startling one, especially in the life and times of the 14th and 15th centuries, a period in history where the world-view was dominated by a harshly negative and dualistic vision, such as that of Anselm. Following *Spiral Dynamics*, we discover in Julian's *Showings* offer a more **INTEGRATIVE** world-view reflective of her ability to 'experience wholeness of existence through mind and spirit.' Compassion, not judgment, is the deepest character of God and creation. Creation is a 'compassionate whole,' (as simple and as beautiful as a hazelnut),[176] where everything that exists is interconnected, with Christ as its soul and life wellspring.

# Invitation: Restoration, Emptiness, Motherhood – A Compassionate Whole

How we perceive ourselves and our world matters. It makes a practical difference in our lives and our ability to live in peace. As human beings we suffer in large part because we insist on clinging to false perceptions. If our world-view is obsessed with judgment, we are unable to experience the healing gift of restoration. If we are driven to obtain status and power, there is little room in our soul to receive the wisdom, love and friendship of others. If God is ever poised in anger to strike us down, then no image of Christ as mother in the end can calm our deepest fears of annihilation.

Cross-cultural studies, interreligious dialogues, and developmental psychology all point to the same awareness as that found in *Spiral Dynamics*: Compassion, not judgment, is the deepest character of the sacred (whom we call God) and creation. The vision of the Second Tier is true: Creation *is* a 'compassionate whole.' We cannot weave a theology of compassionate wholeness simply from the broken First Tier threads of judgment, status and anger.

Micah, Paul, and Julian of Norwich are wise voices from tradition. They are not typical of their cultures. Their experiences of God cannot be contained by the dominant world-views of their times. The Spirit of God speaks to us through their theologies inviting us to experience and know for ourselves the God of boundless compassion who embraces all creation.

## An Integral Theology: The Four Quadrants

Four primary questions continually invite a theology that is integral to ceaselessly inquire into the Truth of life:

Who am I? What am I?

Who are we? What are we?

These questions are deceptively simple, in that they identify the four primary dimensions of all life. When we, as theologians, allow these questions to guide our inquiry, we naturally attend to what it is the Spirit is seeking to reveal. Throughout, we have been exploring the matter of the character of God, as human beings have struggled to understand it unfolding in their lives. The question of the divine character has led us to focus on two of the four quadrants: Who am I? and Who are we?

We have explored these questions as theologians, drawing upon our capacity to reason. Reason is one of the three living sources Anglicans traditionally draw upon when doing theology. We have been careful to clarify that by reason, we are *referring symbolically to the entire self, created in and through the Spirit of God*. Reason is thus a matter of intelligence that includes the head, heart and body. Whether we are aware of it or not, whenever we do theology, we bring our entire self into the act.

An integral approach to theology enables us to embrace both the contributions of modernity, with its focus on science and logic, as well as that of Post-modernity, with its critique of a naïve belief in rationality and its recognition of human bias. We don't have to choose science over religion or spirituality over biology. Every academic discipline reveals an aspect of the larger truth. An integral theology learns to listen and question. By being *receptive* to *all* of the quadrants, an integral theology is able to be a force for restoring wholeness. Everything has a place and belongs. Everything has the capacity to disclose something about who God is, if we develop minds, and hearts and bodies with the ability to listen.

**Receiving God as God Is**
Micah, Paul and Julian are saints because, as much as anything else, they knew (or learned) how to listen. They embody steps in the *evolution* of the human spirit, as it slowly learns to receive God as God is.

A basic and invariable truth of the human journey, which *Spiral Dynamics* captures in its concept of meme (world-view), is that I perceive reality not as it is but as I am. This is also true for a culture: it perceives reality through the lens of its current world-view. The goal of human development, or the invitation by God to humanity, is to develop or awaken so that we might be able to receive God as God is.

In the spirit of Augustine, our hearts are restless until they rest in God; not in our projection of who 'God' is, or who we would like God to be, but in who God truly is.

Micah, Paul and Julian reveal the awakening of the human spirit to a truer understanding of who God is. Each represents a significant development within the tradition to a fuller awakening of the human spirit. 'Who do you say that I am?' With each step, which is the unfolding of a new world-view in human evolution, we *experience more fully* the boundless compassionate embrace of God who is always already present.

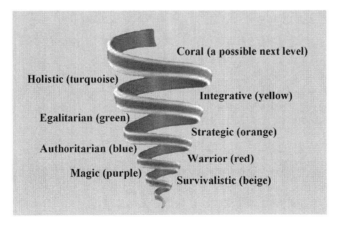

### From Judgment to Restoration: Micah

When we read the book of Micah from the evolutionary perspective of *Spiral Dynamics*, we detect the birth of the **AUTHORITARIAN** world-view. Until now, the **WARRIOR** rulers have been devouring the flesh of God's people. Micah perceives a YHWH who transcends the egoistical needs of the rulers of Israel.

The developmental insight offered by *Spiral Dynamics* is that we perceive God through our stage of development. But our stage of development does not determine who God is in God's own self. **WARRIOR** rulers are going to see a **WARRIOR** God, because that is their stage of personal development embedded in a culture at the same stage. But, we are not totally determined by our culture. The Spirit never ceases to invite us into a truer understanding of who we are and who God is. Human history is graced with persons who have become receptive to the fuller vision and invited the rest of us forward.

Micah is just such a person. For whatever reason, his spirit comes to know YHWH's presence in a way different than his **WARRIOR** culture. He encounters a God for whom sacrifice for the greater good outweighs self-centered behavior. **AUTHORITY** based on right judgment, says Micah, needs to be the standard. And if it is, the rulers can no longer 'skin' their own people. Order and predictability can then replace chaos and corruption.

The book of Micah exemplifies the importance of distinguishing world-views. Micah struggles to proclaim a God who is present and responsive to a people's unjust suffering. He sees that God opposes such crime against humanity. But Micah doesn't *invite* Israel to the God of **AUTHORITY**; he *demands* it with the threat of divine *retribution* if the leaders fail to comply. **AUTHORITY** remains tethered, for Micah, to the means of violence. **AUTHORITY** is still wielded in part by God the **WARRIOR**.

The different world-views sometimes unfold within us over huge expanses of time. However, that need not be the case. In Micah, the editors of the book have written salvation speeches bearing characteristics of the **EGALITARIAN** world-view. They see more clearly than Micah that restoration is a step beyond violent justice. Perhaps we even see here the opening of the human spirit to the Second Tier.

**WARRIOR** God. **AUTHORITARIAN** God. God of Restoration. It is clear that with each development we, as human beings, perceive that the scope of God's mercy and compassion broaden. God is not the one changing, in the sense that previously God's being was that of violence and now it is that of love. Humanity is changing, evolving, and discovering the truth of God in whose image we are made.

### An Empty Lordship: A Loss of Status: Philippians

Simply because a person, or several persons, or even a group within a culture, awaken to a fuller picture of who God actually is, does not mean that the culture as a whole is transformed. Transformation on a large scale, like that of a culture, or of a religious system, happens over time. Several hundred years after Micah and his editors we come upon Paul and the Philippians, and the struggle still has to do with **WARRIOR** and **AUTHORITARIAN** world-views. Whether it be Christ or Caesar, the Philippians' life and piety are still controlled by an egocentric concern with status. They are deathly afraid of losing it.

The paradox with which Paul and the Philippians are struggling is that we do not associate the experience of emptiness with fullness. For the logical mind, emptiness is the opposite of fullness. The issue is by no means unique to the Philippians. We tend to feel full of worth when we have something. We are familiar with the phrase, 'he is full of himself.' When someone is full of themselves they have no room, no space to receive anyone else. Ironically, when we are full of ourselves we are the most lost, the most desperate, and the most anxious. Everything we 'have' can be lost. None of it is permanent: health, occupation, family, wealth.

The Philippians are convinced that status is their salvation. Their hearts are filled with the fear they might lose it. And the truth is, they very well might. The critical question for them to consider is this: are they willing to lose it?

An additional difficulty for the Philippians is that when they look about for role models, they don't see any. This predicament should help dispel any romantic notions we might have of first century followers of Jesus. Baptized into the Christian community at Philippi, these people are still trying to figure out who Christ is and who God is. The Philippians remain much embedded in the **WARRIOR** and **AUTHORITARIAN** world of Rome. They continue to imagine Christ's **AUTHORITY** as minted in the image of **WARRIOR** Caesar. Status is what makes Christ awesome. To be Christ-like is still to be Caesar-like in some ways and full of oneself.

The realization that emptiness is the greatest fullness we can ever know unfolds in us slowly. Paul's letter to the Philippians contains a depth of wisdom not quickly digested. The struggle of the Philippians is not an abstract theological matter for Paul. As a former Pharisee, he knows what it means no longer to be full of himself. Thousands of years before the Enlightenment, Paul's **EGALITARIAN** vision is born: there is no longer Jew nor Greek, slave nor free, male and female.

Paul's **EGALITARIAN** ecclesiology is not deduced from abstract principles. Paul knows firsthand, in the presence of his own heart, a Christ of emptiness and boundless compassion. Emptied of his righteous rage, Paul is no longer on a crusade to purify the faith. With nothing to be lost, the passionate energy of fear has been transformed into courage. Paul embodies the courage of Christ present on the cross.

Paul's own transformation through the cross draws him beyond the vision of an **EGALITARIAN** community of mutual respect. With the absence of egocentric self, and the living through his Christ-self, Paul invites (not the demand of Micah) a Second Tier compassion that is truly boundless. It is in this sense that 'loss *is* life' for Paul. Concern with status is living death. Empty of concerns for status, the Philippians will have the courage, like Paul, to come to the aid of their sisters and brothers.

### The Motherhood of Christ: All is Well – Julian of Norwich

If we perceive ourselves in competition with, or at war with, others, we are not likely to come to their aid. Within the First Tier, competition between the world-views is ongoing. Each world-view, even the **EGALITARIAN** world of **GREEN**, devalues the others.

Francis of Assisi's vision of non-violence; Meister Eckhart's knowledge of the common ground; Teresa of Avila's betrothal to Christ; Gandhi the *Satyagraha* **WARRIOR**: Over and again the mystics experience the Second Tier world-view and invite us to awaken. For Julian of Norwich, her Second Tier world-view is born through her experience of the tender divine love known in the motherhood of God and Christ. Love turns the key that allows the meaning of the parable of the lord and servant, tightly locked within the theology of Anselm, to unfold in unforeseen and unimaginable ways.

Julian's insight is not simply the motherhood of Christ. Anselm can speak eloquently of that. But Anselm's theological vision remains locked within the warring First Tier. His feminine image continues to be shaped by anxiety over damnation and retribution. Fear, not love, shapes the dominant theology we find expressed by Anselm's *Cur Deus Homo*? Fear presupposes an 'us' and a 'them.' Julian changes the entire theological equation. We are not creatures set apart from God. Love does not distance, and love is the 'word summing up the message' of Julian's revelations.

Julian awakens to the Second Tier universality of God's compassion: 'All will be well.' All is well because the Motherhood of Christ speaks of the true intimacy between God and us. Our very will, she says, is our 'godly will by which we never cease to will the good.' Julian's theology deepens the profound words of Paul that we live and move and have our being in Christ. Of course we do. God is our mother. We have not only been 'knit' together within God, we continue to live within the divine embrace. Each and every one of us is 'Christ': anointed with the Spirit of God.

The human vocation shared by each and every human being is the awakening to the truth that we are 'Christ.' Since all that is exists only because it is anointed with Spirit, Julian, in true Second Tier fashion, speaks to us of the salvation of all. Because all is enclosed in God, God's love for creation is endless. Within Julian's Second Tier panentheistic world-view, creation is a 'compassionate whole.' Christ is literally the wellspring of creation. Our suffering, like that of the fallen servant in the parable, stems from our blindness to this Truth. God is Truth and the Truth of God is that all creation lives, moves and has its being in God.

# Restoration, Emptiness, Motherhood: A Compassionate Whole

We began with the recognition that it makes a practical difference in our lives how we perceive ourselves and God. To the degree that 'now we see in a mirror, dimly,' (1 Corinthians. 13.12), we suffer: Our suffering stems largely from our partial vision.

None of the world-views is wrong. Each of them, however, is a mirror, dimming our sight. Each refracts our vision so that it fails to see that 'the greatest [of gifts] is love.' Without the full presence of love within, we react in fear, in anger and in deceit. We deceive ourselves (not from ill will) as to what truly matters, and become fearful, like the Philippians and Anselm, before a divine authority whose power is that of judgment.

Without the full presence of love within, our world-view does easily remain obsessed with judgment. When we are full of our false selves, we are all too easily driven to obtain status and power as the hope of salvation. When anger drives our souls, even if we manage to imagine Christ as mother, She is not a mother of Love, but of retribution.

Micah, Paul and Julian of Norwich do not so much invite us to restore a lost Eden, as together beckon us forward by asking us to experience *now* the restoring, empty lordship of Mother Christ. Only this experience can help us know, as did Julian, that 'all will be well.' And for a world suffering and scared, 'all is well' is truly good news.

# ~Exploring Life as a Compassionate Whole~

### From Judgment to Restoration: Micah
### World-views in Today's World
What world-views can you identify in current events around the world? in conflicts? in leaders? What are examples of all the different world-views? Use colored pencils for each of the colors in the Spiral, and draw/write your ideas on paper. You can also build a multi-colored Spiral with the events you identify.

### An Empty Lordship, a Loss of Status: Philippians
### Status: What Does it Mean?
What does the word 'status' bring to mind for you?

### INTEGRATIVE and WARRIOR/AUTHORITARIAN Visions of God
How would you describe the difference between Paul's theology of divinity as self-emptying (**INTEGRATIVE**) and the Roman theology that saw Caesar as the egocentric 'form of God' **WARRIOR/AUTHORITARIAN**?

### A Self-Emptying God
What are the implications for the church and yourself of following a self-emptying God? You might want to try telling this as a story that is written many years from now, much as the story about our bakers in Philippi.

### The Motherhood of Christ: All Will Be Well – Julian of Norwich

### *Spiral Dynamics* and Christ
Drawing upon the worldviews identified in *Spiral Dynamics*, compare Anselm's and Julian's images of motherhood of Christ.

### Restoration, Emptiness, Motherhood:
### A Compassionate Whole – All Will be Well
Julian knows that 'all will be well' because of her experience of God as the lordship of Mother Christ. How might this theology of God draw the church to restore wholeness to a world twisted and broken by hunger for status and power?

# PART VII

# TRANSFORMATION: GOD'S ABIDING PRESENCE

"The real freedom is to be able to come and go from that center and to be able to do without anything that is not immediately connected to that center. Because when you die, that is all that is left. When we die, everything is destroyed except for this one thing, which is our reality, and which is the reality that God preserves forever. . . .The freedom that matters is the capacity to be in touch with that center. Because it is from that center that everything else comes."[177]
Thomas Merton

> *My God,*
> *my Beloved:*
> *in You,*
> *from You,*
> *as You –*
> *I breathe,*
> *I live,*
> *I die*
> *I am.*
>
> Kevin G. Thew Forrester

We awaken to our at-one-ment as we practice an integral theology. As we practice theology we retell the story of the unfolding of God's presence in creation as the very manifestation and flowering of creation. As Christians, we tell this story of God's abiding presence as the heart of creation and our journey to discover that abiding heart as our own heart, as learning to celebrate and serve the reign of God. And yet the celebration unfolds in and through much difficulty.

If God is the gracious abiding Center of creation, why is it that our journey is indeed a struggle that entails much suffering? We have spoken repeatedly of sin as our human blindness to our goodness. We continually struggle to know the truth of who we are and to live that truth in service to others. As theologians, our blindness continually hinders our own personal and collective unfolding. We begin our life enclosed in God and yet we inevitably lose sight of this immediate divine presence. As a result, too much theology becomes the 'mumble, rumble-dumble' lamented by Rumi. Instead of conversation celebrating who we are, theology is reduced to passion-driven arguments to justify our constricted 'straw' idols (to use the language of Aquinas).

The Enneagram (see Chapter 3 – Theology as Transformative) can help us understand not only why we become blind, and our theology confused and lost. But this ancient wisdom, rooted in the desert tradition, offers a path through the disorienting fog of the human personality that results in so much suffering. The Enneagram, especially as taught by Helen Palmer and A. H. Almaas, reintegrates psychology with spirituality. Even more, authentic psychology is spirituality. As we know ourselves for who we truly are as God's abiding presence, the eyes of our souls begin to open and we become a people who serve not out of duty or fear, but of love, and speak a theology that embodies as well as proclaims celebration.

# CHAPTER 19 – DEVELOPMENT OF PERSONALITY: THE SOUL REMEMBERS

**Enneagram Psychology:**
**How Spirit Manifests within Humanity**

All of creation lives, moves and has its being in Christ. This is theological shorthand for affirming that everything is anointed by the Spirit (which is the meaning of 'Christ'). Spirit is thus the true nature, or essence, of the human being. The spiritual path of transformation is the journey from a constricted, or egoic, expression of our true nature to a life lived freely and spontaneously out of our true essence.

The Enneagram understands spiritual transformation as the conversion from 'personality' to 'essence' (see Figure A). This conversion does not imply a movement from evil to holy or from bad to good. Since Christ is eternally the Mother of all (Julian of Norwich), enclosing all creation in the goodness of God, the conversion is from 'glory to glory' (Gregory of Nyssa). The glory of an existence driven by personality, however, is a pale imitation of the brilliant glory of true essence.

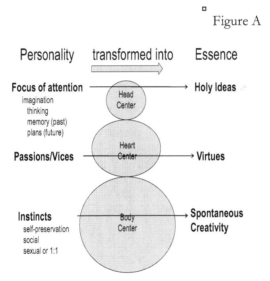

Figure A

Within the human being, the Enneagram distinguishes between the body center, the heart center and the head center. Each and every person has all three centers, and no center is more valuable than the others. It is also true that one of these centers – body, heart or head – will tend to be predominant in us. Thus we will say that someone is a body-type, meaning that she receives life first and foremost through body, while the heart and head tend to play catch-up. To say that one center is predominant, such as the body, does not at all imply that a person doesn't feel or think. 'Predominant' simply, but importantly, identifies the person's *dominant* tendency. We all sense, feel and think. *How* we do all three, however, is important to know about ourselves and others.

**Developing a Personality: The Loss of Essence**

Each Enneagram type (and there are nine of them; *Ennea* is Greek for 'nine') has its own distinct story line. Here are the names of the nine Enneagram types:

| | |
|---|---|
| Type One: | The Perfectionist |
| Type Two: | The Giver |
| Type Three: | The Achiever |
| Type Four: | The Romantic |
| Type Five: | The Observer |
| Type Six: | The Loyal Skeptic |
| Type Seven: | The Epicure |
| Type Eight: | The Protector |
| Type Nine: | The Mediator |

Often the types along with their distinct mental focus of attention are arranged on the Enneagram diagram in this way:

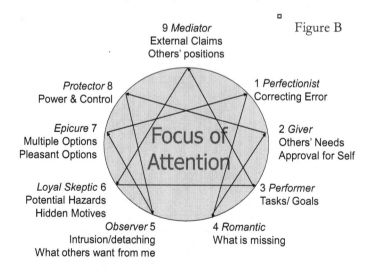

Figure B

Although each type does have its own distinct story line, it is the *same* Spirit unfolding through all the types. Each type refracts a different quality of the

Spirit or a different dimension of God. Julian of Norwich says that 'Peace and love are always in us, living and working but we are not always in peace and in love.' Transformation is awakening to the Divine peace and love always in us. This awakening can be seen in lives lived less from driven-instinct and more from spontaneous creativity.

The Enneagram illuminates how this awakening unfolds. The universal pattern is that as a young child we lose touch with our essence, which is the Divine presence always in us. There are nine distinct faces of this Divine presence, which the Enneagram calls the *Holy Ideas*. This loss is felt but not consciously known. A. H. Almaas describes the result as a kind of hole in the child's soul that cannot be tolerated. The child reacts by filling it in, which is what the *personality* is. The personality, or ego, is how we learn to survive in life in the absence of the direct experience of the Divine. Our personalities are our substitute for essence. More accurately, our personalities are the constricted face of essence.[178]

Each Enneagram personality develops its own *focus of attention*. Instead of freely receiving the peace and love of God, we become convinced, in nine different ways, that our survival depends upon realizing our new focus of attention (such as the agenda of others – 9, control and power – 8, correcting error – 1). Our focus of attention is our new 'god.' We become convinced that only it can satisfy us. We begin to habitually *avoid* whatever we perceive might hinder us from realizing our focus of attention. The life-force of the spontaneous Spirit within us becomes constricted to that particular *passion* which fuels our personality. And so, for example, the Protector-8 is fueled by the passion of lust. Lust for power drives the Protector to deny her vulnerability so as to experience control. Slowly, personality becomes reinforced from the experiences that support our focus of attention, and spontaneous creativity is lost.

## Original Sin: Losing Sight of our Essence

Throughout the history of Christianity the dominant theology has understood original sin as a doctrine (or teaching) pointing to the essential badness of humanity. Augustine of Hippo is credited with formulating the dominant theology of original sin as he struggled with the theology of the British-born Pelagius. Augustine's theology of original sin enabled him to emphasize the necessity of grace for human salvation (or healing) whereas Pelagius, at least as Augustine understood him (perhaps incorrectly), emphasized the capacity of human beings to know union with God through a morally and spiritually upright life.

The theologies of Meister Eckhart and Julian of Norwich offer the possibility for a different understanding of the human spiritual journey; one that invites us to consider anew our theology of original sin. For Eckhart and Julian, the spiritual journey need not be construed as a conversion from essential badness to goodness. Rather, the conversion is a process of restoring our sight, so that we can see clearly the truth of who we are: conceived in grace, all creation groans to know its true essence. Created in and through the Spirit, and held in being in the Spirit, humanity's journey is to taste the divine goodness dwelling deep within.

Through the Enneagram we can reinterpret the dominant theology of original sin consistent with the vision of Eckhart and Julian, which points us to the universal reality of the human condition: each of us gradually becomes blind to our true essence, our Christ-self. This 'fall' is the loss of our ability to see life for what it truly is. Original sin is neither a judgment nor a curse upon us by God. The mythological language of Genesis describes the pain and suffering that results from human blindness. In our blindness we no longer see ourselves, our loved ones, or God, as we or they truly are.

If original sin is not punishment for wrongdoing, how does it develop? Sandra Maitri, in her book, *The Spiritual Dimension of the Enneagram*, identifies three factors contributing to the process of losing contact with our essential nature. She points out that 'everyone who develops an ego goes through it:'[179]

1. Identification with our bodies
2. Reactivity and loss of trust in the environment
3. The essential realm not being reflected back to us[180]

### 1.    Identification with our bodies

The child within the womb and the newborn infant experience themselves in and through union with the mother. To be, is to be through merging. Originally, there is no sense of a separate self. The child's sense of existence is in and through this larger realm of being.

The first stages of separation have to do with a sense of a physically separate self. The child begins to sense that she is not the same as the other who nourishes and sustains. 'The beginning of self-reflective consciousness, then, begins with physical impressions, and so our sense of who and what we are becomes identified with the body. 'The ego,' as Freud said, 'is first and foremost a body ego."

Maitri describes the result of this identification.

> When we are identified with our bodies and thus with our discreteness, instead of experiencing ourselves as unique manifestations of one thing, or as different cells in the one body of the universe, we come to experience ourselves as ultimately separate, and thus cut off and estranged from the rest of reality.[181]

## 2. Reactivity and loss of trust in the environment

None of us is raised in an environment where we experience ourselves as held simply and utterly for who we are. No parent is completely attuned to the being of their child. Parents and others 'react' to the child in light of their own wants and needs. The child is praised not simply for who he is but for who he might become in the eyes of the parents. Love is conditioned, often subtly, and these conditions constrict the naturally expansive soul of the child, leading it to want what it is told is lacking within. A.H. Almaas explains:

> The less holding there is in the environment, the more the child's development will be based on this reactivity, which is essentially an attempt to deal with an undependable environment. The child will develop mechanisms to deal with an environment that is not trustworthy, and these mechanisms form the basis of the developing sense of self, or ego.... Implicit, then, in the ego is *a fundamental distrust of reality*.[182]

The sense of a separate self and the fundamental distrust of reality result in a sense of *duality* at the heart of existence: we begin to take for granted the false division of ourselves from our essence, from God. We believe 'in our inherent separateness.'[183]

## 3. The essential realm not being reflected back to us

To varying degrees, the child is not loved for who she is but for what she can do. When we say that no parent is completely attuned to their child, we are describing the inability of the parents to fully reflect back to the maturing child her essential qualities.

Created in the image of God, knit together in the Spirit by the Spirit, every child embodies Joy, Lovingkindness, Strength, Intelligence, etc. These qualities, or aspects of God, are intrinsically good and beautiful. What the child experiences, however, is that Intelligence, for example, is the result of her grades, looks, or athletic prowess. She is loved 'because of _____.' Each and every conditioned love is remembered in the body of the child and disforms the soul.

> This loss of contact with our depths is called the fall in some of the spiritual schools. It does not happen all at once as some teachings seem to imply, but rather it occurs gradually during the first four years of childhood....Essentially a sort of critical mass is reached, in which the whole of the essential realm fades from conscious awareness. Because Essence is the nature of the soul, the fall is not an actual *loss* of Essence --- rather, we simply lose touch with it. This is an important discernment, because it means that the essential

realm is present all the time; we have just 'forgotten' it or screened it out of awareness.[184]

**A Theory of Holes**

Original sin is a theology reminding us that we forget who we are. We come to believe that we are our personality. We fall asleep to our true selves, our essence, and begin to live as if our egos perceive reality as it actually is. We see through a glass very, very darkly, and don't know it (see 1 Corinthians. 13:12).

Maitri says that 'One way, then, of looking at spiritual development is as a matter of making conscious the unconscious.' Anthony deMello, the Indian Jesuit spiritual master, described the Christian life as one of waking-up. Jesus is Christ because he is fully awake to his true Beloved essence. The way of Jesus is the way of waking up to who we all are: Beloved.

Almaas has developed a 'theory of holes.' 'A hole refers to any part of you that has been lost, meaning any part of you that you have lost consciousness of. Ultimately, what we have lost awareness of is our essence.'[185] Since we cannot tolerate the existence of a hole within us, we fill it in. With each new bit of fill, the personality is slowly created and the distance from essence grows.

Within the Enneagram, 'passions' are emotions that are distorted and misdirected (see Figure C).

> Most feelings, specifically those that are automatic and compulsive, are the result of holes. When there are no holes, there are no such emotions. Sadness, hurt, jealousy, anger, hatred, fear --- all of these are the result of holes. If you have no holes, you don't have these emotions. You have only Essence. That's why such emotions are sometimes called passions, false feelings, or pseudo-feelings.[186]

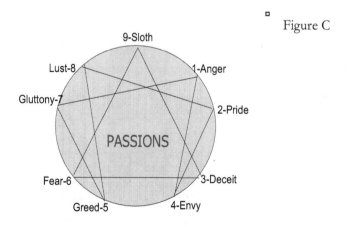

Figure C

The personality is convinced that survival requires avoiding the holes. It does this by following the passions, which are false feelings because they lead us *away* from our essence. It takes energy for us to avoid awakening to our Christ-self and the passions are the source of this energy. For example, in the heart center, the ability of the Performer-3 to continually identify herself with her successes is fueled from her passion to hide from herself why it is she is always doing tasks (deceit): she 'does' constantly because if she was to let up and simply 'be' she would be terrified of finding no one at home. She would experience emptiness. She would see the hole that she has spent a lifetime trying to cover over.

Our personalities are utterly convinced that if we stay away from our holes we will be alright. If the Giver-2 can remain on the offensive, meeting the needs of everyone else, then he will never have to confront the reality of his own sense of deep, deep need. The 2 takes great pride in the ability to feel the needs of others and respond effectively. As long as he can lean into life and be the proud giver, he keeps a safe distance from his own suffering. The Giver-2 has convinced himself that he is without need; he does not know how to receive.

With our focus of attention turned outward, the passions are the fuel enabling us to avoid coming face to face with our holes. Rather than exploring the gaping wound within we are driven to receive satisfaction outside ourselves. We turn away from our own hearts and as we do, the ancient and wise words of the prophets, such as Jeremiah and Ezekiel, sound impossible and alien:

> *I will put my law within them, and I will write it on their hearts.* (Jer. 31:33. NRSV)
> *A new heart I will give you, a new spirit I will put within you...I will put my spirit within you...* (Ez. 36: 26, 27. NRSV)

Our personality is convinced that the God of life is always 'out there,' outside our own hearts, and not 'within' -- especially not within the very holes that elicit such fear in us.

Like the Romantic-4, we have become utterly convinced that we are somehow essentially incomplete. In the wake of original sin we continually focus our attention outside ourselves instead of deep 'within.' We search desperately for the fool's gold, rather than exploring the possibility that the true gold is planted in our own hearts. The Romantic-4 is envious of everyone else who seems to be complete and happy. 'If only I could have what they have,' the 4 wistfully dreams, 'I would be happy.'

**Passion to Virtue Conversion (see Figure D)**
The Enneagram offers a wisdom map of the human ego and the path of transformation. This map provides a frame of reference for understanding

Figure D

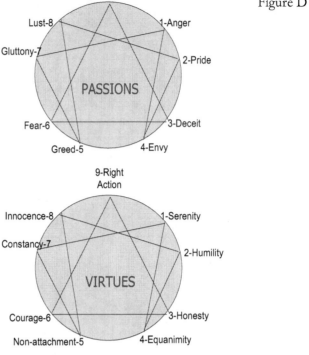

ourselves. It provides an alternative set of eyes through which our soul can begin to see the truth known and proclaimed by Jesus – the reign of God is already in our midst. The journey into the reign of God is indeed demanding, but it is far from impossible. Virtually every one of Jesus' parables is an invitation to awaken to the presence of the reign of God. The reign of God is like impure and smelly yeast. Just a little bit has the power to open and expand the dough, making it rise into something new and fully satisfying.

The smallest insight into the truth that God abides in us, as we are, has the potential to bring the walls of the divided reign tumbling down. It takes enormous energy for our personalities to remain in place and control our lives. Our passions exhaust us because they are continually driving us away from all our fears in search of a safe haven. Yet our souls still remember, however faintly, the sweet taste of rest; the *shalom* of being held faithfully by God.

In the language of the Enneagram, the passion to virtue conversion names the process whereby we begin to know the truth for what it is. This conversion echoes the call of the prophets who used the Hebrew word *shub* 'to call Israel to *turn away from* idols (Jeremiah. 7:9), injustice and immorality (Isaiah. 55:7), and to turn back to God for mercy and salvation.'[187] The first words of Jesus in the gospel of Mark center on conversion: 'This is the time of fulfillment. The reign of God is at hand! Change your hearts and minds, and believe this Good News!' (Mark. 1:15)

The Good News is that that the reign of God is already in our midst and it is possible for us, like Jesus, to know this truth. To know this truth is not to grasp an intellectual proposition. We are speaking about the intimate and direct knowledge of the heart and mind. This knowledge depends upon our *bodily experience* of a changed heart and mind. In the very experience of the change lies the yeast of the reign of God.

Conversion is cradled in grace, since life is lived in God. God's abiding presence within us is what makes the change, or conversion, even possible. God speaks to us through our very sense of dis-ease and fear. The fear is itself the invitation. The personality, or Enneagram type, is not the enemy, it is the gracious door. It is interesting to note that these two ideas, conversion and gracious door, correspond to the insights of Augustine and Pelagius, that we mentioned earlier. All is indeed dependent upon grace, as Augustine realized. All truly creative and good human action is already an expression of grace, as Pelagius realized.

The Gospel of Mathew reminds us:

> *Ask and keep asking, and you will receive. Seek and keep seeking, and you will find. Knock and keep knocking, and the door will be opened to you. For the one who keeps asking, receives, the one who keeps seeking, finds. And the one who keeps knocking, enters.* (Matthew 7:7; see Luke 11:9. The Inclusive New Testament)

The Spirit works in and through the very passions driving us. The conversion is of the passion itself. Our spiritual work is to seek, not by avoiding our passion, but by *understanding* it. Julian of Norwich speaks to this very point when she says, 'And God showed me that sin will be no shame, but somehow honor for humanity...God's goodness makes the contrariness which is in us very profitable for us.' We profit from our sin by allowing it to teach us about our wound or hole. It is through understanding our passion that we experience the path to life.

As our passion points the way to the hole in our soul, it brings us into the desert, where there is no place to hide. Here, in this desolate place, like Francis of Assisi trapped in the jailor's dungeon in Perugia or Gandhi being thrown to the ground from the train, we may finally let go and know the truth: within our passion, at its very center, lies our salvation, our healing. We awaken to discover the integral connection of forsakenness and presence. In the desert of his dying Jesus is able to say, 'My God, my God, why have you forsaken me' (Mk. 15:34). Because Jesus knows and speaks the true fear of his heart he is also able to taste the truth of God's immediate presence, 'Abba, into your hands I commit my spirit' (Luke 23:46). Releasing into the fear of forsakenness is the path into the courage of faithful rest. This is a core wisdom of the Enneagram.

The passion-to-virtue conversion *is* the path of life known by the prophets and Jesus. 'The truth of the matter is, unless a grain of wheat falls on the ground and dies, it remains only a single grain; but if it dies, it yields a rich harvest' (John. 12:24). Passion describes the constricted quality of an ego-centered self. When these passions are transformed the personality or type-structure softens, becoming more receptive and less constricted. The result of the transformation is the conversion of the passion into its essential virtuous expression.

## Holy Essence: The Precious Pearl

> Jesus said, 'The Father's imperial rule is like a merchant who had a supply of merchandise and then found a pearl. That merchant was prudent; he sold the merchandise and bought the single pearl for himself.' (Gospel of Thomas 76:1-2; see Mt. 13:45-46)

The merchant could see what mattered and acted on it: he bought the pearl for himself. All too often we are unable to see what matters most to us. We live a life fogged-in by the fixations of our personality. We continually scan the horizon for what we believe will satisfy us. For some, as they say, the grass is always greener on the other side: 'if only I could have what others have, then I would be happy' (Romantic-4). Others continually give-to-get, staving-off any experience of dependence and need (Giver-2). Some are convinced that salvation lies in what we know, and we can never know enough (Observer-5). And there are those who cling to control and power, staving-off any experience of vulnerability (Protector-8).

Ever since childhood we have been convinced that the ground of our own soul is lacking what it needs to be whole. And so the eternal search commences. Some spiritual traditions advise the 'seeker' to kill their ego, or abandon their personality, because it can only lead to ruin. We have learned that Julian of Norwich advises another path: she encourages us to learn from our personality. Let it show us the way to life. As we have said, the personality is not bad. Indeed, it is inevitable for healthy human development. The issue is that we have become enslaved to its fixations and driven by its desires. We are blind because the personality overshadows and dominates the soul (See Matthew. 12:29).

The Enneagram identifies nine distinct ways the personality comes to dominate our lives, by turning our vision outward. We become transfixed by the things of this world and we desperately hope they will satisfy our deep hunger (see Figure E).

Figure E

According to Enneagram theory, each of the nine foci of attention develops as the result of a loss experienced by the young child. For example, as a child loses touch with Holy Love, she strives to experience the closest thing possible, which is merging with someone else. This is the Mediator-9 -- the child who learns to compensate for her loss of the immediate experience of Holy Love by living in and through someone else.

Each personality type develops as a result of a loss of 'contact' with God. The child cannot tolerate this hole and reacts in the only way she knows how: the child develops a strategy that mimics the very quality of God lost. If we imagine God as a Holy Diamond, magnificently one, but with facets of sparkling beauty, then each facet embodies and reveals a distinct quality of the Divine, such as Faith, Hope, and Love. The Enneagram identifies nine distinct such qualities, which are called 'Holy Ideas' (see Figure F).

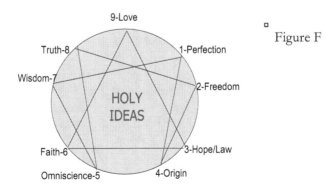

Figure F

The personality is the path to the precious pearl of Christ-within because each personality type is itself a substitute for the very facet of God the child lost touch with. If an adult can become aware of what their habitual focus of attention is, they will discover that lost quality of God for which their soul hungers (see Figure G). They will begin to realize with Julian that 'Peace and love are always in us, living and working,' and God 'is the foundation of our whole life in love...'[188]

Figure G

## Transformation

If I become aware that my habitual focus of attention is correcting error, this awareness can lead me to that hole in my soul, which is the loss of contact with Holy Perfection. The Perfectionist-1 is vainly attempting to make things perfect and acceptable to God, precisely because he lost touch with the truth that God is always already present in all that is and so all that is is already perfect. If I begin to discover that my continual focus of attention is maintaining as many options in my mind as possible, then I am awakening to the reality of being an Epicure-7. I need to have many options because I never want to be trapped in a painful situation with no exit; and so, I've developed the habit of running up and into my mind and trusting it as my savior. The truth that the Wisdom of God is always already present, working its way out through all of life, including pain and suffering, has faded into the distant background for the Epicure-7. Holy Wisdom, planted deep within as the very soil of her soul, is what the Epicure-7 longs to know again.

What the personality finds unimaginable is that God is in this place -- the very soil of the soul from which the personality has sprung as a defense. But the personality cannot see it. This soil of the soul is God, the one in whom we live, move and have being. In the theology of Meister Eckhart, we share a common ground with God, and that ground is God: 'God's ground is my ground, and my ground is God's ground.'

Precisely because this ground never leaves us, it is possible for us to see beyond and beneath our own personality. Learning to see with these new eyes is the reason for the practice of contemplative prayer or meditation. We develop the capacity to see ourselves through the eyes of the soul, rather than the obsessions of the personality. We finally see our own blindness. We can see our blindness because we can see our personality with all its bias. This is why Julian says that 'Our Lord God in his goodness makes the contrariness which is in us now very profitable for us.'

For the awakening soul, the personality is the precise path to the pearl, our Christ-self. The divine gift of the personality is that it is our best teacher. 'And God shoed that sin will be no shame, but honor to (us)...'[189] The journey into Holy essence is in and through our personality, this is the way of eternal life; the road less traveled. Will we follow?

## The Taste of Essence: Only Begotten, Beloved Children

The wealthy young ruler asks Jesus what he must do to inherit eternal life. Jesus responds,

> *There is only one thing left for you to do. Sell everything you own and give the money to those poorer than you – and you'll have treasure in heaven. Then come and follow me.* (Lk. 18:22. The Inclusive New Testament)

Jesus invites each of us to let go and 'sell everything' we own; give it all away for the precious pearl. Why did the young ruler find it so hard to let it all go? Because he truly believed he still needed 'everything' to live. We will only loosen our grasp of the things we clutch to our breast if we know that in the end we will live. The gift of the Enneagram is that it helps us awaken to *why* we cling to different things. *We don't cling because we are bad*, but because the Loyal Skeptic-6 is *afraid* and the Romantic-4 is *envious* of what others possess.

As we awaken to our fixations and the motivations feeding them (fear, envy, anger, etc.), we are graced with the ability to loosen our grip. As we see and understand the truth of ourselves, trust naturally grows and we begin to rest in the embrace of God. God, we gradually rediscover, is already within us as our strength. Like the young ruler, we hunger for words to set us free, but have forgotten what salvation tastes like when it is offered us. But the soul remembers. When Jesus speaks to the young ruler, he is inviting him to discover the most precious of all truths: the young ruler, like Jesus, is the beloved of God. Eckhart describes it wonderfully:

> People think God has only become a human being *there* – in his historical incarnation – but that is not so; for God is *here* – in this very place – just as much incarnate as in a human being long ago. And this is why he has become a human being: that he might give birth to you as his only begotten Son, and as no less.[190]

Everyone, like Jesus, is the sacred word of God, in whom Christ (the anointing Spirit) lives. Each and every one is an only begotten child of God.

To awaken to this deep truth is to arrive home into Holy Essence. The soul, free at last in a creation of endless grace, can only sing in wonder and gratitude, along with Hildegaard of Bingen:

> I, the highest and fiery power, have kindled every living spark and I have breathed out nothing that can die....I flame above the beauty of the fields; I shine in the waters; in the sun, the moon and the stars, I burn. And by means of the airy wind, I stir everything into quickness with a certain invisible life which sustains all....I, the fiery power, lie hidden in these things and they blaze from me.[191]

# Chapter 20 – Transformation: Conversion in the Body Center

> **Psalm 23**
> *Do not be far from me*
> *Be the center*
> *Of the center*
> *Of the circle*
> *Be the strength of that center*
> Norman Fischer[192]

**The Body Center: Mediator-9, Protector-8, Perfectionist-1**

According to Enneagram psychology, the person has three centers: body, heart and head. We begin our discussion with the body center and the three Enneagram types associated with this center. Each of us, regardless of the center that is predominant, will identify with much of what is said. However, for some of us, who are predominately body types, the discussion will clarify the dominant tendencies of our particular personalities. The same can be said of the heart center and the head center.

As we've said, although the content of the story line changes, the features remain constant: loss of contact with the Holy Idea, development of a new Focus of Attention (Fixation), Avoidance of perceived barriers, a distinct Passion that fuels the personality's drive. These constant features enable us to distinguish with clarity between the types, as the *same* Spirit unfolds. Each type refracts a different quality of the Spirit or a different dimension of God.

Each Enneagram personality develops its own *focus of attention*. Instead of freely receiving the peace and love of God, we become convinced, in nine different ways, that our survival depends upon realizing our new focus of attention (such as the needs of others – 9, control and power – 8, correcting error – 1). Our focus of attention is our new 'god.' We become convinced that only it can satisfy us. We begin to habitually *avoid* whatever we perceive might hinder us from realizing our focus of attention. The life-force of the spontaneous Spirit within us becomes constricted to that particular *passion* which fuels our personality. Let us now look at each of the Body Types

# Enneagram – The Body Types  Figure H

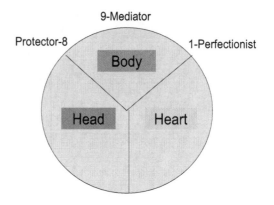

**Mediator-9**

HEAD    Focus of Attention: *Agenda of others*    Holy Idea: *Love*
HEART    Passion: *Sloth*    Virtue: *Right action*
Avoidance – *Conflict*

   In the beginning, this child experienced God as holding her in Love. As time passed, however, the child lost contact with this immediate sense of holding Love; it faded into the distant background. This loss left a hole in the child's soul, which she filled with a new focus of attention: the agenda of others and/or the environment. As the child learned to focus on the claims others made of her, she gradually fell asleep to her own essence – her own true needs, her own true value. She became convinced that her value lie in merging with others. Their needs became hers. Their hopes became hers. Their agenda became hers. She came to habitually identify herself with others, living through their value. By focusing on the agenda of others, she became skilled at avoiding conflict; there is no conflict when someone else's agenda becomes our own. Merging became a substitute for Love; Love is only possible when there is mutual recognition and acceptance. Along with this new focus of attention there also arose a passionate self-forgetting, or sloth. The Mediator-9 child became astoundingly attuned, viscerally, to the agenda of others, and yet deeply asleep (sloth) to her own deepest longing: the experience of being held in Love for who she already Essentially is.

**Protector-8**

HEAD    Focus of Attention: *Power, control*    Holy Idea: *Truth*
HEART    Passion: *Lust*    Virtue: *Innocence*
Avoidance: *Vulnerability*

Originally, this child experienced the divine Truth that God held her in all her innocence and dependence. But this direct perception of Holy Truth faded into the distant background and was lost from the child's awareness. The Protector-8 child filled this hole with power and control. By focusing her attention on power the 8 child came to believe that she was in control of life. She was the one who could and would protect her innocence from being violated ever again. The hole would be covered up for good. At all costs she would avoid being vulnerable, because that only led to being hurt. The new truth became the unassailable power of personal control. Along with this new focus of attention there also arose in the Protector child a larger-than-life passionate energy – lust. This lustful hunger for control and power made the child into an imposing presence. The Protector is someone on the strong offensive in life, not the vulnerable defensive.

**Perfectionist-1**
HEAD   Focus of Attention: *Error*         Holy Idea: *Perfection*
HEART  Passion: *Anger*                    Virtue: *Serenity*
                  Avoidance: *Error*

This child initially always experienced himself as being held Perfectly by God. As time passed, however, the child lost touch with this experience. The immediate sense that life as it is, as always already Perfect, faded away into the distant background. The child filled this hole in the soul with a new focus of attention – that of noticing and correcting error. The child developed a keen sense for perceiving the imperfections in life. Life became an endless task of detecting and correcting error in order to make things worthy and acceptable. Above all, the child's attention was focused on his own lack of perfection. His own being was imperfect and in need of change. *He* was the mistake. Avoiding new error became an obsession. Along with this new focus of attention there also arose a passionate anger, which could be triggered by any perception of error. The Perfectionist is someone driven to make right an inherently blemished world.

**Self-Forgetting and Awakening:**
**Self-Transformation and Theology**
The body types reveal that as human beings we forget who we truly are. The body types are known as the Self-Forgetting personalities, losing touch with their essence as they turn outside themselves in the hope of discovering themselves. The Mediator – 9 desires harmony above all else in a world where he senses being overlooked. The Protector – 8 desires the power to control life thereby assuring him of survival in a world that would certainly hurt him. And the Perfectionist – 1 is on a ceaseless improvement binge, correcting all the errors of life, especially his own.

With all this focus outside themselves, the body types lose touch with 'the center of the center of the circle,' their Christ-self. They forget their ability to act for themselves (9). They forget their innocence (8). They forget their own inherent beauty (1). They develop a spiritual amnesia about their essence, losing sight of God who always resides deep within.

> Inside this clay jug there are canyons and pine mountains,
>     and the maker of canyons and pine mountains!
> All seven oceans are inside, and hundreds of millions of stars.
>     The acid that tests gold is there, and the one who judges
>         jewels.
>     And the music from the strings no one touches,
>         and the source of all water.
>     If you want the truth, I will tell you the truth:
>     Friend, listen: the God whom I love is inside.
>
> Kabir[193]

Transformation begins with what is known in spirituality as the backward or downward step. The personality is always moving forward in an effort to remain in charge. Transformation is a process of dropping down into our essence. We turn our gaze *inside*, courageously asking of our soul, 'who am I?' Like Jonah in the belly of the whale, we realize we can no longer run. We are where we are. The only path to life is to look within.

> There is nothing bad about having a personality. You have to have one. You couldn't survive without it. However, if you take the personality to be who you truly are, then you are distorting reality because you are not your personality. The personality is composed of experiences of the past, of ideas, of notions, of identifications.
>
> If a person believes himself to be the ego, resulting from identifications, ideas and past experiences, then he is said to be 'not in the world, but of it.' He is not aware of who he really is, of his essence.[194]

Our constricted personalities have taken us as far as they can go; we have learned how to act but now the task is learning how to *receive* the 'strength of that center.' Jesus says that the only sign we will receive for this journey is that of Jonah (Matthew 12:39-41). Personal transformation is the path to receiving a new vision of God through a new understanding of ourselves. As each of the body types awakens through this self-understanding, they glimpse a facet of the divine face (Holy Idea) formerly hidden from view. The theologian and her theology are transformed.

## Mediator – 9

When theology is a product of personality, then the divine is reduced to a pale imitation of its true glory. For the Mediator – 9, what is of paramount importance is the avoidance of conflict. God becomes a divine force for harmony among personalities, which is realized through merging with others. The truth of one's own Christ-self is forgotten. God is always 'out there,' not within 'one as insignificant as me.'

The confusion of Love with avoidance of conflict leads to an understanding of the church (ecclesiology), which clings to 'unity' at all costs. The church begins to follow a misguided theology of appeasement that reduces Holy Love to the absence of conflict. Unity, however, can never be lost if God is always already the center. What is often lost is our ability to see this divine center, and to courageously receive its dynamic evolution in history. Because relationships change and sometimes end does not mean that unity is lost.

As the Mediator–9 releases his need to merge with others he begins to awaken from his self-slumber (sloth). Sloth in this context means he is asleep to the truth of his own abiding giftedness; a new divine strength – that of his true center – is rediscovered and draws him forth into spontaneous, right action.

Teresa of Avila is a marvelous example of such awakening. Realizing that she is one betrothed to Christ, she experiences herself as being set free to reform the medieval church. Holy Love, she discovers, is not passive, but spontaneously creative, trusting in its own wisdom: it is Miriam celebrating delivery from Egypt; Ruth venturing forth with Naomi and boldly securing her survival with Boaz; Jesus reading from Isaiah, as he stands before his neighbors (who then threaten his life). The Absolute truth is that right action – action flowing from a soul aware of its own essence – can lead to significant disagreement and disharmony. But, this is *not* the loss of union with God. Holy Love can never be lost.

## Protector – 8

When the personality of the Protector–8 is in charge, stories and images of power and control come to the fore. Theology loses touch with the Holy Truth of divine Innocence. We no longer experience the Absolute Truth that we live forever enfolded in God. *We* must do the work to secure our safety. Vulnerability appears as ridiculous and foolish, since life and God are harsh and cruel – 'vengeance is mine,' says the Lord.

As the Protector–8 lets loose of her tight grip of control, and allows her lustful passion to pass through and not drive her, innocence arises and theology rediscovers Holy Truth. Martin Luther King, Jr. can march on Selma, not to stir a riot, but to awaken the power of non-violence. Theology becomes able to invite us to know the divine Truth that even if our innocence is violated and we are harmed by life, God is with us, in us, and holding us.

Atonement is not an achievement. At-one-ment, as Second Isaiah discovers, is the essential Truth of our existence. The divine omnipotence is known again as the power of universally embracing Love, not control.

## Perfectionist – 1

The theology of the Perfectionist–1 is often that of righteousness and moral purity. This is because the Perfectionist has lost an awareness that everything is always already perfect. God has been reduced to an imposing external authority demanding rigorous purity, as we see in the crusading Saul. The church is constricted to a community of unquestioned orthodoxy, as happened in the Inquisition. There can be no room for error, because error would indicate that we are unacceptable before God. 'Worth' becomes of paramount importance. Are we worthy to stand before God? Are we worthy to come to the table? Serenity is lost on the altar of concern for personal worth. This reduces Jesus to the one who can make us worthy.

As the Perfectionist–1 (such as Saul/Paul) awakens to his own inherent perfection, the energy of anger is transformed into serenity: everything belongs. Serenity means that whoever we are and however we are is perfectly beautiful in God's sight. Theologically, the heart of the good news is that we do not need to be made right. Jesus reveals a creation already made in the image of Holy Perfection. The gospel is no longer seen as a supernatural program for self-improvement, but an invitation into a life of self-awakening, which is being born again, shedding the dead skin of the personality. Perfection is not out there to be found, but already within us to be realized. The passion for cleansing crusades dissipates and the healing power of non-violence emerges.

## Theology as Sacramental

For the Enneagram body types intuition is primarily instinctive. These types know what they know, first and foremost, through their bodily senses; not through their hearts or heads. A body type intuitively knows right and wrong (Perfectionist-1), power and weakness (Protector-8), harmony and conflict (Mediator-9), through highly attuned and calibrated bodily senses. The bodily response is registered (often unconsciously) and the heart and head play catch-up.

On the one hand, we need to remember that our personality, or Enneagram type, is a *constricted* expression of Spirit, being dominated by instinctual desires. The attention of body types is outer- not inner-, directed. The body types are attuned to *re-acting* to what is *out there* in the world. When we are simply reactive to our world, then the instincts are in control and much damage can be done. Our hunger is to satisfy our passions, which we believe will bring us peace.

On the other hand, this re-*activity* also speaks to the fact that the body types are 'doers.' They learn through doing. These are kinesthetic people. When their re-activity is transformed, so that doing becomes creative, then the body types remind all types that we are Essentially created co-creators made in the image of God who is 'spontaneous creativity': Human beings are *incarnate* creatures. The Spirit is manifest as Spirit in and through the spontaneously creative body. Body *is* Spirit alive in history.

If theology is to speak to human beings it must come to us through our senses: through music, dance, painting, poetry, drama, etc. We know what we know because we are incarnate in bodies that feel, taste, touch, hear, see, and imagine. The body types forever remind us that human beings are signs, or *sacraments*, of the Creator. Touch our hearts and you touch Christ. See our paintings and drama and you see Spirit. Hear our poetic cries and laughter and song and you hear God. Since we know through our body, through our senses, the body types insist that all theology be sacramental.

# Chapter 21 – Transformation: Conversion in the Heart Center

**Exploring the Heart Center:**
**The Personality's Desire for Avoidance**

'Our hearts are restless,' cries Augustine, 'until they find their rest in God.' Our hearts are restless because to some degree we are all like Romantic-4s, wistfully fantasizing about someone or something who will ride to our rescue. As with the Performer-3, the heart of this Image-based Triad, we tend to believe the source of our identity and worth lie beyond being our true selves.

The Giver-2, Peformer-3 and the Romantic-4, are the three Enneagram types of the heart center (see Figure G). Image is of paramount importance for these three types, with the core emotional issue being that of 'what am I feeling?' Whereas the intuition of the body types is kinesthetic by nature, that of the heart types is emotional.

Resident in the heart center, the 2, 3 and 4 are the most out-of-touch with their own hearts of all the types. They need to feel needed (Giver-2), successful (Performer-3), or unique and special (Romantic-4). They search in order to feel and through this feel alive. But the source of feeling remains external to the soul. The Giver-2 feels worthwhile by caring for others. The Performer-3 feels a sense of self-worth by compiling success after success. The Romantic-4 feels complete by tasting the unique experiences of others.

Each type is convinced that the source of satisfaction lies outside: by repressing their own needs (Giver-2); by deceiving themselves as to their fear of failure (Performer-3); by introjecting the unique gifts and experiences of others (Romantic-4). Each of the heart types *avoids* having to deal with the suffering of their own soul. But even more, each persists in the illusion that their own soul lacks the Presence of God. The sacred is what lies out there and not within.

There is something in particular that each Enneagram type would rather avoid, which is depicted in the Enneagram of Avoidances (see Figure J). The avoidance identifies the hole of each personality type. Each type expends enormous amounts of energy desperately trying to avoid these holes. The personality is convinced that if it experiences the 'avoidance' it will fall into a hole from which it cannot escape and be annihilated. The passion is the energy fuelling the personality's attempts to avoid these experiences.

## Enneagram – The Heart Types

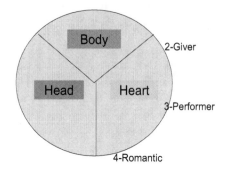

Figure I

From the perspective of the dualism developed in early childhood, the hole is perceived as unholy. We have convinced ourselves that to taste need, or failure, or ordinariness is to be swallowed by death. In a sense, this is quite true. But the death involved is that of the personality, or ego-self, and not that of our Essential self. The irony is that the personality is what is able to lead us home. The spiritual journey begins in earnest through learning to pay attention to our personality, its passion and avoidance. Here we have the chance to learn the path into life. A path, as Jonah discovered, that leads through the belly of the whale; in other words, life is through the hole, which is the tomb for the personality.

In terms of spiritual growth, our primary avoidance is precisely the path the Spirit invites us to travel in order to awaken to our Christ-self. If we are to experience wholeness, then the breach, the dualism, we accepted as a child needs to be mended. More accurately, we need to realize that the breach has never actually existed, except in our own personalities. We come to know this essential theological truth by being willing to fall into the void of the hole.

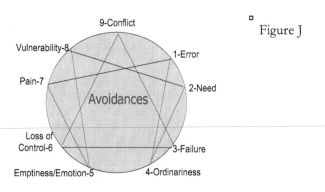

Figure J

## Stepping into the Void

> *My God, my God, why have you forsaken me?*
> (Mk. 15:33. The Inclusive New Testament)

The Enneagram of Avoidances identifies nine different faces to the cross, nine different ways we, like Jesus on the cross, or Jonah in the whale, experience being forsaken by God – the dark night of the soul. To step into the void means being willing to let go of everything we have identified with as giving us a sense of self and worth. For the Perfectionist-1, the invitation is drop the need to improve and perfect. The Giver-2 is asked to let go of the compulsion to take care of others. For the Performer-3, it means letting go of the need to succeed. For the Romantic-4, it means letting go of the necessity of feeling utterly special. The Observer-5's path is that of letting go of the tendency to detach from feeling in order to increase knowledge. The Loyal Skeptic-6 liberation flows from the freedom of having to garner certainty. For the Epicure-7, freedom from future plans and options is the path, whereas for the Protector-8, the challenge is to forgo the desire for control and power. And, finally, for the Mediator-9, the counter-intuitive path of liberation is that of ceasing to merge with others in order to avoid conflict.

For our personalities this letting go is a feeling of being utterly forsaken, because there is nothing left to hold. The Avoidances name precisely what we fear will bring us complete annihilation. For each of the nine types the avoidance is distinct, but the spiritual issue is the same – letting go.

The critical Avoidances of the Heart Types are need, failure, and ordinariness. For the 2, 3 and 4, these name the experience of death. They also name the path to life. Need, failure and ordinariness offer the chance to wake-up and become conscious of our Belovedness. Need, failure and ordinariness are faces of the Spirit beckoning us to follow.

What the personality is unable to see is that need, failure and ordinariness, like all of the Avoidances, name holy ground. If we allow ourselves to sink into this ground new life can be born.

> You can look at your problems as difficulties to be gotten rid of as fast as possible with the least struggle, or you can look at them from the perspective of the part of you that is guiding you to yourself. If you look at them from that more accurate, more finely tuned perspective, the new issues that then arise have a new value. They have the nutrition that you need.[195]

Again and again in the parables Jesus speaks to the central truth of the spiritual journey: life is only through death. At the heart of Pauline theology is the realization that resurrection comes only through the cross. From this perspective, when we let go of our identifications (being helpful, being a success, being unique) we drop our idols and trust in the absolute grace of God to bear us up and guide us when all the personality can see is darkness.

> Ultimately, the struggle with yourself leads to what is called the 'Black Death,' which is the death of the personality, when you wrestle it to the ground, struggling with it [just as Jacob did]. That doesn't mean fighting, punching, kicking, screaming. Struggling and wrestling is the *process of understanding*. It requires persistence and steadfastness. ...When you see through to its source, its center – which is the experience called 'Black Death' – you will recognize that the *heart* of this death is pure compassion.[196]

To die is not to kill. Death-as-transformation, or conversion, graciously happens to us through our struggle with who we are. Death is a process of letting go not only what we habitually focus on as the source of our desires. Death is also the process of letting go of our desire to avoid what our ego believes can *only* bring suffering. Death is the door to life when, with compassion, we seek to understand ourselves. Let us now turn to the Heart types to discover how this process of understanding unfolds.

## Performer-3

HEAD   Focus of Attention: *Tasks/Successes*     Holy Idea: *Hope/Law*
HEART  Passion: *Deceit*                          Virtue: *Honesty*
           Avoidance: *Failure*

In the beginning, this child's 'heart' experienced God's presence as an immediate sense of Hope that naturally held her as she was. Without effort on her part, there was a Law unfolding that simply carried her small being gracefully along. Slowly but surely, this child began to experience life as requiring effort in order to be carried. The sense of Holy Hope dissipated and this loss created a hole the child now sought to fill by becoming herself the guarantor of hope. Since she could not depend on God, on life, to carry her, she learned to focus on task and success, for these were what, in her experience, the world recognized and respected. Doing. Doing. Doing is the eternal internal mantra of the Performer-3. Amazingly efficient, she is finely attuned to what counts as success in the eyes of others. Always anxious to excel, there is no time to kick back and relax. She even forgets why it is her life is a continual performance. She has become utterly convinced that life, especially her own, depends on achievement.

Deceit is the passion sustaining the Performer-3. She no longer remembers why it is that task is of vital importance. She tells herself it is for the good of the family, the company, the church – all of which are socially acceptable motivations. The truth is that she cannot stop doing because she would not know who she is and is unconsciously convinced that to stop would be to lose hope. Her deepest longing is to let go and be and to know once again Holy Hope.

Within the dominant culture of the West, the Performer-3 has an especially challenging spiritual journey. The entire culture, it seems, rests on the assumption that worth is proven through successful doing, not restful being. Holy Hope has been lost. David Daniels describes the Performer-3 as a 'human doing,' not a human being. She has swallowed the lie that her right to exist lies in the ability to perform well. As a result, the Performer-3 is constantly on the run from the next possible failure. Tasks must result in successes. There is no time to rest on a job well done. Since there is no immediate awareness of Holy Hope, the efficiency of the Performer-3 supplies Hope by creating success.

Claudio Naranjo points out that in the psychological literature the Performer-3 is not even recognized as a personality disorder. Our culture assumes that the drive to succeed is healthy and good. Just as it can be good to care for another, it can be good to succeed at a task. The spiritual question concerns motivation. The Performer-3 is *driven* to succeed because if she is not accomplishing something she feels worthless. She feels her being has a right to exist *because of* the tasks being continually completed well. The Performer-3 has swallowed the lie that she is a human doing. She deceives herself as to why she performs. She tells herself she does it for the good of the family, the company, the church, the community, while in truth she is driven to succeed because without that taste of success she fears a black hole of nothingness.

Hope for the Performer-3 three lies in experiencing and understanding failure as the path of life. The theological truth with which the Performer-3 must wrestle is that Jesus the Redeemer is no Caesar. The crown is not a laurel wreath, but thorns of loss. Nor does Jesus search out the cross – the cross comes to him as the cost of utter love.

The Performer-3 is invited to discover that failure has its own way of arriving at our feet: a marriage dies; a job is lost; a child suffers from alcohol addiction. We do not so much bear this cross, as spoken of in popular Christian piety, as allow ourselves to be borne by the cross. Failure has the capacity to carry the Performer-3 into the awareness that Hope lies not in her string of successes, but in self-honesty (the 3's virtue). A Peformer-3 is invited by the Spirit to awaken to the truth that she has been deceiving herself. Through the Black Death she can honestly know she is held in Love as she is, in failure and success. The passion of deceit is transformed into virtuous honesty. No one is ever forsaken by God, which is the heart of the good news.

### Giver-2

HEAD     Focus of Attention: *Needs of others*     Holy Idea: *Freedom*
HEART    Passion: *Pride*     Virtue: *Humility*
               Avoidance: *Need*

In the beginning, this child experienced God holding him, freely giving what was needed. With the passing of time the child's immediate sense of being held in Holy Freedom slowly faded and was lost from experience. The hole in the child's soul was gradually filled by learning to focus on the needs of others. Since, in the child's experience, life did not freely give, the child learned how to give in order to get. He developed a heart keenly aware of the needs of others, especially others who had significance and power in his life. As he became outwardly focused, he lost touch with his own essence, his own true and authentic need as a human being. The rewards for being a perceptive giver were reinforced time and time again. He became the Giver-2, where it is so much more natural to care for others than to be cared for himself.

Pride is the passion fueling the 2. Helen Palmer observes that pride is traditionally seen as the deadliest of sins because it is so hard to identify. Who would ever think to link pride with helping others? What a Giver-2 does is indeed good. But what is deadly, in the spiritual sense, for the Giver-2, is the *motivation* behind the caregiving. Because Holy Freedom has faded into the distant background, the Giver-2 *gives in order to get*. He takes enormous, if subtle and unconscious, pride in his capacity to know what others need – all the while unaware of his own heart's need for tender care.

Freedom for the Giver-2 emerges out of the experience and understanding his own sense of need. On the surface, the personality of the Giver-2 seems perfectly Christ-like. But the Giver-2 struggles to realize that he has been acting from compulsion, not freedom, assisting others in order to keep them at a safe distance from knowing that he also has needs. The Giver-2 is convinced that needs are not met freely by the grace of God but only through his effort.

As the Giver-2 begins to let go of his compulsion, falling into the ground of his own authentic need (which is the meaning of the virtue, 'humility'), he begins to understand the heart of true, pure, compassion. A new theology is slowly birthed: authentic care is *mutual* care. The Giver-2 slowly begins to understand that it is in receiving, as well as giving, that we are born to eternal life. The Giver-2, moving through the Black Death, awakens not only to his own authentically humble sense of need, but of the marvelous giftedness of others.

### Romantic-4

HEAD     Focus of Attention: *What is missing*     Holy Idea: *Origin*
HEART    Passion: *Envy*     Virtue: *Equanimity*
               Avoidance – *Ordinariness and rejection*

This child's sense of the divine is that from the beginning, the Origin, all was present and nothing was lacking. But this immediate sense of completeness soon began to fade and with it a hole in the soul emerged. A new focus of attention arose, born of the sense that something was indeed missing and must be found. The Romantic-4's heart became utterly convinced he was lacking something or someone utterly vital to his survival. Without that quality he was not worthy of being held. There developed within an idealized 'something' for which the child found himself in a desperate search to have. Life, in his experience, did not value and hold the ordinary, and so the Romantic-4 learned to search desperately for something extraordinary. He himself endeavored to become someone utterly unique and thereby worthy to be held. The Romantic-4 is trapped in the illusion that happiness lies with others, who always have that secret 'extra something' his own life is lacking.

Envy is the passion driving the Romantic-4. He doesn't want to take away what makes others happy; he simply wants a taste of it in his own life. But when he finally gets 'it,' in the hope that it will make his life complete and worthwhile, he holds nothing. Essentially complete, the Romantic-4 searches for what has never been lost.

The story is told that the monk and mystic Thomas Merton, a famous 4, experienced his profound transformation while on a city street. He realized, as he watched all the utterly common and ordinary people passing by, that all were acceptable and held by God, exactly as they are. The Romantic-4 reconnects with Holy Origin as he wrestles with falsehood that he is somehow deficient, lacking an essential 'something' that would make him unique and special, and thereby worthwhile for God to hold. The Romantic-4 struggles to see through the conviction that he is not whole and complete as he is. Here we encounter the tragic face of the duality at the heart of human existence from childhood, which results in our desperate search for the fool's gold. Our search brings inevitable suffering, for it cannot be fulfilled. We are discovering that no pot of gold exists out there capable of fulfilling the deepest longing of the human soul.

If the Romantic-4 is persistent and steadfast, he follows the trail of his longing down and in, and no longer up and outside himself. The process of understanding is the inner journey of awakening to the gold deep within. Grace is common, not uncommon. The Romantic-4 slowly becomes conscious of a universe that, *as it is*, lives and moves and has its being in God. Envy is transformed into equanimity. Spirit saturates all that is, *as it is*. Sin has been our blindness to this goodness. Awake, the Romantic-4 discovers a God who resides eternally in the heart of *all* creatures; this divine heart is our common ground and our gold.

**Transformation**

For every type, transformation is a process of letting go, or of dis-identifying with the attachments of our ego, and exploring 'the hole' through inquiry. As we explore, the identifications fall away and our true essence is born again. We finally awaken to the truth that the holy ground we long to stand on is already beneath our feet. The sacred pilgrimage is not to a foreign country but into the alien terrain of our own soul. The dark night through which we each must pass is the journey in and through the holes of our own self. A compassionate heart, or loving-kindness, is the most treasured of all virtues, because without it we are unable to bear the pain we must endure to discover the truth of who we are. Compassion does not remove the pain, but enables us to bear the pain for the sake of the Truth, and thereby discover our Christ-self.

# Chapter 22 – Transformation: Conversion in the Head Center

## The Head Center: Fear & Truth

> *If you live according to my teaching,*
> *you really are my disciples;*
> *then you'll know the truth,*
> *and the truth will set you free.*
> (John. 8:30. The Inclusive New Testament)

As long as we are unaware of who we *essentially* are we remain slaves. To the extent that we are driven by our passions to avoid the hole in our soul, we are held captive by our fears. *Fear* is the passion central to the head center (Loyal Skeptic-6, Observer-5, Epicure-7). Fear, whether it manifests as fight or flight, is a response rooted in the autonomic nervous system. Fear represents the primal human reaction to an environment beyond our control, whether it be through knowledge (5), control (6) or escape (7). To some degree, each and every one us of knows these faces of fear.

Fear presupposes that there is something or someone set apart from us, threatening our existence. Like every passion, or false feeling, fear is a reaction to the dualism we internalized in early childhood. In the language of the Christian Scriptures we experience the kingdom (or reign of God) as divided. Nevertheless, we take this division as the basis of our life and try to build upon it. But a reign divided against itself, a soul split in two, cannot stand (see Luke. 11:17).

The truth shall set you free. The truth, in part, is that the reign of God is already come near, is at hand, and is among and within us (the gospel of Luke). And yet, Luke reminds us (18:24), how hard it is to enter the reign of God. How can this be if the reign of God is already in our midst (Luke. 17:21)?

The journey is made hard in large measure because of our fear. We cannot imagine how it could be possibly true that the reign of God is already in our midst. The most often spoken words in the scriptures have to do with facing our fear. Usually, we do not even know we are afraid, which is why the words need to be repeated again and again – 'be not afraid.' The reign of God is so difficult for us to know directly because the truth of its immediate presence is blocked by our minds. It is blocked by our sense of separateness. It is blocked by our sense of duality. It is blocked by our conviction that who we are, as we are, is essentially defective. How could the reign of God already be in our midst when we 'know' ourselves to be separated from God? The Head types illustrate well how the soul becomes lost as we habitually follow the fixations of the mind.

## The Head Center Types: Loyal Skeptic-6, Observer-5, Epicure-7

### Enneagram – The Head Types

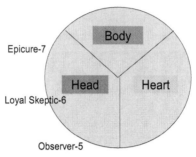

Figure K

### Loyal Skeptic-6

HEAD  Focus of Attention: *Potential Hazards*    Holy Idea: *Faith*
HEART  Passion: *Fear*    Virtue: *Courage*
          Avoidance: *Losing control*

    In the beginning, this child knew God as completely Faithful. To live was to relax into the loving hands of life, which were always there. This child trusted life's fidelity. As the inconsistencies of life's relationships were experienced, however, Faith became a distant memory. This hole in the child's soul drove him to find a substitute, which for the Loyal Skeptic-6 were life's potential hazards. Since life could not be trusted to provide, the child learned to resort to the resources of his own mind. If he could detect the hazard, he could plan accordingly and avoid the danger. By focusing on potential hazards the child had a new source of faith – his mind – and avoided losing control. Whether the child fought against the hazard or fled from it, anxiety governed his heart. Fear is the passion of the Loyal Skeptic-6. Fear is the lens through which life is seen. Fear orients the Loyal Skeptic-6 to the future, producing anxiety over what might possibly go wrong. Fear is also the filter through which memories are retrieved, trapping the heart of the Loyal Skeptic-6 in constant vigilance. Driven by fear, he forgets the truth that he is held from within, for his very essence reflects and embodies divine Faith.

### Observer-5

HEAD  Focus of Attention: *Intrusion/Detachment*    Holy Idea: *Omniscience*
HEART  Passion: *Greed/Avarice*    Virtue: *Non-attachment*
          Avoidance: *Emptiness/emotion*

This child originally experienced the Divine as Omniscient. Life knowingly held the child in warmth, bringing food and security. In a world of inevitable ups and downs, this child slowly lost touch with Holy Omniscience. Lapses and failures were experienced as an inherent lack of knowledge. As the taste of Omniscience faded into the background, the hole created in its wake, intolerable to the growing child, was filled by a new focus of attention: detaching from feelings in order to attend to gathering the knowledge necessary to survive. If life lacked knowledge, this child would step into the breach. She became wary of any intrusion that might distract and tap into her limited supply of energy. All her resources must be applied to the constant pursuit of the knowledge necessary for life. As she matures, the Observer-5 often lives a rather Spartan material existence. Her hunger is for knowledge. Greed, or in the language of the ancients, avarice, is the passion fueling the search out there for the holy grail of knowledge. Having lost touch with the Essential truth that she knows in her soul all things necessary for salvation, she endlessly searches the horizon.

**Epicure-7**
HEAD   Focus of Attention: *Multiple Options*      Holy Idea: *Wisdom*
HEART  Passion: *Gluttony*                         Virtue: *Constancy*
                    Avoidance: *Pain*

In the beginning, this child knew God as the Wisdom to hold, carry, and provide what was necessary. There were no dead-ends, for life's inherent Wisdom knew when to rest and when to move, when to go straight and when to turn. This sense of Wisdom inevitably slipped away, and the Epicure-7 child came to fill the hole by focusing her attention on multiple options. It were as if to say, 'if life doesn't have the sense to move on, I'll be wise enough to take the initiative.' Pain, for the Epicure-7, was being caught with no way out. So often, too often, for this child, life did not provide as she felt was necessary. The pain of being left at a cul-de-sac of some kind was too much to tolerate. She discovered she had the capacity to go up into her own mind and find refuge there. If life was boring, if life was forgetful, if life was hard, then she could escape into her fertile imagination and go wherever she would like. Gluttony is the passion fueling the activity of the Epicure's mind. This hunger leads the Epicure-7 to place trust in her own ability to imagine multiple options. Her mind can always create a plan and split her off from the dead-end of boredom, pain, futility. She becomes lost to the Essential truth that Wisdom is not a product of a creative intellect, but the very nature of her soul, created in the image of God.

**Blind to Our True Selves**

The lie we all swallow as we build our personalities is that God is not, and cannot possibly be, already in our midst. Each of the Enneagram types then fills in the blank: God cannot be within my midst because _____ -- 'all that goes wrong' (Loyal Skeptic-6), 'I do not know enough' (Observer-5), 'all the pain in life' (Epicure-7).

The mind can always find a reason and a theology to rationalize its fear. In the case of the Loyal Skeptic-6, the presence of the reign of God requires first the imposition of orthodox theology and liturgy. Or, proper control is of paramount importance otherwise things will fall apart into deadly chaos. The 6 is convinced that she holds life together. For the Observer-5, the reign of God is not yet among us because I either do not know enough or do not know the right things. With the Epicure-7, the reign of God is never experienced as here, because his mind is always focused on future plans.

Through original sin, what we are blind to is our true selves. We cannot see the reign of God in our midst. What we take as truth – namely, that the reign of God could not possibly be within us already – is false. The journey is difficult because we don't know how to distinguish between truth and falsehood. The truth will set us free *only* if we become able to *actually recognize* the truth. In other words, as Almaas says, what Jesus is driving at is that 'the truth will set the truth free.'[197]

**Soul: Fundamentally Faithful to the Truth**

The Loyal Skeptic-6, Observer-5, and Epicure-7, all react in fear to the truth. Fear, whether it manifests as fight or flight, is a response rooted in the autonomic nervous system. The 6, 5 and 7 embody the three primary ways human beings react in fear: control (6), knowledge (5), and escape (7). To some degree, each and every one us of knows these faces of fear.

The awakening Loyal Skeptic-6 knows a truth that has been acknowledged and understood by all spiritual traditions: 'What finally liberates the soul is to see the false as false and the true as true.' Almaas identifies one simple reason for this, 'Our soul is fundamentally faithful to the truth.' Knowing this, the Loyal Skeptic-6 experiences the courage to let go and trust life, trust God. The Loyal Skeptic-6 is freed from the falsehood that authority is a sword threatening annihilation. Yes, the personality dies, but the essential self is born. The Loyal Skeptic-6 discovers that the true source of authority lies within the soul, for therein resides God. Nothing without threatens her because no-thing is out there. The ruling fear of the personality that originates in infancy is false; there is no place God is not already present.

The presence of God is a knowing presence. All that needs to be known is known and guiding the unfolding of life. The soul of the Observer-5 awakens to life as he realizes the fullness, the completeness, of the reign of God within and all around. There is no need to fear depletion of energy, because life has the inherent capacity to replenish and sustain. When held captive to the passion of greed, the Observer-5 experienced a constant fear of his finite energy source being tapped-out; there was an ever-present anxiety of being depleted and unable to garner the knowledge necessary for survival. But life, the awakening 5 realizes, is not so stingy. Life prodigally provides all the energy ever required for the soul to thrive. The Oberserve-5 begins to feel the strength of knowing all he needs to know, with the result that he is truly and spontaneously free to live, and love, and simply be. Knowledge is not out there to be, but within, waiting to be received.

The Epicure-7 tastes the reign of God rising in her soul as she discovers the falsity of pleasure as ultimate satisfaction. The pleasures of the mind have been a constant source of distraction for the Epicure-7. She has believed that in her creative mind lies her salvation – a safe haven from a cul-de-sac of worldly pain and suffering. The transformed Epicure-7 now knows that when she acts from a sense of insatiable gluttony, there can never be enough – she can never have enough ideas floating around in her mind. She awakens to her true nature: constancy. A constant 7 is someone who can remain settled in the present, however uncomfortable and boring it might be, and not seek escape through her mind. The Epicure-7 recognizes that God is always and only to be found in the here and now.

**Passion to Virtue Conversion**

Through the Enneagram, we now know that there are nine basic passions and nine basic virtues. The spiritual journey of each and every person follows the same path of transformation. What distinguishes one person from the next is the particular passion that is being let go of and the energy being converted.

Each of us begins and ends this life, in the words of Julian, enclosed in God. In the first years of life, however, we lose sight of this immediate divine presence. To compensate for this hole in our soul, we each develop a focus of attention to which we become passionately committed, for it is our new 'god.' Our lives become built around this focus of attention: potential hazards (Loyal Skeptic-6), acquiring data and avoiding emotion (Observer-5), and future plans (Epicure-7). Unconsciously, our minds become constricted and fixated and our hearts desperately driven to stay focused on our new 'god' that gives our lives meaning.

The fixation acts to constrict our vision of our selves, of life, of God. Rather than being open to receive what life has to offer, we become driven to find whatever might reinforce our fragile and restricted view. The fixation is not evil, nor is it wrong. The fixation is inevitably narrow and partial, and we mistake our partial view for the whole. Consequently, theological talk about God, church, liturgy, ethics, becomes for Rumi a 'mumble, rumble-dumble' passion-driven argument to justify our constricted 'straw' idols (Aquinas).

Meditation is the ancient sacred practice that so effectively helps open the self to experience the passion to virtue conversion. Meditation, especially the *via negativa*, is the practice of learning to surrender, receive, and gently ride the divine breath in and down into the center of our being, letting go of all concepts including those of God (described so well by Eckhart). Conversion is not achieved, it is a received transformation that continually and gradually deepens and embraces every aspect of the self. In the words of Gregory of Nyssa (330-395), this is the journey of 'being transformed from glory into glory'.

As we begin to surrender, the barriers erected in our mind from childhood can begin to soften. We become more receptive to the *true* truth. Understanding becomes possible and understanding the truth of who we are is what enables conversion. 'That is why at some point, the most important thing for the soul is to see what the truth really is....Only when the soul recognizes the truth and is certain about it will she change.' We are beings who have been created in the image of God and our souls long for Holy Truth.

As each type begins to understand the truth of who they are, a gracious transformation begins to unfold. The Perfectionist-1 releases the need to correct error. The Giver-2 becomes less driven to give in order to get. The Performer-3 can relax from perpetually doing. The Romantic-4 begins to sense that something is not missing. The Observer-5 lets go of her attachment to knowledge. The Loyal Skeptic-6 begins to surrender his identification with worst-case thinking. The Epicure-7 starts to see through her fixation on options and plans. The Protector-8 can let down his guard and experience vulnerability. The Mediator-9 no longer feels compelled to avoid conflict.

If we lay out the Enneagram numbers in a linear fashion, the conversion for types of the Body, Heart and Head Centers, looks like this.

| Passion | | Virtue |
|---|---|---|
| 8 Lust | *converted into* | Innocence |
| 9 Sloth | *converted into* | Right action |
| 1 Anger | *converted into* | Serenity |
| | | |
| 2 Pride | *converted into* | Humility |
| 3 Deceit/Vanity | *converted into* | Honesty |
| 4 Envy | *converted into* | Equanimity |
| | | |
| 5 Greed/Avarice | *converted into* | Non-attachment |
| 6 Fear | *converted into* | Courage |
| 7 Gluttony | *converted into* | Constancy |

**'The Truth Will Set the Truth Free'**

Through the passion to virtue conversion, we begin to experience and see ourselves and God more clearly and less defensively. For example, the

Observer-5 experiences this conversion as a freedom from his constant need to have to know more in order to feel safe. The reign of God is experienced as a non-attachment to the compulsion to know in order to be saved. Salvation does not lie in knowledge; it does not lie in any achievement. The Observer-5 awakens to the gift of salvation as he realizes that God holds him as he is; acquiring knowledge is not the ticket of admission into the reign of God.

Through the passion to virtue conversion the soul knows immediately and directly the truth of the words of the Johannine Jesus: 'the truth will set you free.' This truth is known because the soul is the very image and presence of God, who is truth. Almaas captures this wonderfully:

> Truth is the fundamental ground of the soul, so the soul is fundamentally faithful to the truth. She [the soul] always lives and acts out what she believes to be true. Yes, we frequently act out of lies and falsehoods, but this is because the soul believes that they are true. ...When we act from anger, we really believe that the truth is that we should act out of the anger. The difficulty is not that the soul loves or likes falsehood, but that she takes a falsehood as truth and lives it out faithfully....The soul is, in a word, ignorant.[198]

This act of spiritual surrender is the same for all types. We will only let go as we understand. This means that meditation is *not* a substitute for understanding. The *via negativa* helps us to let go of our problem-solving intellects so that we may come to know the fullness of Christ already resident in our souls.

Within Christianity, Buddhism, Hinduism, Islam and Judaism, there are many ways of learning to surrender. Yet there is an underlying unity. In the end, conversion flows from an understanding of the truth; and understanding the truth is what sets us free.

> ...all methods produce understanding at some point. If they don't, they won't liberate us. If at some point, through devotion and passionate love, we don't recognize and understand that we are part and parcel of the Beloved, how will we be liberated?
>
> And when we are convinced ... that this truth is really our nature, then we change. So liberation is actually a change [conversion] of mind. At some point, we change our mind about what reality is in a very fundamental way.[199]

# ~Exploring Transformation~

## Development of Personality
### The Hole

The Enneagram identifies a hole characteristic of each personality type. We expend enormous amounts of energy trying to avoid our hole. If we are to experience wholeness, then the breach, the dualism, we accepted as a child needs to be mended, through a process of inquiry, acceptance and understanding. In a sense, we need to be able to let go and fall into the hole, which can feel like a threatening void.

> - For some of us the hole we try to avoid at all costs is failure - especially in the eyes of others. How might this ring true for you?
> - For some of us the hole we try to avoid at all costs is to avoid having needs - which would make you dependent on others. How might this ring true for you?
> - For some of us the hole we try to avoid at all costs is being ordinary and typical and therefore rejected. How might this ring true for you?

Have you ever awoken and *emotionally felt* Christ in your heart and realized how closed-hearted you had been? What was your experience like?

### Following the Path

Following the path of the vice to virtue conversion (Figure C) is one way of discovering the precious pearl or our Essential self. Explore experiences you may have had of

> Anger being converted into serenity
>
> Fear being converted into courage
>
> Deceit being converted into honesty

## Transformation: Conversion in the Body Center
### Jonah

Jonah's habit of running away and hiding eventually ended with him in the dark belly of the whale, with no way out – which means he had to face his suffering or die.

> - For some of us, we develop the habit of avoiding conflict at all costs. How might this ring true for you? (Enneagram 9)

- For some of us, we develop the habit of avoiding vulnerability at all costs. How might this ring true for you? (Enneagram 8)
- For some of us, we develop the habit of avoiding making mistakes at all costs. How might this ring true for you? (Enneagram 1)

Have you ever awoken and *physically sensed* Christ in your body and realized how numb, or asleep, you had been to your self? What was your experience like?

## Transformation: Conversion in the Heart Center
### Identifying our Avoidance

In our fear we tend not to look at – or avoid – certain tendencies. The Enneagram invites us to recognize in these avoidances the very door to lie. If we explore our avoidance compassionately they have the capacity to reveal the path of life. Looking at Figure B, can you recognize something you particularly try to Avoid? What it might mean for you to compassionately recognize this Avoidance as part of your personality. How might you let it go and still be 'ok'?

## Transformation in the Head Center
### Minds that Build Walls

In the life of the child, the power of the mind seems to be the very dynamism of life, capable of creating a world that is secure, predictable and a source of joy. As the child grows, however, she can begin to experience the mind less and less as a safe haven. Rather, the truth is that the mind is obsessed with trying to build higher and thicker walls in an exhausting attempt to protect against an ever-threatening, unpredictable and painful life. The result is that the space for living becomes smaller and smaller.

- For some of us, we are driven to build mental walls of safety in order to avoid at all costs losing control, because life is dangerous and the worst case will happen. (Loyal/Skeptic-6) How might this be true for you?
- For some of us, we are driven to build walls of knowledge in order to avoid at all costs our feelings, because they will deplete our fine amount of emotional energy (Observer-5). How might this be true for you?
- For some of us, we are driven to build a maze of walls in order to avoid being cornered in the experience of pain, because life will become unbearable. (Epicure-7) How might this be true for you?

Have you ever awoken and known that your life in Christ is safe? What was your experience like?

# EPILOGUE

*Beloved God,*
*You are present within us*
*as a fire burning in our hearts.*
*Burn away the shame that imprisons our souls.*
*Burn away the rage that drives us to vengeance.*
*Burn away the fear that despairs of your love.*
*Leave nothing buried in our ashes,*
*but hearts alive to You*
*in Christ.*
Kevin G. Thew Forrester

Evelyn Underhill, in her groundbreaking work, *Mysticism: The Nature and Development of Spiritual Consciousness*, speaks in her final chapter about "the unitive life," following upon "the dark night of the soul." For Underhill, union marks the pinnacle of spiritual development.

In truth, union is the foundation of life's gracious unfolding. Union, or what I have described as at-one-ment, is the gracious font from which all life flows. Because God lives, moves, and has being in time and space as us, we arise and exist only insofar as we are God's incarnate ones. We are God becoming manifest now. Incarnation is the fruit of union. Here we hold Beauty in our soul's arms. Even more, we discover we are Beauty and theology is the exploration of Beauty-unfolding in all its Truth and Goodness.

And yet we struggle mightily to know the Beauty of our gracious essential nature. Jesus says that the only sign we will receive for our journey is that of Jonah (Mt. 16.4). The holy wisdom within this hyperbole is that life is a divine living womb ready to give birth to us, if we learn to trust. The seeming paradox is that learning to trust is the fruit of digging and digging and digging within our soul; learning to see into, through, and beyond, our egoic selves. Such soul-work is the living womb of Christ and is indeed all too often the road less travelled.

But our gracious True Nature in Christ cannot be erased or lost. Our deepest longing is to awaken to the truth realized by Paul: "it is no longer I who live, but it is Christ who lives in me" (Gal. 2.19). As the contemporary contemplative, Bernadette Roberts explains, the spiritual path actually begins with our realization of union with God, and there begins to unfold in ways heretofore unimaginable.[200]

In the end, as in the beginning, all that exists is *I Am*. In between, *I Am* invites us to savor the oil of anointing upon our lips and let that beautiful honey sustain us for the long unfolding journey. We may taste that honey each time we are gathered as the people of God at prayer. In the next volume of this series, *"My Heart is a Raging Volcano of Love for You,"* we will explore collects, blessings, litanies, prayers, and Eucharistic prayers, which embody our living At-One-ment with *I Am*.

**Awakening to At-One-Ment: Volume II**

# My Heart is a Raging Volcano of Love for You!

**Liturgical Explorations
Collects, Blessings, Litanies,
Prayers and Eucharistic Prayers**

Volume II in this series, *My Heart is a Raging Volcano of Love for You*, explores how we may express our unfolding union with God in the prayers and liturgies of the church.

Available from LeaderResources
in print and electronic file with
license to reproduce and use in worship

www.LeaderResources.org

# BIBLIOGRAPHY

Abelard, Peter. "Exposition of the Epistle to the Romans." Thelma Megill-Cobbler, "A Feminist Rethinking of Punishment Imagery in Atonement." *Dialog* 35 [winter 1996].

Almaas, A. H. *Essence with The Elixir of Enlightenment.* Boston: Weiser Books, 1998.

Almaas, A.H. *Diamond Heart Book One: Elements of the Real in Man.* Boston: Shambhala, 1987.

Almaas, A.H. *Facets of Unity: The Enneagram of Holy Ideas.* Berkeley, CA: Diamond Books, 1998.

Almaas, A.H. *The Point of Existence: Transformations of Narcissism in Self-Realization.* Boston: Shambhala, 2001.

Almaas, A.H. *Spacecruiser Inquiry: True Guidance for the Inner Journey.* Boston: Shambhala, 2002.

Anderson, Bernhard W. *Understanding The Old Testament, Fourth Edition.* Englewood Cliffs, New Jersey: Prentice Hall, 1986.

Anselm of Canterbury, *Cur Deus Homos?*

Athanasius, *De Incarnatione* or *On the Incarnation* 54:3, PG 25:192B.

*The Autobiography of St. Teresa of Avila.* Translated by Kieran Kavanaugh and Otilio Rodriguez. New York: One Spirit, 1987.

Bailie, Gil. *Violence Unveiled: Humanity at the Crossroads.* New York: Crossroad, 1997.

Bauerschmidt, Frederick Christian. *Julian of Norwich and the Mystical Body Politic of Christ.* Notre Dame: University of Notre Dame Press, 1999.

Beck, Don Edward and Cowan, Christopher C. *Spiral Dynamics: Mastering Values, Leadership, and Change.* Malden Massachusetts: Blackwell Publishers, 2001.

Benson, M.D., Herbert, Corliss, Julie, and Cowley, Geoffrey. *Newsweek*. September 27, 2004.

Bielecki, Tessaa. *Teresa of Avila: Mystical Writings*. New York: Crossroad, 1994.

Bilinkoff, Jodi. *The Avila of Saint Teresa: Religious Reform in a Sixteenth-Century City*. Ithaca, New York: Cornell University Press, 1989.

Borg, Marcus J. *The Heart of Christianity: Rediscovering a Life of Faith*. New York: HarperCollins, 2004.

Bourgeault, Cynthia. *Mystical Hope: Trusting in the Mercy of God*. Boston: Cowley, 2001.

Bourgeault, Cynthia. *The Wisdom Way of Knowing: Reclaiming an Ancient Tradition to Awaken the Heart*. San Francisco: Jossey-Bass, 2003.

Bradley, Ritamary. *Julian's Way: A Practical Commentary on Julian of Norwich*. London: HarperCollins *Religious*, 1992.

Brock, Sebastian. *The Luminous Eye: The Spiritual World Vision of Saint Ephrem the Syrian*. Kalamazoo, Michigan: Cistercian Publications, 1992.

Brueggemann, Walter. *Hopeful Imagination: Prophetic Voices in Exile*. Philadelphia: Fortress Press, 1986.

Brueggemann, Walter. *An Introduction to the Old Testament: The Canon and Christian Imagination*. Louisville: Westminster John Knox Press, 2003.

Carney, Thomas Francis. *The Shape of the Past: Models and Antiquity*. Coronado Pr, 1975.

Chilton, Bruce. *Rabbi Jesus: An Intimate Biography*. New York: Doubleday, 2000.

*The Collected Poems of W.B. Yeats*. Edited by Richard J. Finneran. Revised Second Edition. New York: Scribner Paperback Poetry, 1996.

Crossan, John Dominic, and Reed, Jonathan L. *In Search of Paul: How Jesus's Apostle Opposed Rome's Empire with God's Kingdom*. New York: HarperSanFrancisco, 2004.

Cusa, Nicholas. "On Learned Ignorance." *Nicholas Cusa: Selected Spiritual Writings.* Translated by H. Lawrence Bond. New York: Paulist Press, 1997.

*Delicious Laughter: Rambunctious Teaching Stories from the Mathnawi.* Versions by Coleman Barks. Athens, Georgia: Maypop, 1990.

Fabian, Richard. *The Scandalous Table.* Unpublished paper, 2010.

Fischer, Norman. *Opening to You: Zen-Inspired Translations of the Psalms.* New York: Viking Compass, 2002.

Fox, Matthew. *Passion for Creation: The Earth-Honoring Spirituality of Meister Eckhart.* Rochester, Vermont: Inner Traditions, 2000.

*Francis of Assisi: The Saint.* Early Documents Volume I. Edited by Regis J. Armstrong, O.F.M. Cap., J.A. Wayne Hellmann, O.F.M. Conv., William J. Short, O.F.M. New York: New City Press, 1999.

Gandhi, M.K. *An Autobiography: The Story of My Experiments in Truth.* South Asia Books, 1994.

Gandhi, M.K. *Non-Violent Resistance (Satyagraha).* Mineola, New York: Dover Publications, Inc., 2001.

*Gandhi on Non-Violence.* Edited by Thomas Merton. New York: New Directions Paperbook, 1965.

Green, Deirdre. *Gold in the Crucible: Teresa of Avila and the Western Mystical Tradition.* Worcester: Element, 1989.

Haight, Roger. *Jesus: Symbol of God.* Orbis Books: Maryknoll, New York, 2000.

Harmless, S.J., William. *Mystics.* New York: Oxford University Press, 2008.

Heschel, Abraham J. *The Prophets.* Volume I. New York: Harper Torchbooks, 1969.

*Hildegard of Bingen: Mystical Writings.* Edited by Fiona Bowie and Oliver Davies. Translated by Robert Carver. New York: Crossroad, 1990.

*Hildegard of Bingen: Scivias.* Translated by Mother Columba Hart and Jane Bishop. New York: Paulist Press, 1990.

*Hildegard of Bingen's Book of Divine Works.* Edited by Matthew Fox. Santa Fe, New Mexico: Bear & Company, 1987.

House, Adrian. *Francis of Assisi: A Revolutionary Life.* New Jersey: Hidden Spring, 2001.

Hudson, Nancy J. *Becoming God: The Doctrine of Theosis in Nicholas of Cusa.* Washington, D.C.: The Catholic University of America Press, 2007.

Irenaeus of Lyons, *Against* Heresies V.

*Julian of Norwich: Showings.* Translated by Edmund Colledge and James Walsh. New York: Paulist Press, 1978.

*The Kabir Book: Forty-Four of the Ecstatic Poems of Kabir.* Versions by Robert Bly. Boston: Beacon Press, 1977.

Keller, Catherine. *Face of the Deep: A Theology of Becoming.* New York: Routledge, 2003.

Lathrop, Gordon. *Holy Ground: A Liturgical Cosmology.* Minneapolis, MN: Fortress Press, 2003.

Lathrop, Gordon W. *Holy Things: A Liturgical Theology.* Augsburg Fortress: Minneapolis, 1993.

Lathrop, Gordon W. *Holy People: A Liturgical Ecclesiology.* Augsburg Fortress: Minneapolis, 1999.

Levine, Amy-Jill. *The Misunderstood Jew: The Church and the Scandal of the Jewish Jesus.* New York: HarperOne, 2006.

Limburg, James. *Hosea—Micah, Interpretation: A Bible Commentary for Teaching and Preaching.* Atlanta: John Knox Press, 1988.

*Love Poems from God: Twelve Sacred Voices from the East and West.* Translated by Daniel Ladinsky. New York: Penguin, 2002.

McBrien, Richard P. *Catholicism* . New York: HarperCollins, 1994.

McGinn, Bernard. *The Harvest of Mysticism in Medieval Germany (1300-1500), Vol. IV of The Presence of God: A History of Western Christian Mysticism* . New York: A Herder & Herder Book, 2005.

McGinn, Bernard. *The Mystical Thought of Meister Eckhart: The Man From Whom God Hid Nothing.* New York: Herder and Herder, 2001.

Maitri, Sandra. *The Enneagram of Passions and Virtues: Finding the Way Home.* Tarcher/Putnam, 2005.

Maitri, Sandra. *The Spiritual Dimension of the Enneagram.* New York: Tarcher/Putnam, 2000.

Matera, F.J. *Galatians, Sacra Pagina Series Volume 9.* Daniel J. Harrington, S.J., Editor. Collegeville, MN: A Michael Glazier Book, 1992.

*Meister Eckhart: The Essential Sermons, Commentaries, Treatises, and Defense.* Translated by Edmund Colledge, O.S.A. and Bernard McGinn. New York: Paulist Press, 1981.

Mitchell, Nathan D. *Eucharist as Sacrament of Initiation.* Chicago: Liturgy Training Publications, 1994.

*Mohandas Gandhi: Essential Writings.* Selected by John Dear. Maryknoll, New York: Orbis Books, 2002.

Murphy-O'Connor, Jerome. *Paul: A Critical Life.* New York: Oxford University Press, 1996.

"The Never-Ending Upward Quest: A *WIE* Editor Encounters the Practical and Spiritual Wisdom of Spiral Dynamics." An interview with Dr. Don Beck. By Jessica Roemischer, 17. See www.wie.org.

*The New Dictionary of Theology,* edited by Joseph A. Komanchak, Mary Collins, Dermot A. Lane. Wilmington, Delaware: Michael Glazier, Inc., 1987.

Newell, J. Philip, *The Book of Creation: An Introduction to Celtic Spirituality.* New York: Paulist Press, 1999.

Nott, C.S. *Journey Through This World: The Second Journey of a Pupil.* Cape Neddick, ME: Samuel Weiser, Inc., 1974.

Nuth, Joan M. *God's Lovers in an Age of Anxiety: The Medieval English Mystics.* Maryknoll, New York: Orbis Books, 2001.

Oakes, Peter. *Philippians: From People to Letter.* Cambridge: Cambridge University Press, 2002.

Ouspensky, P.D. *A Further Record: Extracts from Meetings,* 1928-45. New York: Penguin, 1988.

*Paul and Empire: Religion and Power in Roman Imperial Society.* Edited by Richard A. Horsley. Harrisburg, Pennsylvania: Trinity Press International, 1997.

Porete, Marguerite. *The Mirror of Simple Souls.* Translated by Ellen L. Babinsky. New York: Paulist Press, 1993.

Roberts, Bernadette. *The Path to No-Self: Life at the Center.* Albany: State University Press of New York, 199.

Roberts, Bernadette. *The Experience of No-Self: A Contemplative Journey.* Albany: State University Press of New York: 1993.

Roberts, Bernadette. *What is Self? A Study of the Spiritual Journey in Terms of Consciousness.* Boulder, CO: Sentient Publications, 2007.

Spoto, Donald. *Reluctant Saint: The Life of Francis of Assisi.* New York: Viking Compass, 2002.

Stegemann, Ekkehard, and Stegemann, Wolfgang. *The Jesus Movement: A Social History of Its First Century.* Translated by O.C. Dean, Jr. Minneapolis: Fortress Press, 1995.

Stendahl, Krister. *Final Account: Paul's Letter to the Romans.* Minneapolis: Fortress Press, 1995.

Teresa of Avila. *The Life of Saint Teresa of Avila by Herself.* Translated by J. M. Cohen. London: Penguin Books, 1957.

*The Soul of Rumi.* Translated by Coleman Barks. New York: HarperSanFrancisco, 2001.

*Theosis: Deification in Christian Theology.* Edited by Stephen Finlan and Vladimir Kharlamov. Eugene Oregon: Pickwick Publications, 2006.

White, L. Michael. *From Jesus to Christianity.* HarperSanFrancisco: New York, 2004.

Wiesel, Elie. *Sages and Dreamers: Biblical, Talmudic, and Hasidic Portraits and Legends.* New York: Summit Books, 1991.

Wilber, Ken. *Boomeritis: A Novel That Will Set You Free.* Boston: Shambhala, 2003.

Wilber, Ken. *A Brief History of Everything.* Revised Edition. Shambhala: Boston, 2000.

Wilber, Ken. *The Eye of the Spirit: An Integral Vision for a World Gone Slightly Mad.* Shambhala: Boston, 1998.

Wilber, Ken. *Integral Spirituality: A Startling New Role for Religion in the Modern and Postmodern World.* Integral Books: Boston, 2006.

Wilber, Ken. *No Boundary: Eastern and Western Approaches to Personal Growth.* Shambhala: Boston, 2001.

Wilber, Ken. *Sex, Ecology, Spirituality: The Spirit of Evolution.* Shambhala: Boston, 2000.

Wink, Walter. *The Human Being: Jesus and the Enigma of the Son of Man.* Minneapolis: Fortress Press, 2002.

Winkler, Gabriele. "The Origins and Idiosyncrasies of the Earliest Form of Asceticism." *The Continuing Quest for God: Monastic Spirituality in Tradition and Transition.* William Skudlarek, O.S.B., General Editor. Collegeville, MN: The Liturgical Press, 1982.

Wolpert, Stanley. *Gandhi's Passion: The Life and Legacy of Mahatma Gandhi.* New York: Oxford University Press, 2001.

# ENDNOTES

[1] John of the Cross, "Essence of Desire," *Love Poems from God: Twelve Sacred Voices from the East and West*, translated by Daniel Ladinsky (New York: Penguin, 2002), 314.

[2] John of the Cross, "Dig Here," *Love Poems from God: Twelve Sacred Voices from the East and West*, Translated by Daniel Ladinsky (New York: Penguin, 2002), 327.

[3] Meister Eckhart, quoted in Bernard McGinn, *The Mystical Thought of Meister Eckhart: The Man From Whom God Hid Nothing* (New York: Herder and Herder, 2001), 161.

[4] Angelus Silesius, quoted by Catherine Keller, *Face of the Deep: A Theology of Becoming* (New York: Routledge, 2003), 216. For more, see *The Cherubinic Wanderer*.

[5] William Harmless, S.J., *Mystics* (New York: Oxford University Press, 2008), 228.

[6] Keller, *Face of the Deep*, 203.

[7] Gabriele Winkler, "The Origins and Idiosyncrasies of the Earliest Form of Asceticism," *The Continuing Quest for God: Monastic Spirituality in Tradition and Transition*, William Skudlarek, O.S.B., General Editor (Collegeville, MN: The Liturgical Press, 1982), 26.

[8] Marguerite Porete, *The Mirror of Simple Souls*, translated by Ellen L. Babinsky (New York: Paulist Press, 1993), Chap. 30, 110.

[9] Nicholas Cusa, "On Learned Ignorance," *Nicholas Cusa: Selected Spiritual Writings*, translated by H. Lawrence Bond (New York: Paulist Press, 1997), 135.

[10] Irenaeus of Lyons, *Against* Heresies V.

[11] Elena Vishnevskaya, "Divinization and Spiritual Progress in Maximus the Confessor," Amb 7 (PG 91:1088C; PPS 63-64) quoted in *Theosis: Deification in Christian Theology*, edited by Stephen Finlan and Vladimir Kharlamov (Eugene Oregon: Pickwick Publications, 2006), 144.

[12] *Way of Perfection*, in Egan, "Teresa of Jesus: Daughter of the Church and Woman of the Reformation," 71, quoted in Deirdre Green, *Gold in the Crucible: Teresa of Avila and the Western Mystical Tradition* (Worcester: Element, 1989), 174

[13] Ken Wilber, *Boomeritis: A Novel That Will Set You Free* (Boston: Shambhala, 2003), 340.

[14] Herbert Benson, M.D., Julie Corliss and Geoffrey Cowley, *Newsweek*, September 27, 2004.

[15] Rumi, 'Two Ways of Running,' *Delicious Laughter: Rambunctious Teaching Stories from the Mathnawi*, versions by Coleman Barks (Athens, Georgia: Maypop, 1990), 9-10.

[16] Thomas Aquinas after 6 Dec 1273 mystical experience he ceased writing his *Summa Theolgiae*. See Philosophy of Region website, http://www.philosophyofreligion.info/whos-who/historic-figures/st-thomas-aquinas/.

[17] Rumi, 'What You've Been Given,' *The Soul of Rumi*, translated by Coleman Barks (New York: HarperSanFrancisco, 2001), 230.

[18] Rumi, "Some Kiss We Want," *The Soul of Rumi*, translated by Coleman Barks (New York: HarperSanFrancisco, 2001), 127.

[19] P.D. Ouspensky, *A Further Record: Extracts from Meetings*, 1928-45 (New York: Penguin, 1988), 246; See C.S. Nott, *Journey Through This World: The Second Journey of a Pupil*, (Cape Neddick, ME: Samuel Weiser, Inc., 1974) 87.
[20] Helen Palmer, *The Enneagram: Understanding Yourself and the Others in Your Life* (San Francisco: HarperSanFrancisco, 1991), 51.
[21] Porete, *The Mirror of Simple Souls*, Chap. 30, 110.
[22] Gil Bailie, *Violence Unveiled: Humanity at the Crossroads* (New York: Crossroad, 1997), 7.
[23] Bailie, *Violence Unveiled*, 176, 177.
[24] Bailie, *Violence Unveiled*, 178.
[25] Bailie, *Violence Unveiled*, 179.
[26] Bailie, *Violence Unveiled*, 183.
[27] F.J. Matera, *Galatians, Sacra Pagina Series Volume 9*, Daniel J. Harrington, S.J. editor (Collegeville, MN: A Michael Glazier Book, 1992), 29.
[28] Donald Spoto, *Reluctant Saint: The Life of Francis of Assisi* (New York: Viking Compass, 2002), 23.
[29] Adrian House, *Francis of Assisi: A Revolutionary Life* (New Jersey: Hidden Spring, 2001), 57.
[30] Spoto, *Reluctant Saint*, 44.
[31] House, *Francis of Assisi*, 69, 70.
[32] See Soto, *Reluctant Saint*, 58; House, *Francis of Assisi*, 57.
[33] Spoto, *Reluctant Saint*, 160, 161.
[34] House, *Francis of Assisi*, 226.
[35] Spoto, *Reluctant Saint*, 190-191, 194, 197.
[36] *Francis of Assisi: The Saint*. Early Documents Volume I, edited by Regis J. Armstrong, O.F.M. Cap., J.A. Wayne Hellmann, O.F.M. Conv., William J. Short, O.F.M. (New York: New City Press, 1999), 113-114.
[37] Athanasius, *De Incarnatione* or *On the Incarnation* 54:3, PG 25:192B.
[38] Meister Eckhart, "Sermon Two," *Meister Eckhart: The Essential Sermons, Commentaries, Treatises, and Defense*, translated by Edmund Colledge, O.S.A. and Bernard McGinn (New York: Paulist Press, 1981), 183. Also, Meister Eckhart, quoted in Bernard McGinn, *The Mystical Thought of Meister Eckhart: The Man From Whom God Hid Nothing* (New York: Herder and Herder, 2001), 161.
[39] Krister Stendahl, *Final Account: Paul's Letter to the Romans* (Minneapolis: Fortress Press, 1995), xii.
[40] Stendahl, *Final Account*, 42-43.
[41] Stendahl, *Final Account*, 10.
[42] Neil Elliott, "Romans 13.1-7 in the Context of Imperial Propaganda," *Paul and Empire: Religion and Power in Roman Imperial Society*, edited by Richard A. Horsley (Harrisburg, Pennsylvania: Trinity Press International, 1997), 190.
[43] Stendahl, *Final Account*, 29.
[44] Elliott, "Romans," *Paul and Empire*, 191.
[45] See Jerome Murphy-O'Connor, *Paul: A Critical Life* (New York: Oxford University Press, 1996), 339.
[46] See Elliott, "Romans," *Paul and Empire*, 192-193.
[47] Elliott, "Romans," in *Paul and Empire*, 196.

[48] Meister Eckhart, Ioh. n.185 (LW 3:154.14-155.7), quoted by Bernard McGinn, *The Mystical Thought of Meister Eckhart: The Man From Whom God Hid Nothing* (New York: A Herder & Herder Book, 2001), 3.

[49] See Bernard McGinn, *The Harvest of Mysticism in Medieval Germany (1300-1500), Vol. IV of The Presence of God: A History of Western Christian Mysticism* (New York: A Herder & Herder Book, 2005), 94-107.

[50] Meister Eckhart, "Sermon Two: Creation: A Flowing Out But Remaining Within," in Matthew Fox, *Passion for Creation: The Earth-Honoring Spirituality of Meister Eckhart* (Rochester, Vermont: Inner Traditions, 2000), 66.

[51] Meister Eckhart, "Sermon Nine: Waking Up To The Nearness Of God's Kingdom," Matthew Fox, *Passion for Creation: The Earth-Honoring Spirituality of Meister Eckhart* (Rochester, Vermont: Inner Traditions, 2000), 137.

[52] Eckhart, "Sermon Nine," Fox, *Passion for Creation*, 138.

[53] Meister Eckhart Pr. 103.126-38, quoted in Bernard McGinn, *The Mystical Thought of Meister Eckhart*, 64.

[54] Meister Eckhart, "Sermon Fifteen: How A Radical Letting Go Becomes A True Letting Be," Matthew Fox, *Passion for Creation: The Earth-Honoring Spirituality of Meister Eckhart* (Rochester, Vermont: Inner Traditions, 2000), 217.

[55] Meister Eckhart, "Sermon Twelve: Sinking Eternally Into God," Matthew Fox, *Passion for Creation: The Earth-Honoring Spirituality of Meister Eckhart* (Rochester, Vermont: Inner Traditions, 2000), 180.

[56] Meister Eckhart, Jostes 82 (95.28-36), quoted in Bernard McGinn, *The Mystical Thought of Meister Eckhart*, 146.

[57] Bernard McGinn, *The Mystical Thought of Meister Eckhart*, 148.

[58] Meister Eckhart, Pr. 86 (DW 3:482.17-483.1), Pr. 86 (DW 3:485.5-7), quoted in Bernard McGinn, *The Mystical Thought of Meister Eckhart*, 159, 160.

[59] J. Philip Newell, *The Book of Creation: An Introduction to Celtic Spirituality* (New York: Paulist Press, 1999), 11-12.

[60] Nicholas of Cusa, *De filiatione Dei*, I h 52, Bond, quoted in Nancy J. Hudson, *Becoming God: The Doctrine of Theosis in Nicholas of Cusa* (Washington, D.C.: The Catholic University of America Press, 2007), 167.

[61] Mohandas Gandhi quoted in John Dear, *Mohandas Gandhi: Essential Writings* (Maryknoll, New York: Orbis Books, 2002), 72.

[62] Walter Brueggemann, *Hopeful Imagination: Prophetic Voices in Exile* (Philadelphia: Fortress Press, 1986), 73.

[63] Elie Wiesel, *Sages and Dreamers: Biblical, Talmudic, and Hasidic Portraits and Legends* (New York: Summit Books, 1991), 87.

[64] Walter Wink, *The Human Being: Jesus and the Enigma of the Son of Man* (Minneapolis: Fortress Press, 2002), 25, 26.

[65] Walter Wink, *The Human Being*, 25.

[66] Walter Wink, *The Human Being*, 31.

[67] Walter Wink, *The Human Being*, 26.

[68] Walter Wink, *The Human Being*, 26.

[69] Walter Wink, *The Human Being*, 33-34.

[70] Richard P. McBrien, *Catholicism* (New York: HarperCollins, 1994), 1:462.

[71] Rita Nakashima Brock and Rebecca Ann Parker, *Saving Paradise: How Christianity Traded Love of This World for Crucifixion and Empire* (Boston: Beacon Press, 2008), 268-70.
[72] Peter Abelard, "Exposition of the Epistle to the Romans," quoted in Thelma Megill-Cobbler, "A Feminist Rethinking of Punishment Imagery in Atonement," *Dialog* 35 [winter 1996], 18.
[73] Albert Einstein quoted in *Mohandas Gandhi: Essential Writings*, selected by John Dear (Maryknoll, New York: Orbis Books, 2002), 17.
[74] Stanley Wolpert, *Gandhi's Passion: The Life and Legacy of Mahatma Gandhi* (New York: Oxford University Press, 2001), 23.
[75] Mohandas Gandhi, Vol. 61, July 20, 1931, quoted in *Mohandas Gandhi*, selected by John Dear, 96. See also, M.K. Gandhi, *Non-Violent Resistance (Satyagraha)* (Mineola, New York: Dover Publications, Inc., 2001).
[76] *Gandhi on Non-Violence*, edited by Thomas Merton (New York: New Directions Paperbook, 1965), 36.
[77] Mohandas Gandhi, *All Men Are Brothers*, 77-78, quoted in *Mohandas Gandhi*, selected by John Dear, 96.
[78] *Selections from Gandhi*, December 31, 1934, 17, quoted in *Mohandas Gandhi*, selected by John Dear, 97.
[79] *Gandhi on Non-Violence*, edited by Thomas Merton, 45.
[80] Mohandas Gandhi, *All Men Are Brothers*, 63-64, quoted in *Mohandas Gandhi*, selected by John Dear, 73.
[81] Mohandas Gandhi, Vol. 68, October-November 1938, quoted in *Mohandas Gandhi*, selected by John Dear, 98.
[82] Mohandas Gandhi, *Selected Works*, Vol. 6, 268, quoted in *Mohandas Gandhi*, selected by John Dear, 78.
[83] Mohandas Gandhi, Vol. 63, August 3, 1947, quoted in *Mohandas Gandhi*, selected by John Dear, 78-79.
[84] Mohandas Gandhi, Vol. 74, October 1941, quoted in *Mohandas Gandhi*, selected by John Dear, 79.
[85] Mohandas Gandhi, Vol. 84, June 26, 1946, quoted in *Mohandas Gandhi*, selected by John Dear, 79.
[86] Mohandas Gandhi, *All Men Are Brothers*, 63, quoted in *Mohandas Gandhi*, selected by John Dear, 72.
[87] Mohandas Gandhi, Vol. 28, October 25, 1925, quoted in *Mohandas Gandhi*, selected by John Dear, 81.
[88] Mohandas Gandhi, Vol. 33, March 31, 1927, quoted in *Mohandas Gandhi*, selected by John Dear, 81.
[89] Mohandas Gandhi, Vol. 68, October-November 1938, quoted in *Mohandas Gandhi*, selected by John Dear, 99.
[90] Mohandas Gandhi quoted in *Mohandas Gandhi*, selected by John Dear, 59. See also M.K. Gandhi, *An Autobiography: The Story of My Experiments in Truth* (South Asia Books, 1994).
[91] *Gandhi on Non-Violence*, edited by Thomas Merton, 64.
[92] Mohandas Gandhi quoted in *Mohandas Gandhi*, selected by John Dear. 32.

⁹³ Hildegard of Bingen, *Book of Divine Works*, quoted in *Hildegard of Bingen: Mystical Writings*, edited by Fiona Bowie and Oliver Davies, translated by Robert Carver (New York: Crossroad Spiritual Classics, 1993), 9:2, 103.
⁹⁴ Teresa of Avila, *Meditations on the Song of Songs*, quoted in Tessaa Bielecki, *Teresa of Avila: Mystical Writings* (New York: Crossroad, 1994), 157-158.
⁹⁵ *The Collected Poems of W.B. Yeats*, "The Second Coming," edited by Richard J. Finneran, Revised Second Edition (New York: Scribner Paperback Poetry, 1996), 187.
⁹⁶ James Limburg, *Hosea—Micah, Interpretation: A Bible Commentary for Teaching and Preaching*, (Atlanta: John Knox Press, 1988), 7.
⁹⁷ *The Collected Poems of W.B. Yeats*, "The Second Coming," edited by Richard J. Finneran, 187.
⁹⁸ Abraham J. Heschel, *The Prophets*. Volume I (New York: Harper Torchbooks, 1969), 44 (emphasis added).
⁹⁹ Heschel, *The Prophets*. Volume I, 47.
¹⁰⁰ Heschel, *The Prophets*. Volume I, 68.
¹⁰¹ Heschel, *The Prophets*. Volume I, 44 (emphasis added).
¹⁰² Heschel, *The Prophets*. Volume I, 49 (emphasis added).
¹⁰³ Heschel, *The Prophets*. Volume I, 49 (emphasis added).
¹⁰⁴ Walter Brueggemann, *An Introduction to the Old Testament: The Canon and Christian Imagination* (Louisville: Westminster John Knox Press, 2003), 217.
¹⁰⁵ Brueggemann, *An Introduction to the Old Testament*, 218.
¹⁰⁶ Bernhard W. Anderson, *Understanding The Old Testament, Fourth Edition*, (Englewood Cliffs, New Jersey: Prentice Hall, 1986), 313.
¹⁰⁷ Heschel, *The Prophets*. Volume I, 47.
¹⁰⁸ Elizabeth Schüssler Fiorenza, "The Praxis of Coequal Discipleship," *Paul and Empire: Religion and Power in Roman Imperial Society*, edited by Richard A. Horsley (Harrisburg, Pennsylvania: Trinity Press International, 1997), 236-237.
¹⁰⁹ Elizabeth Schüssler Fiorenza, "The Praxis of Coequal Discipleship," *Paul and Empire*, 237.
¹¹⁰ *The Autobiography of St. Teresa of Avila*, "The Book of Her Life," Chapter 22, translated by Kieran Kavanaugh and Otilio Rodriguez (New York: One Spirit, 1987), 191.
¹¹¹ Jodi Bilinkoff, *The Avila of Saint Teresa: Religious Reform in a Sixteenth-Century City* (Ithaca, New York: Cornell University Press, 1989), 109.
¹¹² Bilinkoff, *The Avila of Saint Teresa*, 112-113.
¹¹³ Bilinkoff, *The Avila of Saint Teresa*, 112-113.
¹¹⁴ Deirdre Green, *Gold in the Crucible: Teresa of Avila and the Western Mystical Tradition* (Longmead: Element Books, 1989), 156-157 (emphasis added).
¹¹⁵ Bilinkoff, *The Avila of Saint Teresa*, 118.
¹¹⁶ Bilinkoff, *The Avila of Saint Teresa*, 121.
¹¹⁷ Bilinkoff, *The Avila of Saint Teresa*, 122. See also Teresa of Avila, *The Life of Saint Teresa of Avila by Herself*, translated by J. M. Cohen, (London: Penguin Books, 1957) 32:9, 236
¹¹⁸ Bilinkoff, *The Avila of Saint Teresa*, 123.
¹¹⁹ Bilinkoff, *The Avila of Saint Teresa*, 127.

[120] Green, *Gold in the Crucible*, 153.
[121] Teresa of Avila, *The Way of Perfection*, quoted in Deirdre Green, *Gold in the Crucible*, 174.
[122] Deirdre Green, *Gold in the Crucible*, 174.
[123] Deirdre Green, *Gold in the Crucible*, 97.
[124] Teresa of Avila, *Meditations on the Song of Songs*, quoted in *Teresa of Avila: Mystical Writings*, 157-158.
[125] Brueggemann, *An Introduction to the Old Testament*, 218.
[126] Sebastian Brock, *The Luminous Eye: The Spiritual World Vision of Saint Ephrem the Syrian* (Kalamazoo, Michigan: Cistercian Publications, 1992), 154.
[127] *Julian of Norwich: Showings*, translated by Edmund Colledge and James Walsh (New York: Paulist Press, 1978), Long Text 5:183, 183.
[128] Brueggemann, *An Introduction to the Old Testament*, 233-234.
[129] *The Access Bible*, General Editors Gail R. O'Day and David Petersen (New York:, Oxford University Press, 1999), 1196.
[130] "The sum of the book of Micah demonstrates the way in which an originary prophetic utterance is transformed into a fuller, coherent theological statement. The test is rooted in the harsh articulation of Micah. The continuing tradition, however, with awareness of the needs of a later context, will not let the harsh judgment of Micah be the last word. The last word, rather, concerns the God who pardons, the God who is unlike any other in *compassion, faithfulness*, and *loyalty* [7.18-20]. The book of Micah has a notable dynamism; clearly its framers felt no need to sort out the tensive relationship between the *initial harshness* of the tradition and the *culminating pardon*. Both belong to the defining relationship with YHWH that Israel came to understand and articulate only through the extended vagaries of their lived experience." Brueggemann, *An Introduction to the Old Testament*, 236.
[131] See Don Edward Beck and Christopher C. Cowan, *Spiral Dynamics: Mastering Values, Leadership, and Change* (Malden Massachusetts: Blackwell Publishers, 2001), 305-06. "[M]y basic role was to reshape the definitions the various sectors of society were using to stereotype each other, replacing the usual racial/ethnic categories with an understanding of these value system or memetic differences, all of which were alive in that global microcosm. The complexity of the South African situation had been simplified down to what is morally right or wrong along race lines, and that was a grave mistake. Much sympathy was lavished on the black 'struggle,' and rightfully so. But getting rid of what they didn't want—apartheid—was not the same thing as getting what they did want—a just and prosperous society. In the final analysis, a black, one-party-state doctrinaire nationalism (as in Zimbabwe today) would be no better than an Afrikaner version of the same." "The Never-Ending Upward Quest: A *WIE* Editor Encounters the Practical and Spiritual Wisdom of Spiral Dynamics," An interview with Dr. Don Beck, by Jessica Roemischer, 17. See www.wie.org.
[132] Ken Wilber offers an important reminder when working with stages and stage models: they are "just conceptual snapshots of the great and ever-flowing River of Life." They are real and they help us better see and understand our personal and cultural dynamic complexity. But, they are also limited frameworks. A helpful presentation of some of the major developmental lines side-by-side (such as

Piaget, Graves, Wade, Kegan, Loevinger, Gebser, Fowler) can be found in Ken Wilber's *Integral Spirituality*, Chapter Two: Stages of Consciousness. 50-70.

[133] "The Never-Ending Upward Quest, 5".

[134] "The Never-Ending Upward Quest," 8. See Beck and Cowan, *Spiral Dynamics*, 197-202.

[135] "The Never-Ending Upward Quest," 8. See Beck and Cowan, *Spiral Dynamics*, 203-214.

[136] "The Never-Ending Upward Quest," 4. See Beck and Cowan, *Spiral Dynamics*, 215-228.

[137] "The Never-Ending Upward Quest," 11. See Beck and Cowan, *Spiral Dynamics*, 244-259.

[138] "The Never-Ending Upward Quest," 3.

[139] "The Never-Ending Upward Quest," 11.

[140] "The Never-Ending Upward Quest," 13. See Beck and Cowan, *Spiral Dynamics*, 2260-273.

[141] Thomas Francis Carney, *The Shape of the Past: Models and Antiquity* (Coronado Pr, 1975), quoted in John Dominic Crossan and Jonathan L. Reed, *In Search of Paul : How Jesus's Apostle Opposed Rome's Empire with God's Kingdom* (New York: HarperSanFrancisco, 2004), 292.

[142] See Peter Oakes, *Philippians: From People to Letter* (Cambridge: Cambridge University Press, 2002), 61.

[143] Gerhard Friedrich, "Der Brief an die Philipper," *Die kleineren Briefe des Apostels Paulus*, 1962), 92 f, translated by and quoted in Oakes, *Philippians*, 211.

[144] See Oakes, *Philippians*, 60.

[145] Oakes, *Philippians,* 89-91.

[146] Oakes, *Philippians*, 101.

[147] Crossan, and Reed, *In Search of Paul*, 291.

[148] Marcus J. Borg, *The Heart of Christianity: Rediscovering a Life of Faith* (New York: HarperCollins, 2004), 111.

[149] Borg, *The Heart of Christianity:*119.

[150] Anselm of Canterbury, quoted in Ritamary Bradley, *Julian's Way: A Practical Commentary on Julian of Norwich* (London: HarperCollins *Religious*, 1992), 142.

[151] Julian of Norwich 6:186 quoted in Joan M. Nuth, *God's Lovers in an Age of Anxiety: The Medieval English Mystics* (Maryknoll, New York: Orbis Books, 2001), 116. Julian of Norwich *Showings* (Long Text) 54:285 quoted in Nuth, *God's Lovers in and Age of Anxiety*, 113. Julian of Norwich, *Showings* (Long Text) 59:295 quoted in Bradley, *Julian's Way*, 140.

[152] Bradley, *Julian's Way*, 142.

[153] Nuth, *God's Lovers in an Age of Anxiety*, 115.

[154] Julian of Norwich *Showings* (Long Text) 51.272 quoted in Nuth, *God's Lovers in an Age of Anxiety*, 114.

[155] Nuth, *God's Lovers in an Age of Anxiety*, 100-101.

[156] Julian of Norwich *Showings* (Long Text) 29:227 quoted in Bradley, *Julian's Way*, 118.

[157] Bradley, *Julian's Way*, 140.

[158] Julian *Showings* (Long Text) 27:225 quoted in Nuth, *God's Lovers in an Age of Anxiety*, 117.
[159] Anselm of Canterbury, *Cur Deus Homos?*, bk.1, ch. 24 [142], quoted in Frederick Christian Bauerschmidt, *Julian of Norwich and the Mystical Body Politic of Christ* (Notre Dame: University of Notre Dame Press, 1999), 132.
[160] Julian of Norwich, *Showings*, 51:267, 268.
[161] Julian of Norwich *Showings* (Long Text) 51.218-221 quoted in Bauerschmidt, *Julian of Norwich*, 161.
[162] Julian of Norwich *Showings* (Long Text) 58.2-8, quoted in Bauerschmidt, *Julian of Norwich*, 158.
[163] Julian of Norwich, *Showings* (Long Text), 86:342.
[164] Julian of Norwich, *Showings* (Long Text), 39:245.
[165] Bradley, *Julian's Way*, 143.
[166] Julian of Norwich, *Showings* (Long Text), 5:183 (emphasis added).
[167] Julian of Norwich, *Showings* (Long Text), 11:198-99.
[168] Julian of Norwich, *Showings* (Long Text), 47:260.
[169] See Julian of Norwich, *Showings* (Long Text), 75:327.
[170] Julian of Norwich, *Showings* (Long Text), 13:201.
[171] Julian of Norwich, *Showings* (Long Text), 49: 263-264.
[172] Nuth, *God's Lovers in an Age of Anxiety,* 112.
[173] Julian of Norwich, *Showings* (Long Text), 60:298.
[174] Julian of Norwich, *Showings* (Long Text), 58:293.
[175] Julian of Norwich, *Showings* (Long Text), 54:285.
[176] Julian of Norwich, *Showings* (Short Text) 4:130.
[177] Thomas Merton, "On True Freedom," quoted in Cynthia Bourgeault, *The Wisdom Way of Knowing: Reclaiming an Ancient Tradition to Awaken the Heart* (San Francisco: Jossey-Bass, 2003), 77. See also Cynthia Bourgeault, *Mystical Hope: Trusting in the Mercy of God* (Boston: Cowley, 2001), 70-71.
[178] See A. H. Almaas, *Essence with The Elixir of Enlightenment* (Boston: Weiser Books, 1998), Chapter Three, "The Loss of Essence," 83-101.
[179] Sandra Maitri, *The Spiritual Dimension of the Enneagram* (New York: Tarcher/Putnam, 2000), 23.
[180] See Maitri, *The Spiritual Dimension of the Enneagram*, 31.
[181] Maitri, *The Spiritual Dimension of the Enneagram*, 26.
[182] A.H. Almaas, *Facets of Unity: The Enneagram of Holy Ideas* (Berkeley, CA: Diamond Books, 1998), 43-44 (emphasis added).
[183] Almaas, *Facets of Unity*, 28.
[184] Almaas, *Facets of Unity*, 30.
[185] A.H. Almaas, *Diamond Heart Book One: Elements of the Real in Man* (Boston: Shambhala, 1987), 15.
[186] Almaas, *Diamond Heart Book One*, 19.
[187] *The New Dictionary of Theology*, edited by Joseph A. Komanchak, Mary Collins, Dermot A. Lane (Wilmington, Delaware: Michael Glazier, Inc., 1987), 233.
[188] Julian of Norwich, *Showings* (Long Text), 39:245.
[189] Julian of Norwich, *Showings* (Long Text), 38:242.

[190] Meister Eckhart, "Sermon Two: Creation: A Flowing Out But Remaining Within," in Matthew Fox, *Passion for Creation,* 66.
[191] Hildegaard of Bingen, *Hildegaard of Bingen: Mystical Writings,* trans. Robert Carver (New York: Crossroad, 1990), 91-93.
[192] Norman Fischer, *Opening to You: Zen-Inspired Translations of the Psalms* (New York: Viking Compass, 2002), 32.
[193] *The Kabir Book: Forty-Four of the Ecstatic Poems of Kabir,* versions by Robert Bly (Boston: Beacon Press, 1977), quoted in Almaas, *Diamond Heart Book One,* opening pages.
[194] Almaas, *Diamond Heart, Book One,* 2.
[195] Almaas, *Diamond Heart, Book One,* 131.
[196] Almaas, *Diamond Heart, Book One,* 131 (emphasis added).
[197] Almaas, *Diamond Heart, Book One,* 136.
[198] A.H. Almaas, *Spacecruiser Inquiry: True Guidance for the Inner Journey* (Boston: Shambhala, 2002), 402-403.
[199] A.H. Almaas, *Spacecruiser Inquiry,* 402-403.
[200] See Bernadette Roberts, *The Path to No-Self: Life at the Center* (Albany: State University Press of New York, 1991); *The Experience of No-Self: A Contemplative Journey* (Albany: State University Press of New York: 1993); *What is Self? A Study of the Spiritual Journey in Terms of Consciousness* (Boulder, CO: Sentient Publications, 2007).

## ABOUT THE AUTHOR

Kevin G. Thew Forrester lives with his wife, Rïse, and their two children, Miriam and Liam, in Marquette, Michigan. He has served the Diocese of Northern Michigan for the past ten years, initially as the Diocesan Ministry Development Coordinator and more recently as the Ministry Developer and Rector with St. Paul's, Marquette and St. John's, Negaunee.

Before coming to Northern Michigan, Kevin and Rïse were Co-Missioners in Central Oregon, nurturing mutual ministry. Kevin also served as the Diocesan Ministry Development Coordinator. While working with St. Michael & All Angels of Portland, Oregon, and serving as the Vicar of Church of the Four Winds, in the mid-1990's, he collaborated with Sonja Miller in the Diocese of Oregon to create the diocesan task force, Ministry of All the Baptized.

Kevin is a past coordinator of Living Stones, as well as a founding member of The Ministry Developers Collaborative, and occasional lecturer at Episcopal Divinity School. Kevin is an editor of and contributor to *LifeCycles: Christian Transformation in Community,* and has travelled throughout the U.S., Canada, Wales, England, and Scotland, to lead workshops on baptismal life and ministry in the post-modern 21st century. He is a certified teacher of the Enneagram in the Narrative Tradition as well as a trainee of the Integral Institute. In 2004, Kevin received Zen Buddhist lay ordination, called *jukai*. He founded the Healing Arts Center at St. Paul's, which hosts Enneagram workshops, weekly meditation, and faith explorations in the spiritual practices of the major faith traditions.

Kevin received his M.A. in Systematic Theology and Ph.D. in Moral Theology from The Catholic University of America, where he was the first non-ordained Resident Minister of Campus Ministry. He engaged in post-doctoral studies at both The Church Divinity School of the Pacific where he received an M.T.S., focusing in the areas of liturgics and bioethics, as well as at Lucille Salter Packard Children's Hospital at Stanford for a 9-month Bioethics Residency.

He is the author of two previous books: *Leadership and Ministry Within a Community of Equals* (published by InterCultural Ministry Development, San Jose, CA) and *I Have Called You Friends* (Church Publishing, Inc.).

Made in the USA
Charleston, SC
02 December 2011